HUMAN RIGHTS
AT WORK

HUMAN RIGHTS
AT WORK

EDITED BY K D EWING

THE INSTITUTE OF EMPLOYMENT RIGHTS
LONDON

Institute of Employment Rights
177 Abbeville Road, London SW4 9RL
020 7498 6919, fax 020 7498 9080
ier@gn.apc.org, www.ier.org.uk

First published 2000

Copyright © Institute of Employment Rights
2000

ISBN 1 873271 81 6

British Library Cataloguing in Publication data
A catalogue record for this book is available from the British Library

Designed and typeset by the Institute of Employment Rights
Printed by Gemini Press Limited, West Sussex

Contents

The authors

Keith Ewing is President of the Institute of Employment Rights. He is Professor of public law at King's College London.

Damian Brown is a Barrister at Old Square Chambers specialising in employment law.

Michael Ford is a Barrister specialising in employment law at Doughty Street Chambers. He is a member of the Institute's Publications Sub Committee.

Judy Fudge is a Professor of employment law at Osgoode Hall Law School, York University, Canada. She has written extensively on matters relating to human rights and employment law, collective rights, equality issues and privatisation.

Conor Gearty is Professor of human rights law at King's College London, and a member of Matrix Chambers. He has published widely on human rights law and on civil liberties, most recently (with K D Ewing) *The Struggle for Civil Liberties. Political Freedom and the Rule of Law in Britain, 1914-45* (OUP, 2000).

Tess Gill is a Barrister at Old Square Chambers specialising in equality matters.

John Hendy QC is a Barrister at Old Square Chambers specialising in labour law; Visiting Professor at King's College London, Chairman of the Institute of Employment Rights; and a Vice-President of the International Centre for Trade Union Rights.

Aileen McColgan is a Reader in Law at King's College London and an Executive Committee member of the Institute. Her interests cover labour law, public law and equality issues.

Sonya McKay is the Employment Law Researcher at the Labour Research Department.

Preface

THE Human Rights Act will introduce major changes to the constitutional landscape of the United Kingdom. The Act has given rise to high hopes and great expectations, and there is no field of law which will be unaffected by it. This volume considers the implications for employment law, and in particular how the Act might be used to extend the rights of workers and trade unions. The volume also considers some of the strategies which may be adopted by workers and unions to ensure that the promises held out by the Human Rights Act are fulfilled. It will be important to move quickly in the period of great uncertainty following the coming into force of the Act, to develop bargaining and litigation strategies to secure the rights which it embraces.

It is clear that the Human Rights Act will have implications for a number of important areas of employment law, and that it provides an opportunity to extend new rights into the workplace and to remove some of the restrictions under which workers and trade unions currently labour. It provides an opportunity to remove some of the Thatcher/ Major restrictions which still occupy a place on the statute book. The new rights relate to privacy at work, freedom of conscience and religion, freedom of expression and freedom of association. There are also important procedural issues which will have to be confronted as a result of the guarantee of a right to a fair trial included among the Convention rights.

The Institute of Employment Rights is delighted to have assembled another outstanding team of leading academic and practising lawyers to contribute to this volume. All are prominent members of the labour law and human rights community, and all are well placed to comment on the possibilities and pitfalls which lie ahead. On a personal note I would like to record my great debt to Carolyn Jones for her brilliant work on behalf of the Institute generally over many years, and on this project in particular; and to Megan Dobney for equally brilliant professional work which ensures that Institute publications are of a standard which are unrivalled in terms of the quality of their production.

KDE 2 October 2000

Chapter 1

The Human Rights Act 1998: an overview

Conor A Gearty

THE Human Rights Act 1998 came fully into force on 2 October 2000[1], though it has already been partly introduced in Scotland, Wales and Northern Ireland as a result of the devolution arrangements that have been put in place for these parts of the United Kingdom[2]. Even in England, the Act has enjoyed a limited applicability since its enactment. For example, all new government bills have had to carry a "human rights check" in accordance with section 19, and public authorities wishing to take proceedings after 2 October have also been bound by its partly retrospective effect[3]. The courts had been preparing for 2 October by accepting human rights arguments far more than they would have done just a few years ago[4] and an intensive training project to prepare the judiciary for the introduction of the legislation has recently been completed[5]. A huge array of conferences has educated legal practitioners up and down the country on the complexities and opportunities that the Act is likely to present. Central government, local authorities, trade unions, schools and members of the wider public are waking up to the huge significance of the legal changes that it will precipitate. Enthusiasts and critics alike agree that the Act represents the greatest alteration in the constitutional balance of this country, at least since 1911 and possibly since 1689[6].

In this chapter, we shall first consider the constitutional and political background to the Act, and we shall then outline its provisions in general terms. We shall conclude with a brief review of the ideological assumptions that lie behind the Act and with some reflections on its broader implications. The Human Rights Act is a radical departure from the style of law-making with which Britain has long been familiar. It is a very general measure, speaking in broad terms about certain ethical values. Its intended effect on the law is pervasive but uncertain. Much will depend therefore on how the Act is interpreted in the courts. The judges will be required to approach this task without the usual detailed set of indicators from Parliament as to the circumstances in which the law should be applied. Instead they will find themselves having to extrapolate a very great deal from the quite minimal raw material they have been handed. There will be more gaps to fill in this legislation than in any other measure with which the courts have ever been confronted, and at the same time there will be far less detailed guidance than usual as to how exactly these spaces should be filled. The courts have been handed something of an open book by Parliament, an ethical guide capable of being deployed in a variety of different ways. How the Act is interpreted, the routes down which the courts find themselves sending the measure, will depend in part on the exigencies of the adversarial process, on the kind of cases that are thrown up and with what kind of factual matrix. But of perhaps even greater importance will be the quality of the principles that the judges will develop to help guide them through the complexities of the measure. This is the issue upon which the future health of the Act depends.

Constitutional and political origins of the Human Rights Act

THE United Kingdom has never had a written constitution in the sense of a single document which has established its structure and institutions of government. Instead as a result of the constitutional revolution effected in England in the seventeenth century, the principle of parliamentary sovereignty was very early confirmed as the basis of the United Kingdom's system of government[7]. Thus it was as a result of primary legislation enacted by successive parliaments that the United Kingdom was gradually democratised, with key reforms along the way including the expansion of the franchise in the nineteenth century[8], the guarantee of secret voting[9], and the eventual acceptance of mass universal suffrage in 1928[10]. The emerging Labour Party of the early twentieth century had reason to be grateful that the principle of parliamentary sovereignty was so embedded in the British constitution, since it was through Acts of Parliament that judicial hostility to the Party and its collectivist goals was tackled and eventually effectively subdued[11]. Throughout the last century, the Labour Party in government was a devout defender of parliamentary sovereignty, believing that it represented the best way of ensuring that the democratic will of the people could be translated into enforceable and effective law. It was through Parliament that the public interest was served and through statutes that the correct balance between the individual and society was sought to be achieved. Under this traditional approach, it was possible to enjoy individual rights, but where these occurred they were the result of specific legislation rather than general constitutional guarantees[12].

It will be obvious however that such a constitutional system left no room for the concept of *human* rights; the idea of inalienable and imprescriptible rights inhering in every human could not co-exist with the principle that Parliament had the power to do whatever it chose, however excessive. Instead the United Kingdom constitution relied on a commitment to civil liberties and a healthy political culture to prevent the lapses into extremism to which the system of parliamentary sovereignty was notionally vulnerable. Though political liberty did not thrive in the United Kingdom in the twentieth century[12], it is by no means obvious that the strains to which the British constitution were occasionally subjected would not have been equally felt had a written constitution been in place[14]. When the European Convention on Human Rights and Fundamental Freedoms was agreed between member states of the Council of Europe in 1950[15], the Attlee government that helped draft the Convention did not make it part of domestic law, not least because it was perceived that the document would undermine the principle of parliamentary sovereignty[16]. For the same reason, the surge in international human rights law that followed in the second half of the twentieth century was not permitted to impinge on British domestic law. An apparently small but as can now see very significant concession was made in 1966, when the Wilson government agreed to allow individuals within the jurisdiction to take cases from the United Kingdom to the European Court of Human Rights in Strasbourg, where a violation of the individual's rights under the European Convention was alleged[17]. This right of individual petition had been an optional part of the Convention when it had been first established, and it had not initially been considered of very great importance. It has however proved itself to be the engine which has driven rights' adjudication in Europe in the last quarter of the twentieth century. There are now forty-one countries signed up to the European Convention, and a huge and ever increasing volume of cases is flowing to the Court, all from individuals whose claim is that their rights have been infringed by their own governments.

The United Kingdom has been in the vanguard of this litigious march to Strasbourg. The 1966 initiative produced little at first but a change gradually came about in the late 1960s and during the 1970s. The scholarly literature on the subject grew in volume and quality, and with it came a new awareness of the domestic legal implications of the Convention and the Convention organs[18]. Cases in Strasbourg involving the United Kingdom drew attention to the new jurisdiction in a way that no journal article on its own could achieve. The first four such decisions by the Court involved: a prisoner denied access to the courts to sue a prison officer for libel[19]; *The Sunday Times'* reporting of the thalidomide litigation[20]; the punishment by birching of a convicted criminal in the Isle of Man[21]; and the finding of breaches of article 3's prohibition of torture, inhuman or degrading treatment made against the authorities in respect of the treatment meted out to certain internees in Northern Ireland in 1971[22]. In the decade that followed, many decisions went against the United Kingdom government in Strasbourg, not least a series of cases provoked by the attempt to ban publication of the allegations detailed in the book *Spycatcher* by the former member of the security service Peter Wright[23]. Despite these and other cases, however, and the effect of successive Thatcher administrations on traditional civil liberties, the Labour Party remained throughout the 1980s opposed to the incorporation of the Convention into United Kingdom law. The Party continued to emphasis that the best way to guarantee rights was through focused and targeted legislation in the traditional way[24], and it was also quick to point out that the Strasbourg court's approach to human rights evinced little sympathy for or understanding of collective rights[25].

This position did not survive the Party's fourth successive election defeat in 1992. Though first suggested by John Smith during his brief term as Labour leader, a commitment to incorporation of the European Convention into domestic law was embraced by Smith's successor Tony Blair as one of the ways in which the Labour Party could under his direction show that it had something new to offer the British electorate. At the same time, the public debate on the need for added rights' protection was being fuelled by senior judges who were increasingly speaking outside the courtroom in support of the case for incorporation[26]. In December 1996, the Labour opposition published a consultation paper on its "plans to incorporate the

European Convention on Human Rights into United Kingdom law"[27]. Its authors, Jack Straw MP and Paul Boateng MP (at the time respectively shadow Home Secretary and shadow Minister for the Lord Chancellor's Department), argued that the proposal would "cut costs, save time and give power back to British courts" and that it was likely to receive wide public support given "the evidence of recent polls showing considerable public support for measures protecting rights"[28]. At the same time, the Party retained its belief in parliamentary sovereignty, "[a] fundamental aspect of the British constitutional tradition" which the proposals outlined in the Paper "would not alter". Following its election victory on 1 May 1997, the new Labour government made the enactment of human rights legislation one of its early priorities, with a white paper on the subject being published in October 1997, together with the draft of the Bill that it was intended would be the basis of the new legislation[29]. It is to an examination of this legislation, and in particular to an analysis of its attempt to reconcile parliamentary sovereignty and human rights, that we now turn.

The Human Rights Act: a general overview

Convention rights

The main purpose of the Act is "to give further effect to rights and freedoms guaranteed under the European Convention on Human Rights"[30]. The rights that are made part of United Kingdom law in accordance with the Act are set out in schedule 1 of the Act[31]. These include such basic entitlements as the right to life (article 2), the abolition of the death penalty (the Sixth Protocol), the right to freedom from torture (article 3) and the right to freedom from slavery (article 4). The scheduled rights also cover such fundamental liberties as the right to free elections (article 3 of the First Protocol), the freedoms of thought, conscience and religion (article 9), freedom of expression (article 10), and freedom of assembly and association (article 11). Also guaranteed are the right to privacy (article 8), the right not to be punished retrospectively (article 7), the right to fair procedures in civil and criminal cases (article 6), and the right to private property (article One of the First Protocol). The rights to marry (article 12), to education (article 2 of the First Protocol) and to freedom from discrimination in the exercise of these various incorporated rights (article 14) complete the list of Convention rights included in the new Act.

This is an extensive menu of new rights to introduce into United Kingdom law in a single piece of legislation. The Convention only unequivocally prohibits "torture" and "inhuman or degrading treatment or punishment" (article 3) and "slavery or servitude" and "forced or compulsory labour" (article 4). The rest of its rights are all to a greater or lesser extent qualified. Some of the rights are rather general and leave much to the national authorities, such as the rights to marriage and to an education. Others contain exceptions setting out ways in which the right in question may be lawfully restricted. The right to property is heavily qualified in this way. The right to life does not apply where it can be said that death results "from the use of force which is no more than absolutely necessary (a) in defence of any person from unlawful violence; (b) in order to effect a lawful arrest or to prevent the escape of a person lawfully detained; [or] (c) in action lawfully taken for the purpose of quelling a riot or insurrection." The right to liberty is also subject to a very wide range of exceptions and many of the other civil liberties protected by the Convention are limited by reference to various ends which can trump the right in question where this is judged in any given situation to be "necessary in a democratic society"[32]. Where an article does not seem on its face to contain any exceptions, such as article 14 and (to a limited extent) article 6, the European Court has been inclined through the process of interpretation to read exceptions into the rights so as to achieve for itself more freedom of manoeuvre when it comes to the application of the right than would otherwise have been available to it. This interpretative process adds a further zone of uncertainty to all the provisions in the Convention; even phrases like "torture" and "inhuman or degrading treatment or punishment" have given rise to sharp differences of opinion as to their true meaning[33].

Apart from these specific and judge-based exceptions, the Convention also allows for more general departures from the rigours of its rights-based demands. Three of these have been included in the Human Rights Act . First, it is possible to derogate from certain provisions of the Convention in situations of public emergency of an exceptionally grave nature[34]. Parliament has done so in respect of certain powers in the terrorism legislation[35]. In a similar way the incorporation of the right to education has been subjected to certain reservations made when the United Kingdom first agreed the right in March 1952[36]. Both derogations and reservations may be withdrawn by the Government in which case they will also cease to apply in domestic law[37]. Second, under article 16, "[n]othing in articles 10, 11 and 14 shall be regarded as preventing the High Contracting Parties from imposing restrictions on the political activity of aliens". This is not a provision around which much jurisprudence has gathered[38]. Thirdly, article 17 states that "[n]othing in this Convention may be interpreted as implying for any State, group or person any right to engage in any activity or perform any act aimed at the destruction of any of the rights and freedoms set forth herein or at their limitation to a greater extent than is provided for in the Convention"[39]. This saving clause has also not been frequently used in Strasbourg[40] and it remains to be seen whether either it or article 16 will develop a dynamic of their own in the context of British incorporation.

As has already been referred to on a number of occasions, the European Convention and its protocols have over the years been subject to a considerable degree of interpretation at the European Court of Human Rights. There have been in the region of one thousand such decisions. In addition, there have been thousands of decisions from the European Commission of Human Rights, a body inferior to the Court which was responsible until very recently for all admissibility decisions on applications to Strasbourg and which in many cases also provided the final opinion on whether the Convention had been breached[41]. A third body that may be mentioned here is the Committee of Ministers of the Council of Europe whose functions used to include the confirmation or rejection of Commission opinions in cases which did not go before the Court but which is now restricted to oversight of the execution of the judgments of the Court[42]. With the coming into force of the Human Rights Act, all this juristic material will become part of United Kingdom law: under section 2 of the Act, a "court or tribunal determining a question which has arisen in connection with a Convention right must take into account" any such material "whenever made or given, so far as, in the opinion of the court or tribunal, it is relevant to the proceedings in which that question has arisen"[43]. The obligation is to "take into account" rather than necessarily to follow Strasbourg jurisprudence. The case-law from the Court will not be "binding" in the way that House of Lords cases are in the English system. Where Strasbourg authority is discounted to the detriment of a non-governmental party, however, it will still be possible to proceed to Strasbourg in the hope of securing the ruling there that has been refused in the national courts. If this were to happen, the United Kingdom government would find itself under an international law obligation to bring the local law into line with the Convention. Though of course the Strasbourg Court is perfectly capable of not following its own earlier decisions, it may be that this awareness of a possible recourse to Strasbourg will operate as a subconscious bar to rejecting too many Strasbourg authorities in the United Kingdom courts.

Three further points of interest arise from section 2. The first relates to quite how important this Strasbourg case law is to a full understanding of the Convention. As noted above, the European Court of Human Rights has read qualifications into apparently unequivocal articles in a way that has now become settled in the case-law and which is therefore very unlikely to be ignored after implementation. The Court has also on occasion interpreted new rights into Convention provisions, most notably in relation to the "right of access to a court" which has now become such a mainstay of article 6 jurisprudence[44]. Again it is unlikely that the British courts after incorporation will wholly disregard such lines of cases. Secondly, the extension of the section 2 duty to tribunals as well as to courts is immensely significant. This is likely to have enormous consequences on the legal system, if only for the reason that such a huge number of cases are dealt with before such a wide variety of tribunals in this country. Now all such bodies must take Strasbourg jurisprudence into account as long as they qualify as a tribunal "in which legal proceedings may be brought"[45]. Thirdly, it is not clear from the Act how a Convention point may arise, and there is already a lively debate as to whether judicial officers and tribunal members may rely on the parties before them to bring the subject up or whether they are duty bound where relevant to raise it themselves. Clearly the latter course has implications for the way in which the adversarial process has traditionally been undertaken in this country. The former approach would however raise serious questions about inequality of arms in relation to proceedings on a complicated but important matter where one side was without legal representation: how would such a person be expected to spot a Convention point, even one of vital importance to their case?

Parliamentary sovereignty after the Human Rights Act

Having dealt with the substance of the incorporated rights, our next area of inquiry must logically be the extent of their impact on United Kingdom law. The Act requires that all primary and subordinate legislation "[s]o far as it is possible to do so... must be read and given effect in a way which is compatible with the Convention rights" (section 3(1)). Significantly this applies to all future legislation as well as to all past Acts and statutory instruments. It affects all legislation regardless of its subject matter or the nature of the litigation in issue, so it will be irrelevant whether a case raising a point of statutory interpretation has a public authority as one of its parties. Section 3(1) represents a far more robust principle of statutory construction than English law has hitherto seen. How far does "[s]o far as it is possible" go?[46] Quite far it would seem, particularly when we note that the government rejected an amendment in the Lords which would have qualified the word "possible" with the word "reasonably"[47]. In doing this, the Lord Chancellor appears to have been content to anticipate certain unreasonable constructions which would nevertheless be possible, and therefore be applied by the courts in preference to other possible (or even probable) interpretations. After 2 October all the old precedents will need to be revisited in relation to all statutes to check their continued relevance in the light of this new, overarching principle of statutory interpretation. Magistrates' courts and tribunals will be able to depart from settled judicial authorities on particular issues if they are satisfied that this is necessary under section 3. This empowerment of lower judicial bodies will be one of the more fascinating features of human rights adjudication, at least until the Act settles down and instructions about the use to be made of the legislation emerge from the courts at the top of the system[48].

While it is commonly assumed that it will be possible to strike down delegated legislation for incompatibility with the Convention[49], the opposite is the case as far as Acts of Parliament are concerned. Under section 3(2)(b), the principle of interpretation discussed above is explicitly stated not to "affect the validity, continuing operation or enforcement of any incompatible primary legislation"[50]. The reference here not only to the protection of legislation as such but also to the "continuing operation" and "enforcement" of such legislation indicates Parliament's determination that its power to legislate in defiance of Convention-based perceptions of what human rights entails should not be restricted. Where a higher court is unable to render a statute compliant with the Human Rights Act by creative interpretation under section 3(1), then it will have the power (but not the duty) to issue a declaration of incompatibility in respect of it (section 4). This will however have no effect on the parties before the court. In particular the party whose litigious energies have produced the declaration will still be bound by the pre-existing rule in respect of which the declaration has been achieved[51]. This may well strike lawyers and non lawyers alike as somewhat paradoxical, but it flows inevitably from Parliament's continuing assertion of its sovereignty. A litigant faced with a declaration of incompatibility will of course still be able to take his or her case to Strasbourg, where the chances of success will be correspondingly higher because of this powerful statement of support from the United Kingdom courts[52]. A second consequence of such a declaration will no doubt be the exertion of political pressure on the government to change the law so as to render it compliant with the Convention, and the Act sets out a complicated procedure for just such an executive response to these declarations of incompatibility[53]. No doubt this is an approach that is likely to be more tempting to pressure groups or well-resourced litigants intent on changing the law in the medium term than it will be to individual litigants. Certainly after implementation of the Human Rights Act, these declarations of incompatibility will equip suitable litigants with a strong weapon with which to undermine – politically and eventually perhaps also legally – primary legislation that is not to their taste. No Home Secretary will want to go into an election as the defiant supporter of "human rights" abuses.

Executive action

Acts of Parliament do not in themselves do anything at all. They require action to give them life. Invariably this is a function performed by the executive branch or by some other kind of public body. It is of immense significance therefore that the Human Rights Act also declares that it "is unlawful for a public authority to act in a way which is incompatible with a Convention right" (section 6(1)). However, as is to be expected in a measure which seeks to protect parliamentary sovereignty, this provision does not apply if "(a) as a result of one or more provisions of primary legislation, the authority could not have acted differently" or "(b) in the case of one or more provisions of, or made under, primary legislation which cannot be read or given effect in a way which is compatible with the Convention rights, the authority was acting so as to give effect to or enforce those provisions"[54]. The probable effect of these saving clauses is that where the terms of an Act are incompatible with the Convention, then what is done under that Act is – like the measure itself – protected from human rights-based scrutiny[55]. This exception apart, section 6(1) looks to be very broad indeed, creating a new cause of action where a person's Convention rights are interfered with by any public authority. The Act provides that any such person may bring proceedings "in the appropriate court or tribunal" or rely on such rights "in any legal proceedings"[56]. Where a court finds that "any act (or proposed act) of a public authority is (or would be) unlawful" it "may grant such relief or remedy, or make such order, within its powers as it considers just and appropriate"[57]. There are however various restrictions designed to prevent the litigation floodgates from being opened too wide. Only "victims" may launch proceedings based directly on the Act[58] a term that is to be understood against the background of the Strasbourg jurisprudence on its meaning[59]. There are reasonably strict time limits within which actions must be launched[60] and Parliament has gone to quite detailed lengths to try to restrict the level of damages that it will be possible to award under the Act[61].

The decision to include in the section 6(1) duty all public authorities, rather than just the more obvious executive arms of government such as the army, the police and so on, is what makes the potential application of the Act so enormous, particularly when the breadth and range of the Convention rights set out in schedule one (discussed above) are taken into account, amplified as these are certain to be by recourse to the Strasbourg jurisprudence under section 2. Though the concept of a "public authority" is not defined, it is clear both from the parliamentary record and the rest of section 6(1) that the term is to be given a wide scope[62]. Clearly government ministers, local authorities, the police, the army etc. are covered. The BBC, the ITC, the Press Complaints Commission and other such bodies would also seem to be within the section. So also are all the regulatory bodies that have been set up under various statutes in recent years, such as inspectors established under the companies and financial services legislation and the serious fraud office. If recent public law cases on the phrase are heeded, even non-statutory bodies (such as the city panel on take-overs in one well-known case[63]) may find themselves within its remit. The Human Rights Act itself provides that any "person certain of whose functions are functions of a public nature" is to be regarded as a public authority[64] but not where the act of such a body which is in issue in any particular case is itself a private act[65]. Thus the door would seem to have been opened to the classification of certain privatised bodies as public authorities for the purposes of section 6(1). After implementation, it can be stated with some confidence that every regulatory body with which trade unions, companies and other legal as well as natural persons come in contact in their day to day lives will need to act in a way which is compatible with the Human Rights Act. Indeed, given the Act's partially retrospective effect (referred to above), to the extent that these bodies desire in the future to initiate litigation on the basis of what they do before 2 October, then such actions would need also to be Convention-compliant[66]. There is likely to be quite an amount of litigation on the question of what constitutes a "public authority" with many bodies seeking to avoid the label so as to escape the new statutory duty imposed by section 6(1). The extent to which this will give rise to a large amount of satellite litigation remains to be seen.

The common law

The common law is a third source of law in this country, separate from statute law and from delegated legislation. It derives its authority from no piece of legislation but rather from the historical power of the courts to assert what the law is by reference to the precedents and authorities to be found in pre-existing case law. Once the main source of English law, the common law has seen its remit narrow as statutes have taken over more and more of the areas that would once have been its exclusive concern. But important subjects remain within its ambit; these include much of contract law and such frequently litigated subjects as breach of confidence, trespass, nuisance and false imprisonment. Where a public authority is involved in these kinds of cases as a defendant, then there can be little doubt that the Human Rights Act will be engaged via that authority's overarching duty to comply with Convention rights under section 6(1) (discussed above). But in cases where the issue before the court is a pure common law matter and both parties are private bodies, the Act's applicability is less easily resolved. There is no statute or piece of delegated legislation upon which the principle of interpretation in section 3 can bite. Viewed from a purely theoretical perspective, it would seem right that the Act should have no engagement in such a situation: the liberal version of human rights upon which this legislation is based has traditionally viewed such rights as being exclusively concerned with the protection of individuals from State rather than from private power. Thus, in the absence of any challenge to official power, the Act has nothing upon which to bite[67].

It will be immediately recognised that the assumption in the liberal theory of rights outlined above is not without controversy. In particular, many proponents of the need for human rights protection are as concerned with the abuse of private power as they are with the restrictions on rights imposed by the State. Socialists have traditionally been especially alive to the danger posed to individuals by private power, particularly in a society which is organised in an unequal way. Those who place as a priority the achievement of a more egalitarian or fairer society will often find themselves advocates of strong government, in order to be able to achieve the goals they desire in the face of much anticipated opposition from entrenched interests. From this perspective a Human Rights Act which operates only against the State not only does not reach the mischief of private power but it also protects exactly that same power from governmental efforts to change its mode of operating. In its bleakest form, this analysis would suggest that a Human Rights Act organised in such a way would buttress rather than challenge the inequalities and injustices that remain at the heart of our society. The question is whether the Act is restricted in this way. On one reading it most certainly is. The whole structure we have outlined above is based on the assumption that only public authorities are caught by its provisions. If this were not the case, why go to the trouble of setting out so much detail about public authorities, and in particular why distinguish between the private and public functions of certain private bodies with functions of a public nature?[68] The scheme for providing remedies under the Act also seems predicated on the same assumption about its remit[69].

A second reading of the Act accepts all this but points to a remarkable provision which it is said undermines all around it. This is section 6(3)(a) under which it is explicitly said that the term "public authority" in section 6 includes "a court or tribunal". What can this mean? On one reading it merely confirms that where a court is presiding in a case (whether involving public or private parties) it must itself behave in a Convention-compatible way, not clearing the court of the public for no reason, not throwing litigants in jail for spurious contempts, not making preliminary orders which are invasive of privacy and so on. This is certainly an effect of the subsection. But it is argued that it also go further than this, and requires the courts to give effect to Convention rights in all common law disputes, regardless of the status of the litigants before them. This is because it is their duty as the relevant "public authority" under section 6(1) not to act in a way which is incompatible with a Convention right and that to act (or omit to act[70]) in such a way by making (or refusing to make) an order required by the Convention will after 2 October be unlawful. Crucially, on this argument such unlawfulness will be established even where the reason for the court acting (or not acting) in the way that it did would have been perfectly justified under the pre-existing common law. Thus on this second view, the whole common law would need after 2 October to be Convention-complaint, and private parties would have a new remedy for breach of Convention rights against other private parties which they could force upon the courts as part of the latter's statutory duty under section 6(1). The public/private divide would be rendered meaningless and the whole common law would be expected slowly to disappear to be replaced by a new kind of judge-made law rooted in the Convention rights and drawing its legitimacy from the application of section 6 to the courts[71].

This eventuality seems extraordinary and it is hard to believe that one subsection in an Act could not only undermine the structure of the legislation in which it appears but also and almost casually transform a system of adjudication that has grown up in Britain over many centuries. But if this is not what section 6(3)(a) involves, why is it in the Act? During the parliamentary debates, the Lord Chancellor took the view that while preventing the courts from "legislating" to create new forms of action, the subsection would enable the judges to develop the common law in Convention-compliant directions in situations where it was suitable so to do[72]. While the difference between the courts legislating on the one hand and developing the common law on the other can sometimes be a difficult one to make, it seems that the expectation is that the Act will indeed open up certain common law remedies in Convention-oriented ways while not permitting private actions between parties rooted solely in the breach of Convention rights. Thus the law of nuisance may be expanded by reference to the Convention right to privacy[73] to give a remedy to a litigant without a proprietary interest in land[74]. The torts of false imprisonment and liberty may draw support from the Convention's protection of liberty and its prohibition on inhuman and degrading treatment. In the employment field, tribunals might find themselves reinterpreting contracts of employment in appropriate cases in a way which infuses into the relationship a new respect for the employee's Convention rights[75]. If adopted, this middle way may in due course prove to be an interpretative route as radical as the second position outlined above. Certainly its potential for infusing the common law with a new ethical dimension should not be underestimated[76].

Human rights ideology and constitutional principle

THE likely impact of the Human Rights Act on United Kingdom law is truly staggering. The right to life in article 2 can be expected to produce challenges to the abortion legislation[77] and to police conduct where death results from alleged operational failures[78]. Article 3 will probably have an effect on the burden of proof in cases in which allegations of brutality have been made against police officers[79], just as its extra-territoriality has already had a profound impact on United Kingdom extradition and asylum law[80]. Article 5's right to liberty has raised questions about United Kingdom law on bail[81] and its terms can be expected to be frequently raised in legal challenges to the exercise of power under legislation like the recently enacted Terrorism Act[82]. The police and the courts will need to be equally mindful of their duties under article 6's guarantee of procedural fairness, and it may be that a challenge to recent changes in legal aid provision will be mounted under its aegis[83]. Articles 7 (on retrospective laws) and 8 (on privacy) will have an obvious impact on police investigations[84] and the criminal process as a whole[85], particularly in relation to the requirement that police intrusions be prescribed by law[86]. Article 10's guarantee of freedom of expression has already been widely welcomed by the media as an important guarantor of press freedom[87]. No doubt articles 8 and 14 (on non-discrimination) will underpin challenges to pre-existing law considered inconsistent with contemporary attitudes to sexual orientation[88].

Dramatic though these changes undoubtedly would be, they are all in areas where some Convention impact could reasonably confidently have been predicted. It is in the sudden delivery of the unexpected that the Human Rights Act is likely to excel. Scotland, with its early experience of the Act, is instructive. The dramatic finding that answers to compulsory questions about whether a suspect was driving a car cannot be used in subsequent criminal proceedings is under appeal to the Privy Council[89]. The collapse for incompatibility with article 6 of the system of temporary sheriffs which had grown up in that jurisdiction as a way of dealing with criminal cases also came as a surprise to many[90]. The same kind of question has already arisen in relation to employment tribunals in England[91]. Though the precise issue in this couple of cases may have already been addressed by the government[92], others will no doubt emerge from unexpected quarters after 2 October. The implications of the Act for administrative law, for commercial law and for financial regulation have begun to engage the attentions of practitioners and academics unaccustomed to describing their practices as human rights-based[93]. Insolvency law[94], the rules of civil litigation[95], insurance law and even pensions law are among the areas that are likely to be affected to an not insubstantial degree.

It is interesting to consider why the Act should have such far reaching implications. At one level it is of course because its terms point towards such pervasiveness. But at a deeper level it is explained by the ideological assumptions that underpin the measure. The Act and the Convention which it largely incorporates are committed to a very particular version of "human rights". The Council of Europe is a creature of the political settlement that followed the end of world war two, and the Convention on Human Rights and Fundamental Freedoms that was one of its earliest achievements reflects the concerns of its time. Primarily these related to the fear that fascism would return, with the Convention's provisions being designed as a bulwark against the danger of such catastrophic regression. This explains the prohibition of torture and slavery and the emphasis on liberty, non-discrimination and the civil liberties of thought, expression, association and assembly. But it seems now reasonably clear that the Convention was also seen by its architects as one of a range of constitutional instruments which would inhibit the emergence of any democratically-legitimised communist or socialist government in Europe[96]. Certainly the document's emphasis on the individual sits uneasily with the collective goals that any such elected government would necessarily have wanted to pursue. Article 6(1) sets out to guarantee individuals due process where any of their civil rights are determined by a public authority. Even more clearly, article 1 of the First Protocol on property rights, agreed on 20 March 1952[97] guarantees that "[e]very natural or legal person is entitled to the peaceful enjoyment of his possessions" and that "[n]o one shall be deprived of his possessions except in the public interest and subject to the conditions provided for by law and by the general principles of international law". It is true that the article does go on to declare that it is not its intention "in any way [to] impair the right of a State to enforce such laws as it deems necessary to control the use of property in accordance with the general interest or to secure the payment of taxes or other contributions or penalties". Even with this caveat, what this provision would seem to involve is the declaration of a political purpose, presenting itself as a constitutional norm.

The jurisprudence of the Court and Commission has over the years reflected the concerns of those whose efforts produced the Convention and its protocols. In *Kommunistische Partei Deutschland v Federal Republic of Germany*[98], the suppression of the German Communist Party was found not to involve an infringement of the Convention, with (unusually) article 17 being the key provision, providing (as we have seen) that Convention protection be withheld from those who "engage in any activity or perform any act aimed at the destruction of any of the rights and freedoms set forth or at their limitation to a greater extent that is provided for in the Convention". The Commission found that this was the position with regard to the applicant Party, with the fact that power was being sought via constitutional means not being regarded as conclusive evidence pointing in the other direction. Similarly, strong German restrictions on free speech which affected political activists on the left for much of the Cold War survived challenge not only before the German constitutional court but also in Strasbourg[99]. In case after case in the first decades of their juristic life, both the Court and the Commission interpreted the freedom of association guarantee in article 11 in a way which has undermined the principle of collective bargaining in favour of greater protection for individual conscience[100]. In a way this was inevitable; the Convention invited just such a prioritisation and at a time of great international tension, with the world divided into two antagonistic blocs, it was unlikely that the Strasbourg bodies would have been inclined to have acted in any other way. With the end of the Cold War and a lessening of anxiety about the threat to European institutions from the left, there has been a noticeable relaxation in attitude in some of the more recent cases[101].

In its contemporary manifestation through the case-law, which pours in ever-increasing volume from Strasbourg, the Convention has shown itself to be a protector not only of human rights *simpliciter* but also and more particularly of the possessive individual. This is evident not only in the property clause discussed above but also in the more general extension of Convention protection to corporate entities[102] and in the application of the procedural safeguards in article 6 to persons where their pecuniary rights have been adversely affected[103]. This is why all State regulation of business, across sectors as diverse as financial regulation, pensions and insurance, will in due course be required to be analysed for compatibility with the Human Rights Act: it is of the essence of state policing of these areas that pecuniary rights are sometimes adversely affected by official decisions. In contrast to its robust line on pecuniary interests, and perhaps somewhat surprisingly, the Strasbourg Court's record on the protection of personal autonomy in such central human rights areas as sexual privacy and artistic expression has been somewhat patchy, with certain conduct being powerfully protected[104] and other apparent manifestations of free expression and sexual identity being denied support[105]. Where the Court has been consistently strong has been in the insistence that restrictions to freedom be prescribed by law[106] and in its distaste for general rules that appear to deny litigants the chance to argue their cases before independent tribunals[107]. The first of these requirements has the strongly democratic-reinforcing effect of requiring governments to articulate their repressive powers in the form of visible law[108]. The latter commitment is more controversial since there may be good administrative reasons why "the right to adversarial proceedings"[109] should not be extended to a particular set of circumstances.

More than perhaps anything else, the Human Rights Act presages a dramatic legalisation of the United Kingdom constitution. Uniquely among member States of the Council of Europe, the United Kingdom introduces the European Convention into a domestic law which contains no written constitution against which it can be compared and where appropriate contextualised. The Act will be expected to perform the role reserved in other member States to an indigenous constitution. This quasi-normative status will derive further potency from the other constitutional statutes that have been passed since 1997, particularly those on devolution and house of lords reform. The overall impression is of a nation that has embarked on a process of constitutional reform which will gather rather than lose momentum in the future. At the forefront of this tentative revolution will be the judiciary, invited by Parliament to step much closer than ever before to the centre of Britain's political process. It is already clear that a result of this reallocation of power from the legislative to the judicial branch will be a huge increase in the attention paid to judges and a far closer scrutiny of their conduct, both generally and in relation to particular cases. Lord Hoffmann's embarrassing travails in relation to the *Pinochet*[110] case showed how potent and unexpectedly intrusive judicial accountability is likely to be after the Human Rights Act comes fully on stream. That case is also a reminder that the language of human rights is a larger presence in our modern law than even the Human Rights Act would suggest.

Significant though it is, the Act is in some ways merely part of a larger process, involving the recasting of much of our political process in the language of rights and responsibilities. Thus, with civil and political guarantees having succeeded in securing a degree of primacy for the values that they represent, the pressure is beginning to grow for the introduction of internationally guaranteed social and economic rights into United Kingdom law on the same basis[111]. The Foreign Office has since 1997 sought famously to practice its diplomacy with an ethical dimension. The oversight of United Kingdom human rights by international officials has become more noticed and more politically important than in the past[112]. The European Union promises a new charter of rights by the end of the year, and Parliament seems to be committed to a joint select committee on human rights. In an article in a popular Scottish newspaper, a Scottish judge Lord McCluskey recently likened the imminence of the implementation of the Human Rights Act to "an avalanche; all we can hear at the moment is a distant roar; but it is coming and we are going to have to struggle to avoid being buried in new claims of rights"[113]. Whether he is also right that the Act will produce "a field day for crackpots, a pain in the neck for judges and legislators, and a goldmine for lawyers" only time will tell.

Notes

1 See Home Office, News Release, 12 July 2000.

2 See the Scotland Act 1998, the Government of Wales Act 1998 and the Northern Ireland Act 1998.

3 s 22(4). See further *R v DPP, ex parte Kebilene* [1999] 4 All ER 801.

4 The background case-law is in C A Gearty (ed), *European Civil Liberties and the European Convention on Human Rights: A Comparative Study* (1997), ch 2.

5 See P Collins, "The Judicial Studies Board and the ECHR" in University of Cambridge Centre for Public Law, *The Human Rights Act and the Criminal Justice and Regulatory Process* (1999), ch 4.

6 See K D Ewing, "The Human Rights Act and Parliamentary Democracy" (1999) 62 MLR 79.

7 It is technically right to regard the United Kingdom of Great Britain as a new nation which resulted from the unification of England and Scotland in 1707, effected through parallel legislation being passed by both the English and Scottish parliaments providing for a new Parliament of Great Britain. The principle of parliamentary sovereignty never quite took root in Scottish soil with the same intensity as it did in England. For an excellent review of the whole subject see N MacCormick, *Questioning Sovereignty. Law, State and Nation in the European Commonwealth* (1999), ch 4 and more generally J Goldsworthy, *The Sovereignty of Parliament: History and Philosophy* (1999).

8 The reform legislation of 1832 and 1867 in particular.

9 The Secret Ballot Act 1873.

10 Note however that some plural voting lingered on until 1948.

11 See Trade Union Act 1871; Trades Disputes Act 1906; Trade Union Act 1913.

12 See for eg. Race Relations Acts 1965-76; Sex Discrimination Act 1975.

13 See K D Ewing and C A Gearty, *The Struggle for Civil Liberties. Political Freedom and the Rule of Law in Britain, 1914-45* (2000).

14 For a discussion of this point in relation to the 1980s see K D Ewing and C A Gearty, *Freedom Under Thatcher. Civil Liberties in Modern Britain* (1990), ch 8.

15 European Treaty Series No 5 (4 November 1950).

16 G Marston, "The United Kingdom's Part in the Preparation of the European Convention on Human Rights, 1950" (1993) 42 ICLQ 796.

17 See K R Simmonds, "The United Kingdom and the European Convention on Human Rights" (1966) 15 ICLQ 539; R Beddard, "The Status of the European Convention of Human Rights in Domestic Law" (1967) 16 ICLQ 206. See also United Kingdom Committee for Human Rights Year, *Human Rights: A Study Guide for the International Year for Human Rights, 1968* (1967).

18 See particularly A Lester, *Democracy and Individual Rights* Fabian Tract 390 (1968) and L Scarman, *English Law – the New Dimension* (1974).

19 *Golder v United Kingdom* (1975) 1 EHRR 524.

20 *The Sunday Times v United Kingdom* (1979) 2 EHRR 245.

21 *Tyrer v United Kingdom* (1978) 2 EHRR 1.

22 *Ireland v United Kingdom* (1978) 2 EHRR 25.

23 *The Observer and The Guardian v United Kingdom* (1991) 14 EHRR 153; *The Sunday Times v United Kingdom (No 2)* (1991) 14 EHRR 229.

24 Thus is a speech to the Fabian Society on 6 January 1990, the then deputy leader of the Party and Shadow Home Secretary Roy Hattersley MP said: "What we propose amounts to a Charter of Rights. But if the rights which it

includes are to be written into law – as distinct from forming a statement of principle and a declaration of intent – they have to be enacted by specific Acts of Parliament which are precise, detailed and capable of only limited interpretation by the courts."

25 See generally on social rights, K D Ewing, *Britain and the ILO* (2nd edn, 1994).

26 See particularly the late Lord Taylor (in his Dimbleby lecture, "The Judiciary in the Nineties" on BBC1, 30 November 1992) and Lord Bingham (see his "The ECHR: Time to Incorporate" (1993) 109 LQR 390).

27 *Bringing Rights Home* (December 1996).

28 For a critique of the paper see K D Ewing and C A Gearty, "Rocky Foundations for Labour's New Rights" [1997] EHRLR 146.

29 See *Rights Brought Home: The Human Rights Bill* (Cm 3782, 1997).

30 See the preamble to the Act.

31 See HRA, s.1(1)-(3).

32 See eg. articles 9, 10 and 11.

33 See in particular *Tyrer v United Kingdom,* above note 21.

34 HRA, s.14.

35 See HRA, sched 3, part I; *Brannigan and McBride v United Kingdom* (1993) 17 EHRR 539.

36 HRA, s.15, sched 3, part II.

37 The procedure is set out at HRA, ss.14-17.

38 See P van Dijk and G J H van Hoof, *Theory and Practice of the European Convention on Human Rights* (3rd edn, 1998), pp 747-50.

39 Cf article 18: "The restrictions permitted under this Convention to the said rights and freedoms shall not be applied for any purpose other than those for which they have been prescribed".

40 The limited case-law is surveyed by van Dijk and van Hoof, above note 38, pp 750-55.

41 The Commission's role has been taken over by the Court: see Protocol No 11 (11 May 1994).

42 See A Tomkins, "Civil Liberties in the Council of Europe: A Critical Survey" in Gearty (ed), above note 4, p 1. Of great interest is Parliamentary Assembly, Committee on Legal Affairs and Human Rights, *Execution of Judgments of the European Court of Human Rights, Draft Report* (AS Jur (2000) 39, 26 June 2000).

43 HRA s.2(1). Further details on this new duty are at ss.2(2) and 2(3).

44 See *Golder v United Kingdom op cit,* note 19. For a recent and controversial case on the point see *Osman v United Kingdom* (1998) 29 EHRR 245.

45 HRA, s.21(1).

46 The literature on the subject is already vast: see in particular: Lord Lester of Herne Hill QC, "The Art of the Possible: Interpreting Statutes under the Human Rights Act" in The Centre for Public Law at the University of Cambridge, above, note 5 (1999), 25; G Marshall, "Interpreting Interpretation in the Human Rights Bill" [1998] PL167; D Pannick, "Principles of Interpretation of Convention Rights under the Human Rights Act and the Discretionary Area of Judgment" [1998] PL 545; G Marshall, "Two Kinds of Compatibility: More about Section 3 of the Human Rights Act 1998" [1999] PL 377; and F Bennion, "What Interpretation is 'possible'

under Section 3(1) of the Human Rights Act 1998?" [2000] PL 77.
47 See in particular the comments of the Lord Chancellor at HL Debs, 3 November 1997, cols 1230-1, 1294.
48 See for an early example *R v Central Criminal Court, ex parte Bright; R v Central Criminal Court, ex parte Alton, R v Central Criminal Court, ex parte Rusbridger, The Times*, 26 July 2000.
49 No such power appears explicitly in the Act but it seems to have been assumed, by eg. ss 3(2)(c), 4(3), s.4(4) and particularly s.10(4).
50 Subordinate legislation which is required by primary legislation is similarly protected: s.3(2)(c). For the definition of primary and secondary legislation see HRA s.21(1).
51 See HRA s.4(6).
52 And in Strasbourg, a litigant will also be able to rely on the right to an effective remedy in article 13 of the European Convention, a provision which has not been incorporated into United Kingdom law but by which the United Kingdom continues to be bound as a matter of international law. It is unlikely that the declaration of incompatibility will be considered by the Court to be an effective remedy, at least when viewed from the perspective of the applicant.
53 See HRA, s.10 and sched 2.
54 s 6(2). Note also that neither House of Parliament nor any parliamentary proceedings are to be classed as public authorities: HRA s.6(3).
55 The issue is however rather complicated where the incompatible Act allows a range of conduct, some of which is compatible and some incompatible with the Human Rights Act: in such a situation is the Convention-incompatible conduct of the authority protected under s.6(2) even where it had the option of acting in a Convention-compatible way but chose not to?
56 See HRA, s.7(1).
57 HRA, s.8(1).
58 HRA, s.7(3).
59 HRA, s.7(7).
60 HRA, s.7(5).
61 See HRA, ss.8(2)-(6), 9(3)-(4).
62 See HL Debs, 16 November 1997, cols 1231-2 (Lord Chancellor); *ibid*, 24 November 1997, col 784 (Lord Chancellor).
63 *R v Panel on Take-Overs, ex parte Datafin plc* [1987] QB 815.
64 HRA, s.6(3)(b).
65 HRA, s.6(5).
66 HRA s.22(4) and 7(1)(b), on which see *R v DPP, ex parte Kebilene*, above note 3.
67 See R Buxton, "The Human Rights Act and Private Law" (2000) 116 LQR 48.
68 HRA, ss.6(3) and 6(5).
69 HRA, s.8.
70 HRA s.6(6).
71 See H W R Wade, "Horizons of Horizontality" (2000) 116 LQR 217.
72 HL Debs, 24 November 1997, col 784.
73 Article 8.
74 On which see *Hunter v Canary Wharf Ltd* [1997] 2 All ER 426.

75 See A Lester and D Pannick, "The Impact of the Human Rights Act on Private Law: the Knight's Move" (2000) 116 LQR 380, at pp 384-5.

76 See M. Hunt, "The Human Rights Act and Legal Culture: The Judiciary and the Legal Profession" (1999) 26 JLS 86.

77 See *Paton v United Kingdom* (1980) 3 EHRR 408.

78 *McCann v United Kingdom* (1995) 21 EHRR 97.

79 *Ribitsch v Austria* (1995) 21 EHRR 573.

80 See *Soering v United Kingdom* (1989) 11 EHRR 439; *Chahal v United Kingdom* (1996) 23 EHRR 413.

81 See Law Commission, *Bail and the Human Rights Act 1998* (Law Commission No. 157).

82 See Lord Lloyd, *Inquiry into Legislation Against Terrorism* (Cm 3420, 1996); Home Office and Northern Ireland Office, *Legislation Against Terrorism. A Consultation Paper* (Cm 4178, 1998).

83 *Airey v Ireland* (1979) 2 EHRR 305.

84 See D Mead, "The Likely Effect of the Human Rights Act on Everyday Policing Decisions in England and Wales" (2000) 5 JCL 5.

85 See *Welch v United Kingdom* (1995) 20 EHRR 247.

86 *Halford v United Kingdom* (1997) 24 EHRR 523.

87 The leading case is *Lingens v Austria* (1986) 8 EHRR 407. See further HRA, s.12.

88 *Smith and Grady v United Kingdom* (1999) 29 EHRR 493; *Lustig-Prean and Beckett v United Kingdom* (1999) 29 EHRR 548.

89 *Brown v Procurator Fiscal, Dunfermline*, 4 February 2000, Appeal Court, High Court of Justiciary.

90 *Starrs v Ruxton*, 2000 JC 208.

91 *Smith v Secretary of State for Trade and Industry* (EAT, 11 October 1999)

92 See the statement of the Lord Chancellor on the point, 12 April 2000.

93 There are already a large number of textbooks designed to meet the needs of such practitioners. See *The Human Rights Act and the Criminal Justice and Regulatory Process*, above note 5, for an up-to-date general survey which usefully indicates the breadth of the subject.

94 See C A Gearty, "Insolvency... and Human Rights" [2000] *Insolvency Lawyer* 68.

95 Law Society, *Civil Litigation Newsletter* (March 2000).

96 See M. Mandel, "A Brief History of the New Constitutionalism, or 'How We Changed Everything so that Everything Remained the Same'" (1998) 32 *Israel Law Review* 250.

97 ETS No 9.

98 (1955-7) YECHR 222.

99 *Glasenapp v Germany* (1986) 9 EHRR 25. Cf *Kosiek v Germany* (1986) 9 EHRR 328.

100 The leading United Kingdom case is *Young, James and Webster v United Kingdom* (1981) 4 EHRR 38.

101 See particularly *Vogt v Germany* (1995) 21 EHRR 205.

102 The cases are now too many to mention but see as one good example *Air Canada v United Kingdom* (1995) 20 EHRR 150. For an interesting domestic discussion of the issue see *R v BSC, ex parte BBC, The Times*, 12 April 2000.

103 *Editions Periscope v France* (1992) 14 EHRR 597.

104 See eg. *Norris v Ireland* (1988) 13 EHRR 186; *Smith and Grady v United Kingdom op cit* note 88; *Lustig-Prean and Beckett v United Kingdom op cit*, note 88.

105 See eg. *Cossey v United Kingdom* (1991) 13 EHRR 622; *Müller v Switzerland* (1988) 13 EHRR 212.

106 See *Halford v United Kingdom* (1997) 24 EHRR 523.

107 See esp *Osman v United Kingdom op cit*, note 44.

108 On the assumption of course that the democratic system is geared to provide proper accountability: see however the Regulation of Investigatory Powers Act 2000.

109 *Van Orshoven v Belgium* (1998) 26 EHRR 55, para 41.

110 *R v Bow Street Metropolitan Stipendiary Magistrate, ex parte Pinochet Ugarte* (No 2) [1999] 2 WLR 272.

111 K D Ewing, "Social Rights and Human Rights: Britain and the Social Charter – the Conservative Legacy" [2000] EHRLR 91.

112 See United Nations Economic and Social Council, Commission on Human Rights, *Civil and Political Rights, including the Question of Freedom of Expression.* Report submitted by Mr Abid Hussain, Special Rapporteur, in accordance with Commission on Human Rights Resolution 1999/36 (11 February 2000).

113 The article appeared in *Scotland on Sunday.* The piece led to Lord McCluskey being taken off a human rights case in which he was involved at the time: *Hoekstra v HM Advocate.* For a full report see *Guardian* 8 May 2000, G2 p 8.

Chapter 2

Article 8 and the right to privacy at the workplace

Michael Ford

ARTICLE 8 of the ECHR states that:

1. Everyone has the right to respect for his private and family life, his home and his correspondence.
2. There shall be no interference by a public authority with the exercise of this right except as is in accordance with law and is necessary in a democratic society in the interests of national security, public safety or the economic well being of the country, for the protection of disorder or crime, for the protection of health and morals, or for the protection of the rights and freedoms of others.

Like many articles of the ECHR, article 8 first sets out a right, or rather rights, and then specifies in what circumstances infringements are justified. But precisely what interests are protected in article 8(1) is a matter of uncertainty, probably reflecting a lack of clarity about what is encompassed in the concept of private life.

Privacy as a political concept

THAT uncertainty should not surprise us, for privacy is a contested political concept. Its emergence as a recognised interest is often linked and counterposed to the emergence of the public sphere as the realm of debate and discussion. Closely connected with prop-

erty ownership, the private sphere was one in which the public –
made concrete in the form of the State and the law – should not
intervene. Historically, privacy has been linked with three distinct
interests: the sphere of moral and religious conscience; economic
rights in the market place; and the domain of the household, of sexuality and daily life[1]. So conceived privacy can be used to justify and
reinforce existing inequalities. For feminists the treatment of the
household as the private sphere, free from state regulation, has permitted injustice in domestic relations to persist. Likewise the exclusion of private contracts from State regulation in the name of privacy has been used as a means of legitimating the deregulated,
exploitative labour market.

But against those conservative views of private life stand more
progressive conceptions. Spheres of life free from intrusion are, it is
convincingly argued, necessary for individual self-development.
Most of us, for example, need areas where we know we are not being
watched in which we can rehearse and prepare ourselves for our
public lives. So too to develop and form meaningful relationships
with others we need guarantees that what we say is not being overheard (imagine the chilling effect on free debate if all conversations
were taped). It may be that these more radical conceptions of privacy are better seen as aspects of or pre-conditions for deeper political
values – autonomy, both individual and collective, and dignity. But
they illustrate the continuing political disagreement about what the
right involves.

As a result definitions of privacy are likely to be controversial,
vague or thin. For some the right to privacy has been defined as the
right to know about and to control what information is held on an
individual[2]. For others much wider interests have been included.
The Lord Chancellor's Department, for instance, recently proposed
a definition including matters relevant to health, family and personal
relationships, together with rights to be free from harassment and
molestation, and it saw privacy as encompassing rights to seclusion,
secrecy, anonymity and solitude as means of protecting personality,
independence, integrity and dignity[3]. Others have defined it as
meaning the right to be left alone; but this only makes sense against
an understanding of in what contexts one should be left alone, and
from what interferences one has the right to be isolated[4]. The
absence of any clear consensus on the meaning of privacy was one of
the reasons why the Younger Committee rejected proposals to introduce such a right in the United Kingdom[5]. In practice definitions
tend to obscure more than they clarify, as they wave away the political disagreements with a definitional wand.

Chapter 2 : Article 8 and the right to privacy

The lack of consensus as to what privacy does or should encompass is reflected in the case law of the European Court of Human Rights. The Court has tended somewhat unreflectively to determine that some interests do fall within article 8 and others do not. But the reasons behind this and the core principles of privacy are, unfortunately, not set out. In part this is no more than a product of the general lack of reasoning in ECHR cases, in turn perhaps caused by the need for the judgment to set out the conclusion of what is in essence a committee rather than the views of individual judges. Another reason may be that exploring the deeper justifications of privacy would simply expose how little consensus there is as to its scope. But a consequence is that it is not easy to predict how privacy will apply in more controversial areas.

One such area is the workplace, in which there is little guidance as yet how workers' private lives are to be reconciled with management's private right to property. At best it is possible to identify two competing strands of privacy in this context, one more progressive than the other. But before turning to private interests at work, a few words about the general nature of article 8.

Article 8 and the European Court of Human Rights

Private life

The case-law of the European Court does not display a principled approach to what is privacy, nor to the values which underpin it. What general indications there are show that the right is not confined to freedom from interference in a restrictively-defined area of activities. In *Niemietz v Germany*, which concerned the search of a lawyer's office, it stated:

> The Court does not consider it possible or necessary to attempt an exhaustive definition of the notion of "private life". However, it would be too restrictive to limit the notion to an "inner circle" in which the individual may live his own personal life as he chooses and to exclude therefrom entirely the outside world not encompassed within that circle. Respect for private life must also comprise to a certain degree the right to establish and develop relationships with other human beings[6].

Regrettably there is little guidance as to exactly what this approach entails in practice and how far it guarantees individual and collective autonomy in particular contexts, though it opens the way to a radical conception of private life in the future.

In the absence of clearer principles, the subject is best approached through examples. Physical integrity receives a high degree of protection, so that even relatively minor interventions engage article 8, such as the taking of blood or urine samples[7]; the same will, presumably, apply to bodily searches. Sexual activities are generally protected and with them sexual identity[8]. But the filming or photographing by the police of demonstrators in a public place has been held by the Commission not to breach article 8 because not intruding into "the inner circle" of his or her life[9]. The general trend is a widening of the scope of the article, so that it can protect against noise and pollution[10].

Article 8 protects against secret surveillance of, for example, telephone conversations and postal communications[11]. As regards the collection of information, so far it has offered little protection against the processing of information about persons which is not closely related to their family or "inner circle". In *X v United Kingdom* the British census was held by the Commission to violate article 8(1) because it asked questions about sex, marital status, place of birth and other personal details, although it was justified on the ground of the economic well-being of the country under article 8(2)[12].

In some circumstances article 8 requires that individuals have a positive right to be told what information is held on them, or be told information relevant to their making decisions about their private life. In *Guerra v Italy*[13] the Court held that individuals, who lived near a chemical factory, were entitled to know sufficient information about the pollutants for them to assess the effect on their health. And individuals exposed to nuclear tests conducted by the United Kingdom government had a right derived from article 8 to know all relevant and appropriate information relevant to the effect on their health[14]. This case-law opens the way to duties of disclosure, up to now alien to English law.

Home, correspondence and family life

In some circumstances business premises may be treated as a "home". In the *Niemietz* case the Court said:

> to interpret the words "private life" and the "home" as including certain professional or business activities or premises would be consonant with the essential object and purpose of article 8, namely to protect the individual against arbitrary interference by public authorities[15].

The justification for this extension was that some business and professional activities may be conducted from a private residence, and private activities may be conducted from an office, reflected in the

French text and the use of the term "domicile". It follows that business premises probably only amount to a "home" where the activity can just as well be carried on at home as at the office. Once premises are deemed to be a home, then occupants have a right to peaceful occupation which may include freedom from unreasonable levels of noise, pollution and harassment, though in each case the threshold for engagement of article 8 is high and, correspondingly, article 8(2) is more easily met[16]. But forms of search or secret surveillance clearly invade the sanctity of the home and will require compelling reasons for justification.

"Correspondence" has been extended to protect against secret tapping of telephone messages[17]. The same should apply to e-mail messages and other forms of sending messages made possible by technological developments. But the degree of protection required may depend upon how secure is the method of communication[18]. "Family life" has been interpreted in accordance with changing times, extending to forms of parent-child relationship wider than those arising from marriage.

Positive duties to ensure respect

Article 8 gives a right not simply to private and family life, to the home and correspondence but also to "respect for" these rights. The Court has interpreted this as requiring the State positively to intervene in order to protect against interference by private agencies[19]. Accordingly the State may have to take positive measures to ensure, for example, that child care decisions properly take account of all the family members affected by them[20]. The Commission has even gone so far as to recognise a duty positively to intervene to protect a woman against harassment by a former partner[21]. As we have seen, in certain circumstances public authorities may owe a duty to disclose information which concerns matters relevant to private life, such as the affect of pollution on health[22].

As a consequence of these positive obligations public authorities, including the courts by virtue of s.6 of the Human Rights Act, are under a duty to act in order to prevent one private party infringing the privacy of another, though the duty is not as strict as when the State itself commits an infringement of privacy. One means of meeting that duty will be the development of the horizontal application of article 8, so that legal remedies will be available for infringements by private sector employers.

Justification for interference

Any interference under article 8(1) can only be justified if it meets the strict criteria of article 8(2). For an interference to be in "accordance with law" there must be a measure of legal protection against arbitrary interferences with privacy. With regard to secret interferences with privacy, such as phone tapping, an individual should be able to foresee under what conditions privacy may be infringed[23]. While it would defeat the purpose of secret surveillance if an individual were told that he was to be watched, this entails that the rules "indicate with reasonable clarity the scope and manner of exercise of the relevant discretion"[24]. In the employment context, the Court accepted that the Ministry of Defence policy banning gays and lesbians from the armed forces satisfied the requirement, as did the Commission in relation to an employer's internal policy on dress code[25]. To satisfy the second qualification, that the interference must be "necessary in a democratic society", the interference must correspond to a pressing social need and be proportionate to the legitimate aim pursued. Both of these issues have been explored in Chapter 1.

Article 8 and working life

SO far there has been little case law on private life in the workplace. Reflecting the competing political conceptions of privacy and no doubt the difficulty of translating a right historically derived from the home into the workplace, the case-law exhibits two competing strands to the right, neither of which has been developed in detail. Nor has the tension between the conceptions been properly explored.

The first strand emerges from the *Niemietz* decision, in which the Court stated:

> Respect for private life must also comprise to a certain degree the right to establish and develop relationships with other human beings. There appears, furthermore, to be no reason of principle why this understanding of the notion of "private life" should be taken to exclude activities of a professional or business nature since it is, after all, in the course of their working lives that the majority of people have a significant, if not the greatest, opportunity of developing relationships with the outside world[26].

This conception recognises a collective dimension to privacy: a right to develop our relationships with others, free from outside interference. Translated into the workplace it probably requires private spaces at work – spaces in which workers can develop their relationships with each other, guaranteed free from employer intrusion.

The *Niemietz* conception should be contrasted with how privacy was articulated in *Halford v United Kingdom*[27]. That case concerned a complaint by Ms Halford, a former Assistant Chief Constable, that Merseyside Police Force had tapped her office phone. Not only had she been supplied with a phone designated for private use, but she had also been given an assurance that she could use her office phone for the purpose of her litigation against Merseyside Police. Finding that article 8 was engaged, the Court rejected the United Kingdom government's argument that an employer was free to monitor calls made by an employee on phones which it had provided. But the language of the decision was perhaps more cautious than in *Niemietz*: in the absence of a warning and because of the assurances she had been given, the Court considered that she would "have had a reasonable expectation of privacy"[28]. (In the absence of any system of regulating the interception of phone calls on a private network, the government conceded that the infringement was not "in accordance with law" for the purposes of article 8(2).[29])

The difference between the two conceptions of privacy is illustrated by how they relate to management prerogative. A conception of privacy which draws upon the right of workers to form relationships with each others ought to be resistant to attempts to remove private spaces at work. It may well require that workers are provided with locations or times when they can be sure that they are free from surveillance. But a conception based upon a reasonable expectation of privacy is, at least on its face, more easily overridden by management decisions. An employer who informs employees at the workshop door that they have no right to privacy, and may be watched or listened to at any time, may argue that it has removed any prior expectation they had of privacy. Take, for example, CCTV: on the *Niemietz* conception one would expect that the employer would be under a duty to provide areas free from such surveillance; on the *Halford* conception the matter is much less clear, for it may be argued the very presence of cameras removes any expectation of privacy. It is significant that US case-law on the Fourth Amendment, which has drawn on a reasonable expectation test, has offered little resistance to management prerogative[30].

The few other cases involving article 8 and the working relationship have done little to clarify how private interests are to be reconciled with ownership rights. In *Smith v United Kingdom*[31] the Court held that the United Kingdom armed forces' ban on gays and lesbians infringed article 8. The United Kingdom government conceded that dismissals for reasons of sexual orientation interfered with the right to respect for private life. Though the dismissals were in accordance with law (the Ministry of Defence internal policy) and pursued a legitimate aim (national security and the prevention of disorder), they were not proportionate. In this regard the Court noted that "particularly serious reasons"[32] were required to justify such interferences, which concerned "a most intimate part of an individual's private life". Recognising that the effect on employment prospects was a material consideration, the Court pointed out that the applicants would find it hard to obtain civilian posts of equivalent status and seniority[33]. And the Court rejected an argument that the Ministry of Defence was entitled to rely on the negative attitudes of heterosexual personnel towards gays and lesbians:

> To the extent [the attitudes] represent a predisposed bias on the part of a heterosexual majority against a homosexual minority, these negative attitudes cannot, of themselves, be considered by the Court to amount to sufficient justification for the interferences with the applicants' rights... any more than similar negative attitudes towards thus of a different race, origin or colour[34].

Rightly the Court makes clear that prejudices and stereotypical assumptions are, therefore, not a sufficient justification.

In a recent decision the Commission considered the effect of article 8 on dress codes. In *Kara v United Kingdom*[35] a male Training Administrator employed by Hackney Borough Council wore female clothing at work. He was instructed to desist. Accepting that choice of mode of dress was an aspect of private life, the Commission went on to find that the requirement of "in accordance with law" was met because the employer had a written dress policy. The interference was not disproportionate: the requirement "that employees dress 'appropriately' to their gender may reasonably be regarded by the employer as necessary to safeguard their public image". There is a certain tension here with the reasoning in *Smith*: attitudes of the general public to cross-dressers were a permissible justification, whereas prejudices of the heterosexual majority were not. As the view of the Court and because it has a more rationale basis, *Smith* is to be preferred: irrational prejudices should not be relevant factors to justification.

The right to privacy in English law

AS yet English law does not clearly recognise a right to privacy, though even before the introduction of the Human Rights Act one member of the House of Lords indicated that the matter might require a close examination in the future[36]. Instead English law offers a patchwork of different laws which in some circumstances may provide protection similar to that required by article 8. But important gaps remain: the failure of English law to provide any effective redress in *Halford* and *Smith* are two obvious examples. The existing position under English law is set out in an earlier Institute of Employment Rights publication, *Surveillance and Privacy at Work*. Below attention is drawn to some of the more significant provisions.

Up to now the law on unfair dismissal has not focussed on whether dismissals interfere with private life. A notorious example is the decision of a tribunal, upheld by the EAT, that it was fair to dismiss a gay man working with children because of the unfounded prejudices of other employers:

a considerable proportion of employers would take the view that the employment of a homosexual should be restricted... Whether that view is scientifically sound may be open to question but there was clear evidence... that it exists as a fact[37].

Similarly the implied term of trust and confidence owed to all employees has not up to now offered any significant protection. An employer has an implied right to introduce new technology into the workplace[38]. If employees continue to work with knowledge of privacy infringements – for example, CCTV or phone call monitoring – a court may infer that they have affirmed any breach of the term. An action for breach of confidence may protect against the disclosure of confidential information (eg. health information) about employees to third parties but otherwise is restricted in scope[39].

If past criminal activities are an aspect of private life, then English law does little to shelter them from disclosure. The Rehabilitation of Offenders Act 1974, concerning "spent" offences, is inapplicable to sentences of more than 30 months[40] and many professions are exempt[41]. Once the provisions in Part V of the Police Act 1997 come into force, under which individuals and employers will obtain various forms of criminal conviction certificates going beyond actual convictions[42], the position will probably worsen. Pressurised by their insurers, many employers will no doubt insist on such certificates as a condition of employment.

There is, however, some drift in the opposite direction, towards recognising private interests generally and in the workplace in particular. Perhaps most significantly, the Data Protection Act 1998 applies to a wide category of information held on individuals, including that held by employers in relation to their workers. Not restricted to information held on computers, it will usually apply to information in personnel files (for example)[43]. It requires that personal data is only obtained and recorded in accordance with various principles, including that it should only be obtained for specified and lawful purposes and that the data should be adequate, relevant and not excessive, thus echoing the ECHR concepts of "in accordance with law" and proportionality. A concern with privacy is illustrated by the special protection given to what is termed "sensitive personal data", defined to include matters such as an individual's political opinions, religious belief, trade union membership, physical and mental health and sexual life[44]. It accords individuals significant rights, such as rights of access to the data and rights to prevent processing likely to cause damage or distress[45]. Expressing concern about the threats to privacy in the workplace caused by new technology, the Data Protection Registrar is to issue a code of practice on the use of personal data in employment which will introduce tighter controls on employee surveillance (eg. CCTV and e-mail), automated processing and collection of sensitive information (eg. drug, alcohol and genetic testing)[46].

Following the decision in the *Halford* case the Home Office introduced new legislation, the Regulation of Investigatory Powers Act 2000, which makes it a statutory tort to intercept communications on a private telecommunications system[47], so catching phone and e-mail monitoring by employers. Regulations will specify the circumstances in which such interception may lawfully be made in the course of business[48]. The Health and Safety (Display Screen Equipment) Regulations 1992 prohibit the use of "quantitative and qualitative" checking facilities unless the display screen operator or user has been informed of this[49].

Outside the areas covered by this legislation, the protection of privacy (however conceived) largely depends upon whether private interests happen to coincide with an interest which the law does recognise. The common law offers virtually no protection in practice against drug testing by employers, for instance. While invasive tests are technically an assault, such an action is invariably ruled out by the fact or fiction of employee consent. The tort of breach of confidence remains tied to the intimate sphere of the home and personal relationships.

Article 8 and the Human Rights Act

HOW article 8 will translate into the employment relationship in the United Kingdom is uncertain for at least three reasons. The first is that, as we have seen, the ECHR case law itself is lacking in clear reasons or principles. Whether United Kingdom courts, or the ECHR, build upon the *Niemietz* conception of private life or limit intervention in the name of the *Halford* doctrine of "reasonable expectation" is hard to say. Certainly a note of caution is required. The jurisprudence of the USA on workplace privacy, perhaps closer to the English legal tradition than the laws of European countries such as France, has had a limited effect. As one commentator puts it:

> The law remains deferential in assessing the justifications advanced by employers for invasive management practices and downgrades the value of candidates'/employees' private interests through principles such as "a reasonable expectation of privacy", "ordinary" business practices and consent[50].

But the potential for a more radical development of privacy exists, illustrated by the *Niemietz* decision. In France, for example, the incorporation of the right to privacy through article L.120-2 of the French labour code[51] has led to decisions banning blanket drug testing of employees and prohibiting the use of evidence obtained through secret surveillance in order to discipline employees[52]. Demonstrating the relatively high degree of scrutiny of management practices under French law, the cases confirm that infringements of employees' family, religious or political life must be proportionate[53].

The second source of uncertainty is that it is unclear how English courts will try to give effect to a right to privacy. As against a public authority employees whose privacy is infringed will be able to bring proceedings under s.7 of the Human Rights Act, coupled with s.6[54]. Similarly, there is little doubt that an employment tribunal, faced with a dismissal which infringes private interests of the employer and will be able, in accordance with s.3 of the Human Rights Act, to interpret s.98 of the Employment Rights Act 1996 to ensure that the test of unfairness makes it unfair to dismiss in circumstances caught by article 8. Elsewhere the position is hazy. In particular it remains to be seen what horizontal remedies will be forged for actions against private employers, and how the law will develop to protect employees who are not dismissed but continue to work. If, for example, the courts develop a new tort of a right to privacy, drawing on the hints in the *Khan* case[55], in future employees will be able to bring an action based on it when their privacy is infringed. Alternatively, the courts may seek to develop the implied duty of trust and confidence so that it gives effective protection to privacy. As one philosopher remarked in the context of whether there is life after death, one can but wait and see[56].

The third reason for uncertainty relates to the intersection of employees' privacy and management legitimations of surveillance. Each kind of surveillance technique or technology may have a justified reason for its use; but whether that is the reason it is used for in fact and whether its use is proportionate will vary from employer to employer. Take the example of compulsory drug testing. It may be introduced to protect colleagues' health and safety; or it may simply be used to monitor what are perceived as undesirable lifestyles. CCTV may be used to protect against theft; or it may be relied on just to keep tabs on the workforce. Consequently, generalisations are often impossible to make. Whether privacy is infringed and whether article 8(2) is met need to be considered in the context of the particular industry.

Against that uncertain background, predictions are necessarily tentative. Many of the areas considered below will tie in with duties under the Data Protection Act.

It is likely that English law will gradually shift to give much greater protection to decisions based on life outside work. Decisions taken on the basis of sexual life and political activities (which would also be protected under article 10 of course) are obvious candidates. The prejudices of other workers, customers or employers should not, following *Smith*, provide a sufficient justification. It may be that the courts will recognise, too, that private life should encompass more controversial areas, such as criminal records and drug taking. Only if an individual's past history indicates that their performance at work is likely to be affected should reasons of this sort be relied upon for dismissal or for placing the worker at a detriment.

Secret surveillance should require tighter safeguards. The Regulation of Investigatory Powers Act 2000 will regulate interceptions of communications, presumably in accordance with the principles of article 8. But surveillance is wider, extending for example to hidden cameras, secret customers and concealed listening devices. For such interferences to be in accordance with law, it seems that an employer must specify with reasonable clarity the purposes for and circumstances in which secret surveillance may be used[57]. In the absence of written policies such surveillance may fall at the first hurdle of article 8(2). In addition, it is arguable that article 8 should restrict the use of video evidence when employees are filmed at home or outside work in secret as a means (for example) of detecting malingering, just as the right to privacy has in France. Secret surveillance for one purpose (eg. to guard against theft) which gives rise to information which was used for another purpose (eg. to discipline an employee who was abusive of management) might infringe article 8 – though quite how the existing legal mechanisms would be developed here is not clear.

How the law will apply to CCTV and other forms of visual or aural surveillance which are not secret is harder to say. The Court has not yet developed any clear basis for regulating video surveillance[58]. Even based on the weak "reasonable expectation" test, some restrictions on constant surveillance may be required. As Lord Reid put it in *Post Office v Crouch*, "it is common knowledge... that every day there are periods when a worker is on his employer's premises but is not expected or required to be actually working"[59]. Surveillance of private areas, such as changing rooms, canteens and toilets, would require compelling reasons to justify it. Again article 8 may require that employers specify why surveillance is taking place and for what purposes the information obtained will be used to satisfy the requirement of "in accordance with law". Parallel duties are imposed under the Data Protection Act: it requires, for instance, that the reasons for which data are collected are specified and that the data is relevant and not excessive to those purposes[60]. In this manner the purposes of surveillance will be exposed to more open scrutiny than they have been hitherto.

Drug testing will also be the subject of closer scrutiny, since most tests will engage article 8[61]. Instead of the simple defence of consent to assault (or disciplinary action for failing to consent to the test), employers will probably be forced to explain clearly the reasons for such tests and to demonstrate how they are proportionate. Too weak a connection between performance and the drugs for which testing is made will mean that article 8(2) is not met. (In many cases the Data Protection Act will guard against unauthorised disclosure, particularly if the tests reveal health problems[62]). The French case law shows the degree of scrutiny of management practices which may be required.

The collection and disclosure of information about workers – and there has been an explosion in the amount and kind of information employers collect – will also receive protection from article 8, again running in tandem with the duties under the Data Protection Act. It may be that English law will gradually reach the position under French law, by which personal information may only be collected if it is necessary for assessing professional competence[62]. At the same time the duties to disclose information which the Court has found flow from article 8 may require the adoption of novel legal duties. At present an employer is not obliged to inform its workers about, for instance, the information it holds on them – there is no requirement of disclosure under the Data Protection Act, only a right of access – and what are the purposes of its techniques of monitoring. Because article 8 requires in some circumstances the disclosure of information so that individuals know how their private interests are being or may be infringed[64], it may be that some kind of duty of disclosure will be developed as part of the contract of employment.

Article 8 may well also have some restraining influence on the numerous methods of surveillance, often assisted by technological developments, used by employers and which will appear in the future. Some of these border on the bizarre. Chair sensors and infrared badges have appeared in the USA. Secret customers are a growing feature of many service industries, such as hotels. New computer systems offer the possibility of an intensification of the monitoring of employees (eg. through network office systems). Genetic testing will almost certainly be used by some employers in the future. It is clear that some of these techniques potentially will engage private interests, though in some cases the issue is open to doubt (does an infrared badge, tracking a worker at work, engage article 8?).

No doubt all these technologies may have a legitimate aim; but there is a risk that they will be used for other, illegitimate purposes. It is to protect against the possibly damaging effects these new practices and the intensification of monitoring systems in general that a progressive conception of privacy coupled with close attention to the test of proportionality are needed. It is to be hoped that the courts, drawing on the ability of the ECHR to change in line with modern developments, will recognise the importance of working relationships as an aspect of private life and ensure that article 8 offers some shelter from the emergence of working practices based on "hyper-surveillance". But it would be foolish to see this as an inevitable development or even a likely one. Conflicts about technology, it can confidently be predicated, will not be subsumed in the legal process.

Conclusion

EXACTLY how article 8 will effect the workplace is a very open question. In particular it is not clear how private interests are to be reconciled with employer property rights and management prerogative. A more sophisticated analysis of the justifications for the protection of private interests is needed than the one so far developed by the Court.

Such an analysis will need to recognise that privacy is perhaps no more than an aspect of deeper rights: rights to dignity and autonomy. Constant monitoring and forms of intrusive surveillance diminish workers' dignity and, at the same time, inhibit their ability to decide for themselves how they will, individually and collectively, run their lives. That deeper values are at stake is neatly put by an American judge in a case concerned with whether or not the installation of CCTV on the production floor violated a contractual provision requiring the maintenance of conditions beneficial to workers:

> The [constant filming by CCTV] is not only personally repugnant to employees but it has such an inhibiting effect as to prevent the employees from performing their work with confidence

and ease. Every employee has occasion to pause in the course of his work, to take a breather, to scratch his head, to yawn, or otherwise be himself without affecting his work. An employee, with reason, would hesitate at all times to so behave, if his every action is being recorded on TV. To have workers constantly televised is... reminiscent of the era depicted by Charlie Chaplin in "Modern Times" and constitutes... an affront to the dignity of man[65].

If English courts evolve out of article 8 rights to autonomy and dignity, then it may begin to have a radical effect on the working relationship. But it is fair to say that the existing case-law on the ECHR only hints at such a development. The tradition of deference to property rights in the common law world favours a narrow conception of privacy, tied to interests connected with the home and intimate life outside work, rather than a conception which begins to undermine management prerogative over monitoring systems. On that narrow conception, the right to individual and collective privacy depends upon how much privacy at work management is content to allow. There is a kind of perverse logic to this: the more workers are subject to constant intrusive surveillance and the less autonomous they are at work, the easier it is on a conservative analysis to argue that they leave behind their private interests when they enter the sphere of work.

Dignity and autonomy are also concepts which go beyond article 8, even when stretched to its conceptual limits. It is notable, for instance, that a collective dimension is largely lacking from article 8, save for its passing recognition of a right to develop relationships with others. By contrast the ILO, in its Code of Practice on the Protection of Workers' Personal Data[66], requires that workers representatives are informed and consulted about the introduction or modification of automated or electronic monitoring systems, and the purposes, contents and manner of using questionnaires and tests.

For these reasons and accepting always that article 8 is capable of more radical development, it would be poor strategy to anticipate that article 8 will replace individual and collective struggles against forms of intensive and unwelcome surveillance and monitoring. With that in mind the Institute of Employment Rights has produced a draft Code of Practice on surveillance at work which is included as an appendix to this chapter. While the Code aims to ensure that work practices comply with article 8, it is also designed to include rights to collective information, consultation and participation which in the long run offer a better pragmatic means of resisting management practices which infringe workers' dignity and autonomy. Article 8 is a means but not the end.

Notes

1 See S Benhabib, "Models of Public Space" in C Calhoun (ed), *Habermas and the Public Sphere* (1992), at pp 91-92.

2 See J Michael, "Privacy" in D Harris and S Joseph (eds), *The International Covenant on Civil and Political Rights and United Kingdom Law* (1995), pp 267-272.

3 See Lord Chancellor's Department, *Infringement of Privacy* (1993).

4 Is there a right to be left alone at work, for example? And in the home, is there a right to be free from pollution and noise?

5 See Report of the Commission on Privacy (Cmnd 5012, 1972).

6 (1992) 16 EHRR 97, at p 111.

7 See *Peters v The Netherlands* (1994) 77A DR 75 (compulsory urine sample from prisoner); *X v Austria* (1979) 18 DR 154 (blood test pursuant to court order).

8 See *Dudgeon v United Kingdom* (1981) 4 EHRR 149 (criminalisation of homosexual conduct in Northern Ireland breached article 8(1)); but cf *Laskey, Jaggard and Brown v United Kingdom* (1997) 24 EHRR 39 (criminalisation of sado-masochism justifiable under article 8(2) because it involved physical harm). In the "gays in the military" case the United Kingdom government conceded that dismissal on grounds of sexuality amounted to an interference with the right to respect for private life: see *Smith v United Kingdom* [1999] IRLR 734.

9 See *Friedl v Austria*, A/305-B Comm Rep (1995); unreported.

10 See *Rayner v United Kingdom* (1986) 47 DR 5; *Guerra v Italy* (1998) 26 EHRR 357.

11 See *Klass v Federal Republic of Germany* (1978) 2 EHRR 214. See also the *Halford* decision, discussed below.

12 Application 9702/82.

13 (1998) 26 EHRR 357. See similarly *Gaskin v United Kingdom* (1989) 12 EHRR 36: article 8 breached when adult formerly in care not given access to his social services file.

14 See *McGinley and Egan v United Kingdom* (1999) 27 EHRR 1.

15 (1992) 16 EHRR 97, at p 112.

16 See *Arrondelle v United Kingdom* (1982) 26 DR 5: noise from Gatwick airport.

17 See *Klass v Federal Republic of Germany, op cit; Malone v United Kingdom* (1985) 7 EHRR 14.

18 See D J Harris, M O'Boyle and C Warbrick, *Law of the European Convention on Human Rights* (1995), p 320.

19 See *X and Y v Netherlands* (1985) EHRR 235.

20 See *Hokannen v Finland* (1994) 19 EHRR 139.

21 *Whiteside v United Kingdom* (1994) 76A DR 80.

22 See *Guerra v Italy op cit.*

23 See *Malone v United Kingdom, op cit*, and *Kruslin v France* A 176-A (1990).

24 *Huvig v France* (1990), 12 EHRR 528, at p 545.

25 See *Smith v United Kingdom, op cit*, and *Kara v United Kingdom*, Application No. 36528/97.

26 *Op cit* at p 111.

27 (1997) 24 EHRR 523.

28 At p 543. For discussion, see J Craig and H Oliver, "The Right to Privacy in

the Workplace: Should the Private Sector be Concerned?" (1998) 27 ILJ 49.

29 (1997) 24 EHRR 523, at p 544

30 See eg. *National Treasury Employees Union v Von Raab,* 489 US 656 (1989): compulsory drug testing of all customs employees who applied for transfer of promotion permissible because they could reasonably expect inquiry into their fitness and probity. The case is discussed in J Craig, *Privacy and Employment Law* (1999), at pp 65-68.

31 [1999] IRLR 734.

32 *ibid.*

33 *ibid.*

34 *ibid.*

35 Application No. 36528/97.

36 See *R v Khan* [1997] AC 558, per Lord Browne-Wilkinson at p 571. On the general absence of such a right see *Kaye v Robertson* [1991] FSR 62, and cf *Helewell v Chief Constable of Derbyshire* [1995] 1 WLR 804.

37 *Saunders v Scottish National Camps Association Ltd* [1980] IRLR 174.

38 See *Cresswell v Inland Revenue* [1984] ICR 508.

39 See eg. *Helewell v Chief Constable of Derbyshire, op cit*: in context of photography person must be engaged in a "private act" for doctrine to apply. On the disclosure of information, see *Dalgleish v Lothian Borders Police Board* [1991] IRLR 422.

40 Rehabilitation of Offenders Act 1974, s.5

41 See the Rehabilitation of Offenders Act 1974 (Exceptions) Order 1975, SI 1975/1023.

42 A criminal record certificate can include cautions (s.113) and an enhanced criminal record certificate can include wider relevant information held by the police (s.114).

43 See the definition of data in Data Protection Act 1998, s.1(1).

44 See Data Protection Act 1998, s.2 and the conditions applicable to processing in Schedule 3 (which apply in addition to the eight principles in Schedule 1). See further the Data Processing (Processing of Sensitive Personal Data) Order 2000, SI 2000/417.

45 See Data Protection Act 1998, ss.7, 9 and 10.

46 See Data Protection Registrar. Press Release, 14 July 1999.

47 See Data Protection Act 1998, s.1(3). Previously only public networks were covered by the Interception of Communications Act 1985.

48 See Data Protection Act 1998, s.4(2).

49 SI 1992/2792. See reg 3 and Schedule 1 para 4(b).

50 See Craig, *Privacy and Employment Law, op cit,* p 84.

51 Law of 31 December 1992. See generally J Rivero and J Savatier, *Droit du Travail* (1993).

52 See *Ministre du Travail v Societe Peintures Corona* (1980) 6 Dr Soc 317 and Noecel Cass. Soc.20 November 1991 (RDS 1992(2), 77). The cases are discussed in Craig, *op cit,* at pp 92-94.

53 See Riverao and Savatier, *Droit du Travail, op cit,* pp 536-7.

54 This may not apply to "mixed function" bodies in relation to their employment decisions: see Human Rights Act 1998 s.6(5).

55 *R v Khan* [1997] AC 558.

56 Or, as he put it, not see.

57 See *Huvig v France op cit*, at p 545. Note that the Data Processing (Processing of Sensitive Personal Data) Order 2000, *op cit*, permits some forms of processing without an employee's consent where it is (for example) in the substantial public interest and for detecting an unlawful act, and where seeking the employee's consent would prejudice those purposes.

58 See S Naismith, "Photographs, Privacy and Freedom of Expression" [1996] EHRLR 150.

59 [1974] ICR 378

60 See Schedule 1, second and third principles. See too the "fair processing code" in paras 1-4 of Part II of the Schedule.

61 *Peters v The Netherlands* (1994) 77A DR 75 (compulsory urine sample from prisoner), *X v Austria* (1979) 18 DR 154 (blood test pursuant to court order).

62 See First Schedule, para 1(b) and seventh principle.

63 See article L 121-6, L. 900-4-1 and L.900-6. The methods used must be disclosed to the individual: see article L.121-8. See generally, Rivero and Savatier, *op cit*, at pp 539-40.

64 See *Guerra v Italy op cit.*

65 *Re Electronics Instrument Company and International Union of Electrical Workers* (1965) LA 563 (Delaney)

66 Adopted at the Meeting of Experts at Geneva, 1-7 October 1996.

Appendix

Draft Code of Practice on Surveillance of Workers

Introduction

1. This Code of Practice offers guidance on the use of surveillance at work: when it should be used, the procedures for its introduction, and controls over the use of the information obtained. It is intended to help employers as well as trade unions and workers in drawing up more detailed provisions applicable to particular forms of employment and particular forms of surveillance. It aims to strike a fair balance between employer use of surveillance and the workers' interests which surveillance may harm and to ensure fair procedures for the introduction of new methods of surveillance.

2. The forms of surveillance are diverse and are constantly changing with developments in technology. In addition, the same form of surveillance may serve different purposes and affect different interests in individual workplaces. For some workers CCTV, for example, may be a useful protection against assaults, while for others it may be seen as a serious infringement of privacy. For these reasons, this Code aims to set out basic principles of fairness rather than laying down specific duties applicable to particular forms of surveillance, although some practical examples are given in the Code.

The meaning of surveillance

3. It is impossible to define all the forms of surveillance and this Code does not attempt to do so. It is intended to apply to methods used by employers to monitor workers, whether while they are working or outside work, and the collection and use of information about workers. These

include the use of computers and other technologies to monitor and assess performance; drug testing; health screening; the use of CCTV, videos and other forms of visual or sound recording equipment; monitoring phone calls and other forms of communication such as e-mail; the use of psychometric and personality testing; the use of private detectives and secret customers; and methods of tracking workers. The list is not exhaustive, of course, and the principles of the Code should assist in ensuring a fair balance in the use of new forms of surveillance (eg. genetic testing).

Legal/international standards

4. There is growing legal and international recognition of the need to protect privacy, and the potential for harm of some new techniques of surveillance. The law already offers some control of surveillance of workers and the information it generates. Recent and forthcoming legislation will impose tighter regulations. Some of these duties are the following:

5. The Data Protection Act 1998 controls the processing of information which is organised in such a way that specific information relating to an individual is readily accessible. Most personnel and other employer records are therefore caught. The Act applies especially strict duties in relation to the processing of "sensitive personal data", such as an individual's political opinions, religious beliefs, trade union membership, physical or mental health and criminal record. A Code of Practice is to be issued under s.53(1) of the Act imposing specific controls on the use of information relating to employees.

6. The Human Rights Act 1998 gives effect to the right to privacy in Article 8 of the European Convention on Human Rights. It has already been established that the right to privacy extends to the workplace, so that it can be infringed eg. by tapping workers' telephones. As a consequence this Act will no doubt have an important effect on surveillance by employers.

7. Regulation 3 and Schedule 1 paragraph 4(b) of the Health and Safety (Display Screen Equipment) Regulations 1992 prohibits the use of quantitative or qualitative checking facilities without the knowledge of computer operators or users.

8. A Code of Practice is to be issued under s.122 of the Police Act 1997, regulating the use by employers of criminal conviction certificates.

9. The Regulation of Investigatory Powers Bill 2000 will make the interception of communications on private or public systems a statutory tort, actionable by the sender or recipient. It will apply to interceptions by employers of workers' telephone calls or e-mails, for example.

10. International standards additional to Article 8 of the European Convention on Human Rights, include the Code of Practice on the Protection of Workers' Personal Data issued by the International Labour Organisation and the European Directive on data protection which led to the Data Protection Act 1998. Other countries, such as France, already recognise the right to privacy at work.

11. The principles and guidance in this Code draw upon these international standards. They are also intended to assist in ensuring that the existing and future legal duties under domestic law are met.

The importance of the Principles and Guidance

12. There is growing evidence that some forms of surveillance can have damaging effects on worker health, dignity and morale. This is especially so in relation to workplaces which use intensive and constant forms of workplace monitoring or workplaces in which workers suspect they may be the target of secret methods of surveillance. With the arrival of the Human Rights Act 1998, some forms of surveillance (particularly those carried out in secret) risk breaching the right to privacy.

13. Of course surveillance often fulfills important functions. It may serve the interests of efficiency, protect against fraud, be used as a method of training or assessing performance, protect workers' health and safety, or be required to meet other legal duties. But its potential for harm and for infringing privacy demands that care is taken to ensure that it is required for a legitimate purpose and that its use does not breach basic standards of fairness. The principles and guidance set out below aim to assist in meeting that end, and to ensure that forms of surveillance do not infringe the Human Rights Act.

The Key Principles

14. The key principles for guaranteeing fairness and protecting against infringements of privacy are:

15. *Transparency.* Save in relation to those rare circumstances in which secret surveillance is justified, workers are entitled to know what forms of surveillance are being used and what they are being used for. Hidden surveillance or the use of the information it produces for covert purposes destroys trust in the workplace.

16. *Consent.* Supporting the principle of openness is the principle of consent. If a worker is to be the subject of a particular form of monitoring, he or she should have specifically agreed to it, either through a clause in a contract or through a separate form of agreement.

17. *Consultation.* So far as is reasonably practicable, new forms of surveillance should not be introduced without meeting standards of procedural fairness. Informing and consulting with workers and/or their representatives is the most appropriate means of ensuring that surveillance is appropriate for a particular workplace. Where a union is recognised, consultation should be with it. Consultation is already a legal duty in relation to the introduction of new technologies which may affect health and safety; the same should apply to new techniques of surveillance.

18. *Private Spaces.* Worker privacy and dignity requires that workers are not constantly subject to surveillance or in fear that they may be. All workers should be guaranteed areas, means of communication and periods dur-

ing the day in which they can be sure they will not be monitored.

19. *Proportionality.* In keeping with the principles of Article 8 of the European Convention on Human Rights, a fair balance should be struck between the purposes of surveillance and the protection of worker privacy, dignity and autonomy. To that end: (1) surveillance should meet a legitimate aim; (2) it should be necessary to meet that aim; and (3) it should be the least harmful means of meeting that aim.

20. Below is set out more detailed guidance on how these principles operate in practice.

Information and consultation

21. *Information.* Workers and their representatives should be informed in advance of any proposal to introduce new forms of surveillance into the workplace or to change the uses which are made of existing methods (including any changes in the use of the information generated by surveillance). If, for example, in the past an employer has monitored workers' phone calls as part of their training but intends in the future to use the information for other purposes (eg. disciplinary), the workforce should be informed of this as part of good industrial relations practice.

22. *Consultation.* For similar reasons the employer should consult with the workers and their representatives about any new forms of surveillance or changes in the methods of existing use. The consultation should be with a view to reaching agreement and should include many of the topics listed below – for example, the purposes of the surveillance, the uses which will be made of the information so generated and individual rights of access to that information.

23. *Regular information.* In addition to informing workers when changes are made to surveillance, employers should also inform them at regular intervals what information is held on them, the purposes for which it is held and to whom it may be disclosed.

Consent

24. *Specific agreement.* It should be a prior requirement of subjecting a worker to surveillance that he or she has specifically agreed to it. This may be through a clause in a contract of employment or through another form of written agreement as negotiated with a union. Such agreements will assist in focussing attention on the need for information.

25. *Content of agreement.* To be meaningful the agreement should give sufficient detail for the workers to know what they are agreeing to. It should set out what form the surveillance takes and in what circumstances it is to be used, what are its purposes, and what will be done with the information produced. If the surveillance or refusal to submit to surveillance (eg. refusal to submit to a drug test) could give rise to disciplinary consequences, it is particularly important that this is clearly specified.

A fair balance

26. The following guidelines seek to ensure that surveillance is proportionate, striking a fair balance between serving lawful employer aims and the protection of workers' interests.

27. *Legitimate purpose relevant to employment.* Surveillance should pursue a legitimate interest of the employer which is part of its lawful business. Such interests include efficient production, guarding against fraud or theft, the protection of health and safety, and fulfilling duties imposed by law. These interests should be directly relevant to the employment of the worker and the business for which he or she is employed. The use of surveillance as a means of "fishing" for information – to see what it may turn up – is not a legitimate aim. On the other hand, surveillance which is necessary to protect important interests of other workers or the public clearly does serve such an aim. An example would be the use of alcohol or drug testing on those employees who occupy safety-critical functions, the impaired performance of which may pose a threat to worker or public safety.

28. *Irrelevant purposes.* Obtaining information about workers' out of work activities is not a legitimate employer aim, unless that information is directly relevant to their performance at work. Information about sexuality or political, religious or other beliefs will rarely (if ever) be justified for this reason. The same applies to data on trade union membership or activities, which should only be collected if the individual worker and union agree. Information about criminal convictions should not be obtained as a matter of course, but should be subject to the same test of direct relevance: the employer should consider the nature of the offence, the length of time which has elapsed and whether the person has reformed. Health information should only be collected if it is necessary for tightly circumscribed purposes, such as assessing fitness for work, meeting legal duties or determining entitlements to sickness benefits.

29. *Least restrictive means.* The form of surveillance adopted should be necessary to the end pursued. If there is an alternative and reasonably practicable method of meeting the same goal which does not infringe significant worker interests such as privacy or health to the same extent, that method should be adopted. Suppose workers' phone calls are monitored to assist in training them in their communications with customers, but that on occasions the supervisor will overhear private phone conversations. Informing the workers of the period during which their particular phone calls will be monitored, or providing the worker with some other means of knowing which calls will be overheard, may meet the same end but with a reduced impact on privacy. By the same token, surveillance should be restricted to those workers or categories of workers necessary to meet the goal. If drug testing of workers is justified to protect the health and safety of others, the employer should test only those workers whose performance is reasonably likely to affect others' safety. Forms of continuous monitoring will often infringe this principle.

30. *Private spaces and times.* Workers should be guaranteed spaces and means of communication where and times when they are free from intrusive surveillance. If CCTV is used in the workplace, workers should be provided with areas in which they can talk and relax where they are not observed. Similarly, workers subjected to phone monitoring should be provided with private phones for those occasions when they need to make private phone calls. Save in the most exceptional circumstances, for example to protect against assault, workers should not be subject to surveillance during meal and other breaks from work. Wherever practicable, there should be regular breaks from methods of continuous monitoring.

31. *Use only for that purpose.* Information obtained through surveillance should only be used for the purposes which justify the surveillance in the first place.

32. *Regular assessment.* To ensure compliance with the above guidance, employers should regularly review their practices as a means of restricting the intrusive effects of surveillance and of redressing any infringements of privacy.

33. *Training of supervisors/processors.* Employers should ensure that those who are responsible for surveillance and for processing the information obtained as a result are aware of their responsibilities and duties. These persons should, for example, be subject to a duty of confidentiality in relation to confidential or private information about workers, such as health information.

Secret surveillance

34. Forms of secret surveillance include phone interceptions or tapping, bugs, hidden cameras and secret customers. Because this form of surveillance will frequently individuals' rights to privacy, its use should be tightly circumscribed.

35. Secret surveillance should only be permissible if there is a genuinely held suspicion based on reasonable grounds of crime or serious wrongdoing. It should not be used as a means of assisting in obtaining information for a disciplinary hearing alone unless that disciplinary matter amounts to a crime or serious wrongdoing. It should never be used to "fish" for information without a reasonable suspicion.

36. The information obtained through secret surveillance should not be used for any purpose other than that which justified its collection in the first place, unless that information discloses a crime or serious wrongdoing. In particular, the information should not be used for disciplinary purposes.

37. Where practicable, employers should still inform and consult with unions and workers about the use of secret surveillance. An employer may be able to make clear that secret surveillance may be used in the case of certain events occurring (eg. repeated theft) without undermining its purpose.

Chapter 2 : Appendix

The use of the information

38. Surveillance inevitably gives rise to information, typically about identifiable individuals and often of a sensitive nature. The following principles seek to ensure protection of the individual's interests while recognising the legitimacy of employers obtaining information. Employers are reminded of the duties under the Data Protection Act 1998 which in many respects are more detailed than this guidance.

39. *Security.* Information on workers, and particularly information which may contain details about an individual's private life, should be secure. The employer should protect against unauthorised access or unintended disclosure so far as is reasonably practicable.

40. *Rights of access.* Workers should be entitled to know what information is held on them and to have access to it. To support this right in practice employers should keep workers regularly informed of the sort of information which it holds about them and what use is made of it, even without requests from the workers (see above). Workers should be entitled to have access to the information during working hours and to be accompanied by a union representative or colleague of their choosing. They should be entitled to take copies of such records. No charging for access should be made and copying should be free or at reasonable rates.

41. *Inaccurate information.* Workers should be entitled to insist that inaccurate or out-of-date information be amended or deleted. Where the information consists of matters of opinion, it is good practice to permit a worker to add comments of his own disagreeing with that opinion, to be retained with the original information.

42. *Health information.* Information about an individual's health is particularly sensitive and its disclosure can cause great harm. It should be processed only by persons who are bound by duties of medical confidentiality. If practicable it should be kept separate from other information.

43. *Restrictions on communication to third parties.* Personal data should not be disclosed to third parties without the worker's consent unless it is necessary to meet legal duties, to protect against serious harm or for a purpose necessary for the individual employment relationship.

44. *Limit on period of retention.* Information on workers should be retained only for so long as is justified by the purpose for which it was obtained. It should not be stored indefinitely unless this is a legal requirement.

Chapter 3

Article 10 and the right to freedom of expression: workers ungagged?

Aileen McColgan

ARTICLE 10 of the European Convention on Human Rights provides that: 'Everyone has the right to freedom of expression...'. Employment-related restrictions upon freedom of expression are commonplace, ranging from dress-codes through express or implicit prohibitions on the display of sectarian, racist or sexist material, to obligations of confidentiality and fidelity imposed both by express contractual terms and by the common law. Some restrictions are regulated by statutory provisions – action taken by employers to suppress advocacy in favour of union membership is prohibited by the Trade Union and Labour Relations (Consolidation) Act 1992, for example[1], and some forms of dress code will breach the provisions of the Sex Discrimination Act 1975 or the Race Relations Act 1976 (further discussed below). But domestic law, both common law and statute, preserves a wide measure of managerial prerogative in this area as in others[2].

The enactment in domestic law of the right to freedom of expression provides a possible basis for challenge to a variety of workplace practices. The main concern of this chapter is with the protection of confidential information and, in particular, the problems surrounding 'whistleblowing'. But in order to give a flavour of the scope for challenge provided by the incorporation of article 10, and the limitations inherent within that provision, some consideration will be given to the issue of dress-codes.

Dress codes and the Human Rights Act

PRIOR to the implementation of the Human Rights Act, dress codes could be challenged in the domestic courts only where they discriminated directly on grounds of race or sex; where they discriminated indirectly and unjustifiably on either of these grounds; or where their enforcement resulted in a potentially unfair dismissal (the actual or constructive dismissal of an employee with adequate qualifying service who had not exceeded the normal retirement age and who had not disqualified him or herself from unfair dismissal protection by, for example, engaging in unofficial industrial action).

Decisions such as those of the EAT in *Schmidt v Austicks Bookshops Ltd*[3] and, more recently, of the Court of Appeal in *Smith v Safeway plc*[4], illustrate the difficulties of proving unlawful discrimination even in the case of dress codes which differentiate between men and women. And where dress codes impact on employees' sexual orientation (as in *Boychuck v Symons*), or disadvantage those whose religious affiliation is not sufficiently connected with their racial origin to qualify for protection under the Race Relations Act 1976 (as in *Dawkins v Department of the Environment*[5]), the only domestic protection available prior to incorporation was that provided by the unfair dismissal legislation[6].

Even where the expression forming the subject matter of the dispute was one connected with a worker's religion and that religion was sufficiently linked to 'race' to qualify for protection under the Race Relations Act, that protection is generally subject to the uncertainties of indirect discrimination. In *Kang v R F Brookes Ltd*[7], for example, a tribunal ruled that a prohibition on the wearing of jewellery did not, when applied to prevent the wearing by a Sikh woman of a bracelet of religious significance, contravene that Act. Though Sikhs are accepted as a 'racial' as well as a religious group (*Mandla v Dowell Lee*[8]), the tribunal found that only six per cent of Sikhs observed the religious obligation to wear the bracelet and that the proportion of Sikhs able to comply with the no-jewellery requirement was not, accordingly, significantly smaller than that of non-Sikhs (100 per cent) who could so comply.

The potential significance of incorporation for these and other issues of freedom of expression (further discussed below) lies in the fact that workers (as well as others) may challenge interference with their freedom of expression in the domestic courts. This is not, of course, to say that such challenges will necessarily succeed – the limitations on article 10, and its interpretation by the European Court of Human Rights (whose jurisprudence must be taken into account in the application of the Human Rights Act), are considered below. But the Human Rights Act provides at least the possibility of direct challenge where the employer is the State, s.6 providing that 'It is unlawful for a public authority to act in a way which is incompatible with a Convention right' save where primary legislation requires such action. Perhaps of more significance in the long term are the interpretive obligations the Act imposes on the judiciary both in relation to statute and to the common law, and regardless of whether the respondent to legal action is the State or (in this context) a private sector employer[9]. Section 6 defines 'public authority' to include courts and tribunals, thus rendering unlawful judicial decision-making in breach of the Convention provisions[10]. Further, s.3 provides that 'So far as it is possible to do so, primary legislation and subordinate legislation must be read and given effect in a way which is compatible with the Convention rights'.

It is at least possible that article 10, read in conjunction with article 14 and article 8 (where the issue concerns sexual orientation) or article 9 (where it concerns religion) will result in increased protection of employees in situations such as those which arose in *Schmidt, Boychuck, Dawkins* and *Kang*. In the first of these cases it could be argued that article 10 read with article 14 ('The enjoyment of the rights and freedoms set forth in this Convention shall be secured without discrimination on any ground such as sex, race, colour, language, religion, political or other opinion, national or social origin, association with a national minority, property, birth or other status') demands that the Sex Discrimination Act 1975 be interpreted to preclude the imposition of a requirement that women workers wear skirts. Such a requirement could be seen as demanding that women present themselves in a stereotypically female fashion which has overtones of sexual availability.

In the case of *Boychuck* it could be argued that a prohibition on a lesbian making her sexual orientation visible through the wearing of a badge interfered with her article 10 rights read with article 8 ('Everyone has the right to respect for his private and family life...'). In *Smith v United Kingdom* and in *Lustig-Prean v United Kingdom* the European Court of Human Rights ruled that dismissals pursuant to the ban on gays in the British military breached the applicants' right to a private life[11]. This could be taken to indicate that the Convention prohibits discrimination based on sexual orientation (though it is suggested below that this is probably an over-expansive interpretation of the judgments). It might be difficult to run an argument that the restriction of manifest display of sexual orientation, as distinct from the attachment of penalty to its fact, raised issues of 'private life'. On the other hand, unless *Smith* and *Lustig-Prean* are read to provide protection only in respect of the bare fact of sexual orientation, as distinct from its behavioural manifestation (which would include, for example, the forming of sexual relationships and the exchange of physical displays of affection) article 8 should, perhaps, be read to require (subject to the exceptions thereto) some form of protected 'space' around the person which would surely extend at least to that, such as the display of badges, which is within the sphere of another ECHR provision (article 10). If this were accepted, the Human Rights Act may provide protection against detriment meted out by the State itself, and would require that the courts interpret existing legislation (whether the unfair dismissal provisions of the Employment Rights Act 1996 or the definition of sex discrimination under the Sex Discrimination Act), so far as possible, to provide a remedy for the infringement of the applicant's 'Convention rights' by private individuals[12].

Most straightforward of the examples mentioned above are those in *Dawkins* and in *Kang*. Article 9 provides that 'Everyone has the right to freedom of thought, conscience and religion; this right includes freedom... either alone or in community with others and in public or private, to manifest his religion or belief, in worship, teaching, practice and observance'. Article 9, like articles 8 and 10, is subject to exceptions (further discussed below). But, taken with article 10, it does suggest that some protection is required in respect of the outward expression, whether through the wearing of Rastafarian dreadlocks (as in *Dawkins*) or of a piece of jewellery (as in *Kang*). How that protection might be provided will depend, again, on whether the respondent is the State or a private sector employer and whether the plaintiff has been dismissed. If this is the case, a remedy might be made available by a finding of unfair dismissal under the Employment Rights Act. In other cases, a purposive approach might be taken to the interpretation of 'racial group' or 'substantially smaller proportion' under the Race Relations Act. This would not be capable of interpretation to cover all religious groups and, in the case of an English Catholic nun refused employment in the private sector on the grounds of her insistence on wearing a veil, it is hard to see how the Human Rights Act might assist. It would be possible for such an applicant to challenge to the European Court of Human Rights the State's failure adequately to safeguard her article 9 and article 10 rights. But, as we shall see, the approach of the Court to positive obligations and, in particular, to employment-related cases, would render success unlikely in that sphere.

Employment and the ECHR

THE discussion above is intended to give some introduction to the possibilities of incorporation. Here it is useful to consider in a little more depth the approach of the Convention organs (the European Court of Human Rights and, until recently, the European Commission of Human Rights[13]) to employment-related cases concerned with article 10. It is useful to note at this point that the limitations here discussed will impact on the interpretive obligations imposed on the domestic courts (for example, in determining a claim under the Race Relations Act 1976 or the Employment Rights Act 1996, above or, below, a claim at common law). Section 2 of the Human Rights Act provides that 'A court or tribunal determining a question which has arisen in connection with a Convention right must take into account', *inter alia*, European Court of Human Rights and European Commission of Human Rights decisions.

The first limb of article 10 has been mentioned above. The second goes on to provide that:

The exercise of these freedoms, since it carries with it duties and responsibilities, may be subject to such formalities, conditions, restrictions or penalties as are prescribed by law and are necessary in a democratic society, in the interests of national security, territorial integrity or public safety, for the prevention of disorder or crime, for the protection of health or morals, for the protection of the reputation or rights of others, for preventing the disclosure of information received in confidence, or for maintaining the authority and impartiality of the judiciary.

It is clear that the right to freedom of expression is not unlimited, that it carries with it 'duties and responsibilities' and that it is subject to exceptions, particularly relevant in the employment sphere, relating to the protection of 'the reputation or rights of others' and of 'information received in confidence'. The approach taken by the Convention organs to article 10(2) are considered below. First, however, it is useful to address a much more fundamental limitation on the application of article 10 and other ECHR provisions to the employment sphere.

Establishing an 'interference'

In *Glasenapp v Germany*[14] and in *Kosiek v Germany* the Strasbourg Court rejected complaints made under article 10 by a left-wing and a right-wing teacher respectively who were dismissed because of their politics. In each case the Court ruled that no article 10 right had been interfered with, permanent positions having been denied them because they failed to meet the 'personal qualifications' for appointment to the 'civil service' (such qualifications including, in Germany, commitment to 'the principles of the free democratic constitutional system' of West Germany and the non-membership of any organisation 'actively opposed to those principles').

The decisions in *Glasenapp* and in *Kosiek* turned in part on the exclusion from the ECHR of any right of access to the public service (including teaching jobs – *Glasenapp* and *Kosiek* and, in the United Kingdom, *Ahmad v United Kingdom*[15]). But those decisions required a very broad interpretive approach by the courts to the scope of 'access'. Both applicants had actually been dismissed from posts, albeit during their probationary periods. Further, the Court's rulings that the restrictions imposed did not even amount to a interference (justifiable or otherwise) with the applicants' rights to freedom of expression (rather to 'personal qualifications' for the particular jobs) points to a huge gap in the protection afforded to workers by the ECHR. It suggests that access to public sector jobs could turn, without breach of the ECHR, on satisfaction of 'personal qualifications' relating, for example, to personal appearance, or willingness to work particular hours.

Of even more general importance are the decisions of the European Commission of Human Rights in *Ahmad v United Kingdom* and in *Stedman v United Kingdom*[16]. These applications concerned article 9 challenges to employer rules which prevented employees from complying with their religious obligations. In both cases the Commission ruled the complaints inadmissible on the grounds that no interference with the relevant right had occurred, the employees having voluntarily 'contracted-out' of protection by undertaking the employment in question[17]. In *Ahmad* the Commission ruled that a Moslem teacher who was refused time off to attend the Mosque on a Friday afternoon 'remained free to resign if and when he found that his teaching obligations conflicted with his religious duties'. And in *Stedman* the Commission ruled that a woman sacked for refusing, on religious grounds, to agree to have her contractual terms varied to require Sunday working had been dismissed for 'failing to agree to work certain hours rather than her religious belief as such and was free to resign and did in effect resign from her employment'. In neither case did the Commission accept that there had been any interference with the article 9 right[18].

This is not to say that workers have never succeeded in establishing employment-related violations of their ECHR rights. *Vogt v Germany*[19], for example, concerned a challenge to the dismissal from her teaching post of an active member of the German Communist Party who, like *Glasenapp* and *Kosiek*, denied that her political affiliations prevented her from fulfilling the 'personal' qualifications for her position. In *Vogt* the Court rejected the German government's argument that the dispute concerned recruitment to the public service, rather than an interference with the rights protected by article 10. It distinguished *Glasenapp* and *Kosiek* on the grounds that *Vogt* had had permanent status prior to her dismissal and that, therefore, 'there was indeed an interference with the exercise of the right protected by article 10)[20].

Kosiek, *Glasenapp*, *Ahmad* and *Vogt* all mounted challenges to action taken by the State itself, albeit in its role as employer. Only the State can appear as respondent in the ECHR. But the Convention organs have accepted that at least some of the its provisions impose obligations on the State to secure the protected rights against violations by private individuals (including private sector employers), and challenge can be made to the State's failure so to do. In *Young, James & Webster* the Commission (with which the Court agreed) stated that 'there are articles of the Convention which oblige the State to protect individual rights even against the action of others... Art. 11 is such a provision as far as dismissal on the basis of union activity or as a sanction for not joining a specific trade union is concerned... the State is responsible under the Convention if its legal system makes such dismissal lawful'[21]. In *Stedman*, too, the Commission accepted that, had an interference with the applicant's article 9 rights been found on the assumption that she had been employed by the State, some protective obligations would arise even in the case of private sector employment[22].

Justifying employment-related interferences

Assuming that an interference with article 10 rights has been established, the question which arises concerns whether any such interference is (a) prescribed by law (b) in pursuit of a legitimate aim and (c) necessary in a democratic society for the pursuit of that aim, this in turn requiring an assessment of the proportionality of the interference with the end pursued.

The first of these requirements has not given rise to any significant difficulties in employment-related cases, extending as it does to cover that which is permitted (the disciplinary powers of employers) as well as that which is expressly provided for. The approach taken by the Convention organs to (b) has been less than rigorous in employment related cases. Article 10(2), as we saw above, provides an apparently closed list of the ends in pursuit of which freedom of expression may be curtailed. These are generous and have permitted the European Commission of Human Rights to dismiss, as 'manifestly unfounded', complaints concerning dismissal or subjection to disciplinary action of employees who had spoken out about safety fears at a defence installation (*B v United Kingdom*[23]), and accused employers of discrimination on grounds of sexual orientation (*Morissens v Belgium*[24]). In these cases the Commission found that interferences justified in connection, respectively, with the employers' rights and reputation. Nor has the Court restricted the aims which may be pursued by the restriction of freedom of expression to those which appear on the face of article 10(2). In *Vogt* the legitimate aim accepted by the Court appeared to be the protection of the Constitution. In *Ahmed v United Kingdom*[25], the Court accepted that the Local Government Officers (Political Restrictions) Regulations 1990 (which restrict political activity on the part of certain categories of local government employees) were justified 'on account of the need to protect the rights of others to effective political democracy'. And in *X v United Kingdom*[26] the Commission accepted that a teacher's colleagues had a protectable interest in avoiding exposure to his evangelising posters and stickers. As Bowers and Lewis point out, in whistleblowing cases 'there will usually be a legitimate aim which can be said to be pursued by the interference'[27].

The Convention organs have been particularly content to accept restrictions on freedom of expression in the employment sphere because of article 10(2)'s reference to the 'duties and responsibilities' incorporated therein. Thus the freedom of the local government politician employed at Aldermaston defence installation to speak out about the safety concerns relating thereto had to give way to the interests of his employer in silence (*B v United Kingdom*). The freedom of expression of the devoutly religious teacher had to give way to the interest of his employer in not having his other employees bothered by this expression (*X v United Kingdom*). And the freedom of the lesbian teacher to protest against the discrimination she believed she had been subject to had to give way to her employer's interest in not being thought to have discriminated against her (*Morissens*)[28].

Some workers have succeeded in article 10 cases. In *Vogt* the Court accepted that the employers had acted disproportionately to what was accepted as their legitimate aim. There the Court paid particular regard to the 'absolute nature of th[e] duty [of fidelity] as construed by the German courts'; its uniqueness amongst European States; the fact that membership of the German Communist party was legal and that prolonged investigations had failed to uncover any incident involving Vogt herself which belied her 'emphatic assertion that she upheld the values of the German constitutional order'; the impact of dismissal on Ms Vogt – she was permanently prevented from following her profession; the absence of any suggestion that Ms Vogt had been either a security risk or a bad influence upon her students[29]. Nine of the nineteen members of the Court dissented, all but one on the grounds that the dismissal was 'proportionate and could be considered necessary in a democratic society'[30].

It was significant in *Vogt* that the applicant had actually been dismissed. The same was true in *Young, James & Webster* (in which the European Court of Human Rights ruled that the imposition of a closed shop on non-union members already in employment breached article 11) although not, apparently in *Stedman* (in which the Commission also appeared to ignore the fact that the requirement for Sunday working had been imposed on the employee after she was already in post). In *Smith v United Kingdom* and *Lustig-Prean v United Kingdom* the European Court of Human Rights ruled that dismissals in pursuit of the 'no gays in the military' rule breached article 8 of the ECHR. It is possible that less severe action might not have been regarded as disproportionate to the legitimate aim (the 'maintenance of the morale of service personnel and, consequently, of the fighting power and the operational effectiveness of the armed forces') pursued by the ban.

The limitations on the protection afforded by article 10 are particularly apparent in cases concerning private sector employers. Even where they have been recognised, positive obligations on the State to protect against violations of ECHR rights by private individuals tend to be weaker than the corresponding restrictions on State action, with the effect that interference with those rights is more readily justified. In *Rommelfanger v Germany*[31], for example, the Commission required only that there was a 'reasonable relation between the measures affecting freedom of expression and the nature of the employment as well as the importance of the issue for the employer'. The applicant, a doctor, had been sacked from his position at a Catholic hospital having put his name (one of 50) to a letter concerning domestic abortion legislation. There the Commission accepted that the doctor had not fully contracted out of his right to freedom of expression on the abortion issue by accepting employment at a church-run hospital. But it found on the facts that no breach of article 10 had occurred.

Confidential information and the Human Rights Act

THE obligations of confidentiality and fidelity imposed on employees were mentioned briefly above. It is common practice in some types of employment to impose express contractual restrictions on the use to which 'confidential' information can be put during and after the termination of employment. Information properly categorised as 'confidential' (that is, according to the Court of Appeal in *Faccenda Chicken Ltd v Fowler*, 'trade secrets or their equivalent'[32]), is protected from disclosure both during the course of employment and, with or without any express contractual provision, after the termination of that employment. 'Confidential' information of a lesser degree is protected during employment (again with or without express contractual provision) by duties of good faith and fidelity the extent of which, according to Neill LJ in *Faccenda*, 'vary according to the nature of the contract[33]. But such information may not be protected, after termination, by action for breach of confidence[34] although the obligation, during employment, in respect of such information would be broken 'if an employee makes or copies a list of the customers of the employer for use after his employment ends or deliberately memorises such a list'[35].

The limitations on the duty of confidentiality after employment are such that employers generally have to protect information falling short of trade secrets by means of restrictive covenants (regulating, for example, approaches to, dealings with or employment by particular persons or in particular fields for a period of time after termination) or 'garden leave' clauses to isolate the employee from such information for a period after notice of termination is given. These give rise to other questions as to compatibility with ECHR rights, notably article 11 (freedom of association). But they are outside the scope of this chapter.

As far as the issue of injunctions to prevent breach of confidentiality after the termination of employment is concerned, it is unlikely that the implementation of the Human Rights Act will have any significant effect. Article 10(2) provides, as we saw above, that the right to freedom of expression is subject 'such formalities, conditions, restrictions or penalties as are prescribed by law and are necessary in a democratic society... for preventing the disclosure of information received in confidence'. One could argue that implied terms, the existence of which may be unknown to the employee, should not be regarded as 'restrictions... prescribed by law'. But the European Court of Human Rights has taken a fairly relaxed approach to this provision (*Sunday Times v United Kingdom*[36]) and, given the restriction of 'confidential' information to that akin to a 'trade secret' (this categorisation in turn depending, inter alia, upon the nature of the employment and 'whether the employer impressed on the employee the confidentiality of the information'[37]), it is likely that the implied term is sufficient to satisfy this requirement. Further, the European Court of Human Rights has adopted a generous approach to the margin of appreciation where commercial information is concerned. Even in cases involving some allegation of wrongdoing (*Jacubowski v Germany*[38], *Markt Intern Verlag GmbH v Germany*[39]), suspicion of malign competitive motive on the part of the discloser has permitted the justification of quite draconian penalties.

Confidential information and the Human Rights Act (2): whistleblowers

GIVEN the narrow approach of the domestic courts to that which is 'confidential' (at least after the termination of employment) and the robust approach of the courts in applying public interest scrutiny to employment-related measures 'in restraint of trade'[40], it is unlikely that the domestic law on confidentiality leaves much room for challenge under the ECHR. Different questions arise, however, concerning disclosures made by those in employment which breach express or implied terms relating to confidentiality[41] or to fidelity. In some cases, such disclosures might be regarded as being in the 'public interest'. The same is true of disclosures made in breach of the Official Secrets Act 1989 whose terms do not permit public interest disclosures.

Whistleblowers have attracted much interest over the last few years, most recently because of the 'culture of silence' among medical staff which has come to light as result of public enquiries into the deaths of babies in the Bristol Royal Infirmary and the malpractice of gynaecologist Rodney Ledward. *The Guardian* headlined its report of the Ledward enquiry (2 June 2000) 'Climate of fear let surgeon maim women' and continued:

> The disgraced gynaecologist, Rodney Ledward, was able to severely maim hundreds of women patients because of a hospital culture in which consultants were treated as 'gods' and junior staff were afraid of 'telling tales'... Mr Ledward botched hundreds of

operations during his 16 years at the William Harvey hospital in Ashford, Kent, because he was protected by a combination of 'failures in senior NHS management', the 'old boys' network' and a 'climate of fear and retribution' which prevented colleagues from reporting their concerns about his surgical skills.

The report recommended an 'open culture' to encourage whistle-blowing together with the creation of channels for complaint and the voicing of concerns. Indeed, the scandalous mortality rates associated with infant heart surgery in Bristol Royal Infirmary came to light only as a result of whistleblowing by anaesthetist Stephen Bolsin who went to the press after repeated attempts to alert hospital authorities to the unusually high death rates. In his evidence to the Bristol inquiry, Dr Bolsin stated that he 'felt he had been blackballed by the British medical community' (*The Guardian* 23 November 1999). He now works in Australia.

Much of the public comment in the aftermath of the Ledward enquiry, conducted by Jean Ritchie QC, focused on the NHS training system in which junior doctors are forced to seek new contracts every six months, this having the effect that many are unable to voice their concerns about senior colleagues without jeopardising favourable references and the chances of future positions. But the fear of retribution which deters many would-be whistleblowers is not confined to junior doctors. Lucy Vickers found evidence of increasing reluctance amongst NHS workers to make public their concerns about the service. This was not explicable 'merely in terms of patient confidentiality', such confidentiality being an 'age old concept'. Rather, she suggested, the changes 'seem to coincide in time with the [internal market] reforms in the NHS', in particular with the increasing trend amongst hospital trusts to introduce 'specific confidentiality clauses for staff, which go much further than traditional patient confidentiality, and which prohibit any discussion of work-related matters with outsiders'. Vickers pointed to a number of cases in which NHS staff were dismissed for raising what were ultimately found to be legitimate concerns about health service practice, noting that those involved 'no longer work in their original posts, and the publicity their cases engendered will have sent a strong message to any other health professionals who contemplate blowing the whistle'[41].

Whistleblowers and the Official Secrets Act 1989

To health service cases such as those of Graham Pink and Helen Zeitlin, discussed by Vickers[42], should be added others in which whistleblowers found themselves subject to prosecution after raising issues of public concern. Perhaps the best known of these is that of Clive Ponting who brought to the attention of an MP ministerial deception over the sinking of the Argentinian ship the *General Belgrano* (the ship was torpedoed while outside the British exclusion zone around the Falkland Islands and, contrary to ministerial insistence, heading away from rather than towards the islands). Ponting, a civil servant, wrote anonymously to Tam Dalyell MP about the circumstances of the *Belgrano*'s sinking[43]. Despite the MP's efforts Ponting was traced as the source of the information and the full force of the criminal law, in the shape of the Official Secrets Act 1911, brought to bear against him. A jury acquitted him in 1985 in disregard of a judicial direction which would have made conviction easier. Sarah Tisdall, who disclosed to *The Guardian* a planned deception on the part of government to avoid anti-Cruise missile demonstrations, was less fortunate. She paid for her breach of the Act with a six-month term of imprisonment the same year[44]. More recently, the government has pursued both David Shayler and those newspapers (notably *The Guardian* and *The Independent*) with whom he has been in correspondence, having injuncted the publication of further allegations by him. The ex-MI5 employee has alleged misdeeds including the planned assassination of Libyan leader Colonel Gadaffi by MI5 and the existence of 'files' kept by the security services on a number of current Ministers.

The Official Secrets Act 1911, under which Ponting and Tisdall were charged, permitted disclosures 'in the interests of the State'. This provision was interpreted by the House of Lords in *Chandler v DPP* to refer, at least in the area of public defence, to the interests of the government of the day[45]. But the then-journalist Jonathan Aitken was acquitted in 1971 in an Official Secrets Act prosecution relating to his disclosures of government misdeeds in the Biafran war, the judge having virtually instructed an acquittal by interpreting the 'State interest' defence as tantamount to one concerned with the public interest. The 1911 Act was replaced in part by the Official Secrets Act 1989 which, while narrower in some respects than the previous legislation[46], contains no defence capable of interpretation to cover the public interest. It is under the 1989 Act that ex-MI5 employee David Shayler is facing prosecution. The absence of any public interest defence in the Act resulted in France's refusal to extradite Shayler (he recently returned to the United Kingdom of his own accord)[47]. Remarkably, the Freedom of Information Act, which has just received Royal Assent, provides for no amendments to the Official Secrets Act.

Whistleblowing and the common law

It is clear that the path of whistleblowers is not smooth, particularly in cases in which they wish to bring government wrongdoing to the attention of the public (or, indeed, MPs)[48]. At the same time, the claim is very frequently made that judicious whistleblowing might have prevented disasters such as Piper Alpha, the Clapham and Southall rail crashes, the Maxwell pension fund fiasco and the Matrix Churchill scandal[49].

It was partly in recognition of this that the Public Interest Disclosure Act 1998, which was implemented in July 1999, became law. Prior to its implementation, whistleblowing employees were relatively unprotected from employer retribution. While the disclosure of criminal and other misconduct might well, in any given case, ultimately be declared to have been in the 'public interest', with the effect that no breach of confidence (express or implied) occurred, little recourse was available against employers who dismissed or otherwise acted to the detriment of whistleblowing employees.

Retribution might amount to a breach of contract or, in the case of a dismissal, to a potentially unfair dismissal. But such protections as predated the Public Interest Disclosure Act were wholly inadequate. Employers are not generally restricted, as a matter of contract, from dismissing for any reason, or for no reason at all. Employees whose whistleblowing was subsequently vindicated by the courts could, in the event of summary dismissal, claim damages in respect of any contractual notice period and, if a contractual disciplinary procedure was not followed, for the period that such a procedure would have absorbed. But injunctions to restrain dismissal (other than, perhaps, for that period) would almost certainly be defeated by the inevitable destruction of trust and confidence between employer and whistleblowing employee.

The dismissal of a whistleblowing employee might be unfair. But external disclosure would almost certainly be regarded as misconduct by the broad range of employers, and even internal disclosure might be regarded as 'some other substantial reason' for dismissal. The 'range of reasonable responses' approach taken by tribunals to the question of fairness stacked the odds against employees, particularly when coupled with the fact that the employer's behaviour had to be assessed at the point of dismissal, rather than *ex post facto* in the light of any decision that the whistleblowing was legally justified. And even if the dismissal (actual or, in the case of detrimental treatment of an employee, constructive) was ultimately judged to have been unfair, compensation was, for the most part, limited (until the implementation of the Employment Relations Act 1999, to a maximum £12,000) and redress available only to those with two years' qualifying employment[50]. In 1996, Bowers and Lewis summed up the position thus:

the whistleblower lives an often lonely and unprotected life. He may be enjoined for abusing the confidential information of his employer. His revelations may well infringe the duty of loyalty that he owes to his employer. A dismissal may be justified on the grounds that trust and confidence have broken down. He may be publicly isolated as a troublemaker or derided as an obsessive. His reputation may be besmirched. He may find himself disciplined over (technical) breaches of the rules. In the public sector his activities may fall foul of the Official Secrets Act[51].

The Public Interest Disclosure Act 1998

The Public Interest Disclosure Act 1998 increased the protections afforded to whistleblowing employees and to other workers, very broadly defined[52]. The Act amended the Employment Rights Act 1996 to protect employees against dismissal and detriment short of dismissal on the ground of 'protected disclosures', further discussed below. It provided (new Employment Rights Act 1996 s.43J) that 'Any provision in an agreement [between a worker and his employer] is void in so far as it purports to preclude the worker from making a protected disclosure' and made available interim relief in respect of dismissals alleged to be by reason of protected disclosures. Compensation payable in respect of detriment or dismissal in connection with protected disclosures is unlimited.

Section 1 of the Public Interest Disclosure Act 1998 defines as a 'protected disclosure' one which (new Employment Rights Act 1996 s.43B) 'in the reasonable belief of the worker making the disclosure, tends to show' the commission of a criminal offence; a miscarriage of justice; failure to comply with a legal obligation; endangerment to health and safety 'of any individual'; or environmental damage. The disclosure may relate to past, present or likely misdeeds in each of these cases, or to the past, present or likely deliberate concealment of any such misdeed. Disclosures must be made 'in good faith' in order to be protected and must be made to a suitable person.

The most straightforward type of protected disclosures are those made to the whistleblower's employer (defined to include any person disclosure to whom is in accordance with a procedure authorised by the employer[53]); to another whose conduct is reasonably believed by the whistleblower to involve one of the types of misdeed listed above; or to a legal adviser 'in the course of obtaining legal advice'. In these cases (Employment Rights Act 1996 s.43C-E as amended), disclosures are protected without more. It is clear from the Act that the preference is for internal disclosure[54].

In the case of disclosure to a regulatory body[55] the whistleblower, in addition to acting in good faith and in the reasonable belief that the disclosure tends to show one of the relevant misdeeds, must also act in the reasonable belief that the misdeed falls within the regulatory body's jurisdiction and that 'the information disclosed, and any allegation contained in it, are substantially true' Employment Rights Act 1996, s.43F. In the case of wider disclosures (for example, to an MP or to the press), the whistleblower must act in good faith, Employment Rights Act 1996, s.43G; the wider disclosure must be reasonable in all the circumstances, and must be made in the reasonable belief that it tends to show one of the relevant misdeeds and that 'the information disclosed, and any allegation contained in it, are substantially true'. The whistleblower must also act other than for purposes of personal gain and will benefit from the protection of the Public Interest Disclosure Act 1998 only where *either* (a) at the time of the disclosure he or she reasonably believes that he or she will be subjected to a detriment by the employer if he or she makes the disclosure to the employer or to a regulator, where relevant; *or* (b) there is no relevant regulator and the whistleblower reasonably believes that evidence of the misdeed is likely to be concealed or destroyed if disclosure is made to the employer, *or* (c) he or she has already disclosed substantially the same information to the employer or relevant regulator. The Act provides that, in determining whether it is reasonable for the worker to make the wider disclosure, particular regard shall be had, *inter alia*, to the identity of the person to whom disclosure was made, the nature of the information disclosed, and (non)compliance with any disclosure procedures established by the employer.

Finally, the Public Interest Disclosure Act provides that, in the case of 'failure[s] of an exceptionally serious nature' disclosure will be protected if 'in all the circumstances of the case, it is reasonable for [the worker] to make the disclosure', the disclosure again being made 'in good faith'; in the reasonable belief that the information disclosed, and any allegation in it, are substantially true and other than for purposes of personal gain. In determining whether the disclosure was reasonable, 'regard shall be had, in particular, to the identity of the person to whom the disclosure is made'.

Where a protected disclosure is made, the Act provides that a worker (as distinct from an employee) is entitled 'not to be subjected to any detriment by any act, or any deliberate failure to act, by his employer done on the ground that the worker has made a protected disclosure'. The 'detriment' prohibited by this section extends to 'dismissal' in the case of non-employees, other dismissals being categorised as automatically unfair (and subject to neither a qualifying period of employment nor a retirement age cut-off) under Employment Rights Act 1996, s.103A (as amended by the Public Interest Disclosure Act). Interim relief is available and compensation, whether for detriment or dismissal in respect of protected disclosures, is not subject to limitation[56].

Effect of the Public Interest Disclosure Act 1998
What the 1998 Act did was to provide significant legal protection to those workers (whether employees or not) whose disclosures fall within its sphere. Prior to its implementation there was no clear legal redress against retribution in respect of such disclosures. Now such retribution will amount to a legal wrong.

This is not to say that the Act is unflawed. Gobert and Punch query whether the 'detriment' prohibited by the Act extends to a refusal by fellow employees to associate with the whistleblower, and whether causation for such behaviour can be traced to the employer where it is on the initiative of the employees themselves, albeit perhaps the result of their perception of the whistleblower as a *persona non grata* and their fear of 'guilt by association'. Further, and given the psychological scarring suffered by many whistleblowers, they highlight the difficulties for tribunals of separating 'internal causative factors' (such as excessive agonising before whistleblowing) from the corporate response to the whistleblowing in attributing causation for, for example, a nervous breakdown. The absence of any cap on compensation:

> may not be as significant as it might appear if 'compensation' is interpreted to be limited to lost income and pensions, and not to include psychological distress or losses resulting from the difficulties in securing comparable employment. In contrast, some American jurisdictions will permit an award of treble damages to a discharged whistleblower. Other proposals advanced in the United States to protect whistleblowers include prison sentences of up to five years for those responsible for any reprisals. The threat of treble damages coupled with criminal liability is a far cry from the modest compensation package likely to be awarded by an employment tribunal... Nor does an employment tribunal have the power under the Employment Rights Act 1996 to order an employer to adopt a policy which protects whistleblowers or to enjoin an employer from practices aimed at discouraging whistleblowing. As long as the employer is prepared to satisfy the com-

pensation award of an employment tribunal, it may take punitive measures against whistleblowers, perhaps with the goal of sending a message to others in the organisation, with virtual impunity[57].

These criticisms deal with employees whose whistleblowing activities fall within the ambit of the Public Interest Disclosure Act 1998. Outside the Act's protection will remain those whose disclosures are not of the appropriate type, those whose disclosure is to the wrong recipient, and those whose disclosures involve them in a breach of the criminal law. Gobert and Punch state that the Act 'is fairly inclusive as to the type of disclosures' covered. But Lucy Vickers points out that, although in the NHS context, 'most concerns... will relate to current, potential or past dangers to health and safety, if not to other listed matters... general discussion of the policies adopted in running the NHS would probably not be covered'. Participation in such discussions (for example, in a televised debate) might contravene express contractual terms or, possible, implied duties of fidelity.

Even internal whistleblowers must, in order to gain the protection of the Act, make their disclosures in good faith and in the reasonable belief that the disclosure tends to show one of the relevant misdeeds. But those who disclose externally must also show a reasonable belief in the substantial truth of the information disclosed and, depending on the identity of the disclosee and the nature of the disclosure, must surmount additional hurdles such as the requirements that the disclosure be reasonable in all the circumstances, that there is a reasonable belief in the possibility of retribution or concealment of evidence of misdeed in the case of internal disclosure or in the likelihood of concealment; and/or that the disclosure not be made for personal gain.

The good faith requirement can be taken to demand that the discloser honestly believes in the truth of his/her allegation[58] and, according to the annotation to the Employment Rights Act 1996, s.43C, to exclude 'disclosure[s]... demonstrably made for an ulterior and undesirable purpose, eg. blackmail'[59]. But, as Gobert and Punch remark:

> The difficulty of proving or disproving 'good faith' will inevitably complicate any subsequent hearing [and]... may also deter whistleblowers who fear that their motivations may be misconstrued, as well as those who are sufficiently self-aware to appreciate that their decision to blow the whistle may be prompted by a combination of factors, [only] some of which may be consistent with good faith... It is certainly arguable that the public interest is best served by the disclosure of all serious malpractice or wrongdoing within an organisation, regardless of whether the person

making the disclosure is acting in good faith.

The same authors suggest that the Act's 'good faith' requirement might be 'strained' by the decision to blow the whistle to a regulator rather than internally, given the possible breach of confidence involved. Certainly, as they recognise, the common law contains no such requirement. Lord Denning in *Initial Services Ltd v Putterill* took the view that disclosures 'out of malice or spite... for reward' might not be in the public interest, it being a 'great evil when people purvey scandalous information for reward'. But in *Re a Company's Application* a disclosure to FIMBRA (the financial services regulator) was, although spitefully motivated, accepted as being in the public interest[60]. So, too, were the financially-rewarded disclosures in *Woodward v Hutchins*[61].

Finally, and of perhaps most significance, is the interrelationship between the Public Interest Disclosure Act and the criminal law – in particular, the Official Secrets Act 1989. The cases of Clive Ponting, Jonathan Aitken and David Shayler have been mentioned above. It is worth repeating that the criminal provisions of the Official Secrets Act are not subject to any exception covering the public interest in disclosure. Disclosures falling within its terms will always be criminal and will not be protected by the Public Interest Disclosure Act 1998.

What the 1998 Act does, in effect, is to reflect much of the previous common law relating to public interest disclosures. It was stated, above, that prior to its implementation, employees were not adequately protected from retribution even in the case of disclosures which were regarded as legally justified. That position has been significantly improved. But the nature of disclosures protected by the Act is not very different from those which would, or might well, have been regarded as in the 'public interest' as a matter of common law[62], save that some disclosures which breached the Official Secrets Act are, nevertheless, protected at common law[63].

In the *Spycatcher* case the House of Lords took the view that a public interest defence was available in civil actions (there breach of confidence) arising from breach of the Official Secrets Act 1989. Lord Griffiths, for example, stated that 'theoretically, if a member of the service discovered that some iniquitous course of action was being pursued that was clearly detrimental to our national interest, and he was unable to persuade any senior members of his service or any member of the establishment, or the police, to do anything about it, then he should be relieved of his duty of confidence so that he could alert his fellow citizens to the impending danger'. And Lord Goff, having accepted that the 'public interest that confidences should be preserved and protected by the law... may be outweighed by some other countervailing public interest which favours disclosure', went on to state that '[t]his limitation may apply... to all types of confidential information', although '[a] classic example of a case where limited disclosure is required is a case of alleged iniquity in the Security Service'[64]. Their Lordships also accepted that confidentiality would be lost as information became public, there refusing to grant a permanent injunction against disclosure of material published abroad and available in the United Kingdom. By contrast, application of the Official Secrets Act 1989 to the intelligence and security services is lifelong.

The ECHR and whistleblowing

The approach of the Convention organs to employment-related cases has been considered above, it being evident that, for the most part, the employment protections afforded by article 10 are slim. Turning specifically to consider the application of the Convention to whistleblowing, it is useful to distinguish (a) those workers whose disclosures are protected by the Public Interest Disclosure Act 1998; (b) those whose disclosures are unprotected in the sense that they involve information falling outwith the scope of that Act, or because they were made to an unsuitable person; and (c) those whose disclosures fall completely outside the protection of the Public Interest Disclosure Act 1998 because they involve the commission of a criminal offence (here, for the purposes of discussion, the Official Secrets Act 1989). A secondary issue which arises in respect of each of these categories concerns whether the employee is in the private or the public sector.

Taking first private sector employees in category (a), it is almost certainly the case that the implementation of the Public Interest Disclosure Act 1998 has satisfied any positive obligations the United Kingdom has in respect of this group. The criticisms made by Gobert and Punch in relation to remedies have been mentioned above. But there can be no doubt, given in particular the availability of interim relief, the absence of any qualifying period of employment, the non-application of any upper limit on compensation to Public Interest Disclosure Act 1998 claims and, perhaps most significantly, the internationally ground-breaking status of the Act[65], that the United Kingdom has satisfied such positive obligations as it bears under article 10. A category (a) public sector employee might, in having been subjected to treatment which resulted in a successful Public Interest Disclosure Act 1998 claim, have had his or her article 10 rights violated. But the question for the Strasbourg Court would, in the event of such an outcome, concern whether under article 13 the employee had been given an 'effective remedy'. Again, it is likely the case that the remedies available under the Public Interest Disclosure Act 1998 would qualify as 'effective', not least in view of the points made above.

As far as category (b) employees are concerned one might argue, for example, that article 10 could protect disclosures of information other than that qualifying as 'protected' under the Public Interest Disclosure Act 1998, or disclosure other than to the persons permitted. In *Fressoz & Roire v France*[66] the Strasbourg Court accepted that information about large pay rises awarded by Peugeot to its managing director was 'of general interest' during an industrial dispute concerning pay demands by the workers: 'The article showed that the company chairman had received large pay increases during the period under consideration while at the same time opposing his employees' claims for a rise. By making such a comparison against that background, the article contributed to a public debate on a matter of general interest.' This type of information, if disclosed by a worker, would not fall within the protective sphere of the Public Interest Disclosure Act 1998[67].

The question in the case of private sector employees would be whether the United Kingdom had taken sufficient steps to protect their article 10 rights from violation by their employers. We saw, above, the willingness of the Convention organs to countenance 'contracting-out' in the employment relationship (*Ahmed, Stedman, Kosiek, Glasenapp*), to emphasise the competing rights and interests of employers and others (*X, B, Morissens*), and to take into account the 'nature of the employment' (*Rommelfanger*). Crucial to the outcome in *Fressoz* was the fact that the plaintiff was a journalist who had been subjected to criminal penalties for handling stolen tax documents which contained the information disclosed. We shall see, below, that the Strasbourg Court's application of article 10 is particularly protective of journalists. Further, subjection to the criminal machinery of the State is regarded, not unreasonably, as a particularly serious interference with protected rights which demands accordingly high levels of justification.

It is true that, as in *Vogt*, employment-related breaches of article 10 are possible[68]. But it is questionable whether its protection would stretch sufficiently far to cover category (b) disclosures, save perhaps where retribution was exacted in a case of internal disclosure. Even there, it is likely that the Public Interest Disclosure Act would suffice to fulfil the State's obligations in respect of private sector employees. We saw, above, that some positive obligations are imposed on the

State by a number of Convention provisions including, it seems, article 10. But *Rommelfanger* illustrates that these obligations are not onerous. So, too, does the decision in *H v United Kingdom*, in which the Commission rejected as manifestly unfounded a complaint to the effect that the non-comprehensive nature of the prohibitions in the Race Relations Act 1996 on race discrimination breached the United Kingdom's obligations under article 14[69].

As far as the position of a public sector category (b) employee is concerned, an example can be posited of a CPS worker dismissed or subjected to other detriment for bringing a concern about a possible miscarriage of justice to the press, rather than to the Chief Executive of the Criminal Cases Review Commission[70], or to an NHS employee similarly penalised for speaking out about national health policies or other matters not 'protected' under the Public Interest Disclosure Act. Assuming that the approach applied was akin to that in *Vogt*, rather than that in *Kosiek* and *Glasenapp*, and the Strasbourg Court acknowledged that an interference had occurred, it is probable in the former case that the employee's failure to go through the proper channels would result in a decision that any interference from the employer both pursued a legitimate aim (protecting the authority of the judiciary or the reputation or other interests of the employer) and (certainly in the case of detriment short of dismissal) was proportional to that aim (*X, B, Morissens*). As far as the latter is concerned, it is at least possible that the Strasbourg Court would accept as a proper price of health service employment some curbs on the expression of opinion by staff. It is certainly true that the Public Interest Disclosure Act renders void any contractual agreements restricting disclosures in the public interest. But it applies only to disclosures covered by that Act which would not, of course, apply in the case under discussion.

The ECHR and the Official Secrets Act 1989

The final area for consideration concerns the position of category (c) workers under the ECHR. Such workers may be members of the security and intelligence services whose disclosures of 'any information, document or other article relating to security or intelligence which is or has been in [their] possession by virtue of [their] position[s] as... member[s] of any of those services' will always breach the Official Secrets Act (s.1). They may also be other persons 'notified that [they are] subject to the provisions of' s.1 or who are or have been Crown servants or government contractors and who (ss.1(3), 2(1), 3(1), 4(1)) 'without lawful authority... make... damaging disclosure of any information, document or other article relating' to security or intelligence, to defence or to international relations, or to any disclosure which results in the commission of an offence, facilitates an escape from or threat to legal custody, impedes the prevention or detection of offences or the apprehension or prosecution of suspected offenders; or is likely to have any of those effects, and which is or has been in his possession by virtue of his position as such'[71]. Finally, they may be persons (generally journalists) to whom disclosure of protected information is made in breach of the Official Secrets Act or in confidence within the terms of that Act, and who themselves disclose the information 'without lawful authority knowing, or having reasonable cause to believe, that it is protected against disclosure by the [Official Secrets Act]' in a case in which disclosure is damaging, and is made in the knowledge, or having reasonable cause to believe, that this is so.

It was pointed out, above, that the Official Secrets Act contains no public interest defence, and that no such defence is to be introduced by the Freedom of Information Act. Article 10 does permit freedom of expression to be restricted in the interests, *inter alia*, of 'national security, territorial integrity or public safety'. But these restrictions must be 'necessary in a democratic society' as well as being prescribed by law. Further, it is clear from the Strasbourg Court's jurisprudence that, as exceptions to 'one of the essential foundations of a democratic society', they 'must be narrowly interpreted and the necessity for any restrictions must be convincingly established' (*Observer and Guardian v United Kingdom*[72]). By contrast, the Official Secrets Act absolutely prohibits the disclosure by those covered by it of information which is protected by it and absent, in the case of disclosures by those who are or have been members of the security and intelligence services and disclosures of security or intelligence information by those who have been notified of their coverage by the Act, any requirement that the disclosure even be damaging, much less contrary to the public interest taken in the round.

We have seen, above, the half-hearted application by the Strasbourg Court of article 10 and other Convention provisions in the employment sphere. The decision in *Observer and Guardian v United Kingdom*, in common with those in *Sunday Times v United Kingdom*, *Sunday Times v United Kingdom (No.2)* and *Goodwin v United Kingdom* (discussed below) owed a significant debt to the fact that the complaints were brought by the press, and to the particular significance accorded by that Court to the freedom of the press. But it is possible that the total criminalisation of disclosures covered by the Official Secrets Act is problematic under article 10.

In *Hadjianastassiou v Greece* the Strasbourg Court ruled that the imprisonment of an air force captain for disclosure (for a fee), to a private company, of a technical report on guided missiles which he himself had written for military purposes did not breach article 10[73]. The report contained military information of 'minor importance'. The Strasbourg Court accepted that 'the freedom of expression guaranteed by article 10 applies to servicemen just as it does to other persons' and that the applicant's imprisonment, accordingly, amounted to an interference with his freedom of expression. But the sentence 'was intended to punish the disclosure of information on an arms project classified as secret, and therefore to protect "national security"' and it was, in the Court's view, 'necessary to take into account the special conditions attaching to military life and the specific "duties" and "responsibilities" incumbent on the members of the armed forces'. In the view of the Strasbourg Court, 'the Greek military courts cannot be said to have overstepped the limits of the margin of appreciation which is to be left to the domestic authorities in matters of national security'. It was significant in the *Hadji-anastassiou* case, however, that no public interest argument was mounted by the applicant and that the information disclosed, though not perhaps of the highest importance, was nevertheless regarded by the Strasbourg Court as having some bearing on Greece's national security.

We will return to the position of employees themselves covered by the Official Secrets Act (generally members of the intelligence and security services, government contractors and other Crown Servants), after considering in more detail the jurisprudence of the Strasbourg Court on article 10.

In *Goodwin v United Kingdom*[74], the Court considered a challenge brought by a journalist to a domestic court order for disclosure of his sources, and to a fine for contempt of court for failure to comply with the order. The material at issue related to financial difficulties being experienced by the company which was at the time engaged in attempting to secure a significant loan. The information was strictly confidential and, it subsequently transpired, had been stolen. An injunction against publication of the material had been issued by the High Court on the grounds that such publication might result in a complete loss of confidence in the company, to problems with its refinancing negotiations and ultimately to liquidation and the loss of 400 jobs.

An order for disclosure was subsequently made against Mr Goodwin under the Contempt of Court Act 1981, s.10 which, although it provides generally that 'No court may require a person to disclose, nor is a person guilty of contempt of court for refusing to disclose, the source of information contained in the publication for which he is responsible', is subject to exceptions where 'disclosure is necessary in the interests of justice or national security or for the prevention of disorder or crime'. Mr Justice Hoffman concluded that the interests of justice required that the company be put in a position to 'bring proceedings against the source for recovery of the document, an injunction against further publication and damages for the expense to which it has been put'. As to Goodwin's contention that the disclosure of the material (as opposed to its source) was in the public interest, the public being entitled to know that the company, whose previous published results indicated that it was prosperous and expanding, was experiencing difficulties, Mr Justice Hoffman declared that nothing in the material 'falsifies anything which has been previously made public' and that the company was under no 'obligation, whether in law or commercial morality, to make that information available to its customers, suppliers and competitors. On the contrary, it seems to me that business could not function properly if such information could not be kept confidential.'

Both Court of Appeal and House of Lords rejected Goodwin's appeals against the disclosure order, largely on the grounds that the injunction on publication by the press did not enable the company to prevent disclosure by the source ('a ticking... time bomb', according to Lord Donaldson in the Court of Appeal). Goodwin's appeal to the European Court of Human Rights succeeded on the basis that, given the importance ascribed to freedom of the press under article 10 and, as an important element of that, to the protection of journalistic sources, the company's interests were not sufficient to outweigh Goodwin's. The United Kingdom was also found wanting by the European Court of Human Rights in the *Observer & Guardian* and *Sunday Times (No.2)*[75] cases, which arose out of the *Spycatcher* litigation. There, the European Court ruled that the maintenance of injunctions against publication of Peter Wright's disclosures regarding the security services, at a point when the material disclosed could no longer be regarded as 'confidential', breached article 10.

Taken alone, these decisions might be taken to indicate a robust approach by the European Court of Human Rights to the rights enshrined in article 10. Such a view would, however, be misleading in the whistleblowing context. In *Goodwin* the Court upheld the journalist's right to protect the identity of his source, despite the implication of that source in wrongdoing (he or she either stole confidential documents or was the recipient thereof) and without consideration of the public interest in the disclosure of the particular material at issue. But the Strasbourg Court also accepted the company's interest in 'unmasking a disloyal employee or collaborator, who might have continuing access to its premises, in order to terminate his or her association with the company'. The determining factor for the court in *Goodwin* lay not in the public interest in disclosure of the material, but in the protection of the press. The *Observer & Guardian* and *Sunday Times* cases, too, turned in part on the freedom of the press.

Despite this proviso, the decision in *Goodwin* is of significance in providing protection to whistleblowers against discovery and subsequent prosecution and/or the risk of employer retribution. Clive Ponting and Sarah Tisdall were both uncovered as a result of disclosure by the recipients of their information, in one case in mistaken good faith and in the other by court order. To the extent that article 10 is adequately applied by the domestic courts, some additional protection might arise.

Whistleblowers and the Human Rights Act

In order to determine the possible measure of article 10 protection in the domestic application of the Human Rights Act, it is necessary to consider the approach of those courts to article 10. In *Attorney General v Observer Ltd (No.2)*[76], Lord Goff expressed his confidence that the position under United Kingdom law with respect to disclosure of confidential information in the public interest complied with the requirements of article 10:

we may pride ourselves on the fact that freedom of speech has existed in this country perhaps as long as, if not longer than, it has existed in any other country in the world. The only difference is that, whereas article 10 of the Convention, in accordance with its avowed purpose, proceeds to state a fundamental right and then to qualify it, we in this country (where everybody is free to do anything, subject only to the provisions of the law) proceed rather upon an assumption of freedom of speech, and turn to our law to discover the established exceptions to it. In any event I conceive it to be my duty, when I am free to do so, to interpret the law in accordance with the obligations of the Crown under this treaty. The exercise of the right to freedom of expression under article 10 may be subject to restrictions (as are prescribed by law and are necessary in a democratic society) in relation to certain prescribed matters, which include 'the interests of national security' and 'preventing the disclosure of information received in confidence.' It is established in the Jurisprudence of the European Court of

Human Rights that the word 'necessary' in this context implies the existence of a pressing social need, and that interference with freedom of expression should be no more than is proportionate to the legitimate aim pursued. I have no reason to believe that English law, as applied in the courts, leads to any different conclusion[77].

A majority of the House of Lords had taken into account article 10 in ordering that the interim injunctions imposed in the *Spycatcher* case be continued until full trial of the issue, Lord Bridge (with whom Lord Oliver concurred) dissenting on the grounds that:

> The present attempt to insulate the public in this country from information which is freely available elsewhere is a significant step down th[e] very dangerous road [to totalitarianism]. The maintenance of the ban, as more and more copies of the book *Spycatcher* enter this country and circulate here, will seem more and more ridiculous. If the Government are determined to fight to maintain the ban to the end, they will face inevitable condemnation and humiliation by the [European Court of Human Rights]...

Lord Templeman, who with Lords Brandon and Ackner formed the majority, declared that the continuation of the injunctions was compatible with article 10, being 'necessary in a democratic society in the interests of national security, for protecting the reputation or rights of others, for preventing the disclosure of information received in confidence or for maintaining the authority and impartiality of the judiciary'. We saw, above, the decision of the Strasbourg Court that the continuation of the injunctions breached article 10. Having accepted that the injunctions were an interference prescribed by law and in pursuit of the legitimate aims of maintaining the authority of the judiciary (this including the protection of the rights of litigants[78]) and protecting national security; the majority judgment continued to the effect that the prohibition on disclosure of information which was already in the public domain was not justified.

The Strasbourg Court in *Goodwin* also ruled against the United Kingdom. The domestic courts in that case (*X Ltd v Morgan-Grampian (Publishers) Ltd*[79]) ruled that s.10 of the Contempt of Court Act 1981, which was itself passed in response to the Strasbourg Court's ruling in *Sunday Times v United Kingdom* that the English law of contempt was inadequate to safeguard freedom of expression, required the disclosure of Mr Goodwin's source. The Strasbourg Court took the view that the order for disclosure breached article 10. But in *Camelot Group plc v Centaur Communications Ltd*[80] the Court of Appeal reached the somewhat surprising conclusion that domestic law in this area reflected the position under the ECHR. There the Court of Appeal imposed an order for disclosure of sources on the grounds that the company's interests in dismissing an employee who leaked financial information to the press in advance of its planned publication was sufficient to out-weigh the public interest in protecting the anonymity of a journalist's sources. The leak had resulted in huge public outrage at 'fat cat' pay-offs and in eventual agreement with the government that the company donate additional sums to 'good causes'.

Schiemann LJ accepted Camelot's argument that the approach taken by the House of Lords in the *Goodwin* case was the same as that of the Strasbourg Court, although the courts had reached oppo-site conclusions on the facts of that case. The Lord Justice interpret-ed both decisions as emphasising the public interest in protecting the anonymity of sources, while accepting that the interest in anonymity was not absolute, and dismissed the different outcomes as 'a no more surprising legal phenomenon than this court conclud-ing that a particular course of conduct amounted to negligence when the court of first instance concluded that the very same course of conduct did not amount to negligence'. Bolstered by this view, Schiemann LJ ordered disclosure on the grounds that: 'there is unease and suspicion amongst the employees of the company which inhibits good working relationships. Clearly there is a risk that an employee who has proved untrustworthy in one regard may be untrustworthy in a different respect and reveal the name of, say, a public figure who has won a huge lottery prize'. Mummery and Thorpe LJJ agreed that there was no material difference, at least on the facts of this case[81] between the approach of the Strasbourg Court and that of the House of Lords[82].

Conclusion

IT is apparent from the foregoing that, while the implementation of the Human Rights Act does provide some scope for challenge to workplace restrictions on freedom of expression, the scope of such challenges will be limited by the ECHR jurisprudence on the exercise of rights in employment, as well as by the terms of the Human Rights Act itself. The Human Rights Act does require that legislation be interpreted, where possible, to give effect to the Convention rights. But even assuming that these rights have horizontal effects, their application in the employment sphere is severely limited. Further, while the courts are constrained by the terms of the Convention in terms of the application of the common law, direct reliance can be placed on the ECHR rights only where legal action is taken against the State itself. Where there is neither a common law nor a statutory action upon which to 'piggy-back' an ECHR argument, the Human Rights Act will not benefit private sector employees.

There is certainly room for argument that the article 10 rights of whistleblowers are not adequately protected in domestic law. The Public Interest Disclosure Act 1998, where it applies, is probably adequate to safeguard the rights recognised by the Convention organs. But the position of those whose disclosures contravene the Official Secrets Act is unenviable indeed. It is arguably the case that article 10, constrained as its application is in the employment field, requires that some public interest defence be recognised within the Official Secrets Act (this in a case where disclosure, though 'damaging'[83], is nevertheless in the broader 'public interest', however defined). David Shayler's return to the United Kingdom was premised on the view that, post incorporation, some such defence would be available to him. It may be the case that a sufficient motivated court could find some way of interpreting the Official Secrets Act to this effect (though it is difficult to see how). But it appears from the decision of the House of Lords in *X v Morgan-Grampian* and that of the Court of Appeal in *Camelot v Centaur Communications* that the domestic courts have some way to go before they afford freedom of expression the same measure of protection as does the Strasbourg Court.

We saw, above, that the application of s.10 of the Contempt of Court Act 1981 could provide some protection to whistleblowers by rendering their identification more difficult. The Court of Appeal in the *Camelot* case showed little enthusiasm for such a course of action. But the more recent judgment of the Court of Appeal (21 July 2000, as yet unreported) in an appeal by *Guardian and Observer* against an order for disclosure of materials relating to allegations by David Shayler may herald a change of attitude in the period immediately prior to incorporation. In what was described by *The Guardian* as 'as robust a statement of the rights and duties of a free press as has been heard in an English court room', Lord Justice Judge (with whom Kay and Gibbs JJ agreed), said that the order would have had a:

> devastating and stifling effect on the proper investigation... Virtually any journalist who made contact with him, and any newspaper publishing an article based on discussions with Shayler, would have been at risk of a similar application'. It was vital that 'inconvenient or embarrassing revelations – whether for the security forces or for public authorities – should not be suppressed'.

It remains to be seen whether the decision in the *Observer* and

Guardian appeal indicates a new approach on the part of the British courts. The *Observer* reported on 23 July 2000 that the intelligence community was 'reeling' from the Court of Appeal's judgment: 'Most whistleblowers come to the press, and it is difficult to see where police will find evidence of breaches of the Act if journalists no longer have to hand over notes'. The same article reported that reform of the Official Secrets Act was planned to take into account the provisions of the ECHR, one source claiming that while 'reform was unlikely to come from inside the Home Office... those in favour of [it] are hoping a high-profile secrets trial [presumably that of David Shayler] will directly challenge the legislation'.

Notes

1 Though see chapter 4 for the shortcomings of this legislation.
2 See, for example, *Boychuck v H J Symons Holdings Ltd* [1977] IRLR 395, discussed below, and (on a related point) *Saunders v Scottish National Camps Association Ltd* [1980] IRLR 174.
3 [1978] ICR 85.
4 [1996] ICR 868.
5 [1993] ICR 517.
6 Save where the employment contract provided otherwise.
7 40 *Equal Opportunities Review*, Discrimination Case Law Digest, p 2.
8 [1983] 2 AC 548
9 Though see the debate on the degree of 'horizontality' implicit in the Human Rights Act: M Hunt, "The 'Horizontal Effect' of the Human Rights Act" [1998] PL 423; R Buxton, "The Human Rights Act and Private Law" [2000] 116 LQR 48, H W R Wade, "Horizons of Horizontality" [2000] 116 LQR 217. A significant degree of horizontal application is assumed for the purposes of this paper.
10 Unless such decisions are required by primary legislation – s.6.
11 Respectively (2000) 29 EHRR 493, and (2000) 29 EHRR 548.
12 The inverted commas are used in deference to the debate referred to at note 9, above. In *Grant v South West Trains* the ECJ ruled that article 141 did not cover discrimination on grounds of sexual orientation. This decision was reached, however, on an understanding of the ECHR position which was subsequently called into question by the decisions in *Smith* and *Lustig-Prean*. For further discussion of this see A McColgan, *Discrimination: Text, Cases and Materials* (Hart, 2000), Chapters 1 and 6.
13 Prior to the implementation of Protocol 11 in November 1998, preliminary decisions on admissibility were taken by the Commission which had the power to dismiss applications as 'manifestly unfounded'.
14 (1987) 9 EHRR 25.
15 (1982) 4 EHRR 126.
16 (1997) 23 EHRR CD.
17 See also *X v Denmark* (1976) 5 D&R 157.
18 A similar decision was reached by the Commission in *Karaduman v Turkey* (1993) 74 D&R 93, which involved the prohibition of headscarves by a Turkish university in pursuit of secularism in education.
19 (1996) 21 EHRR 205.
20 See also *Ahmad v United Kingdom*, discussed below, in which the Strasbourg Court accepted that the prohibition on political activities by certain local government workers constituted an interference with their article 10 rights.
21 *Yearbook* XX 520. The decision of the Court is at (1986) 8 EHRR 123.
22 See also *Fuentes Bobo v Spain*, Application 00039293/98, 29 February 2000, which concerned article 10, available on the web at http://www.echr.coe.int/hudoc http://www.echr.coe.int/hudoc (though currently only in French).
23 (1985) 45 D & R 41.
24 (1988) 56 D & R 127.
25 (2000) EHRR 29.
26 (1979) 16 D & R 101.

---

27 J.Bowers and J.Lewis, "Whistleblowing: Freedom of Expression in the Workplace" [1997] EHRLR 637, p 641.

28 It is arguable that domestic provisions prohibiting victimisation (eg. Sex Discrimination Act,s.4, and Race Relations Act, s.2) provide considerably more protection, certainly after the decisions of the House of Lords in *Nagarajan v London Regional Transport* [1999] 3 WLR 425 and the Court of Appeal in *Chief Constable of the West Yorkshire Police v Khan* [2000] IRLR 324.

29 The interference in *Fuentes Bobo v Spain,* above, was also ruled disproportionate to the aim pursued.

30 The other by refusing to distinguish the case from *Glasenapp* and *Kosiek*.

31 (1989) 62 D & R 151.

32 [1987] 1 Ch 117 *per* Neill LJ. According to *obiter* comments by Butler-Sloss LJ and Staughton LJ in *Lansing Linde Ltd v Kerr* [1991] 1 All ER 418 'confidential' information in this context should extend also to (per Butler-Sloss LJ) 'highly confidential information of a non-technical or non-scientific nature, which may come within the ambit of information the employer is entitled to have protected, albeit for a limited period', citing *Herbert Morris Ltd v Saxelby* [1916] 1 AC 688.

33 Citing *Vokes Ltd v Heather* (1945) 62 RPC 135.

34 See, for example, *Lawrence David Ltd v Ashton* [1991] 1 All ER 385.

35 Neill LJ in *Faccenda op cit.*

36 (1980) 2 EHRR 245.

37 Neill LJ in *Faccenda op cit.*

38 (1995) 19 EHRR 64.

39 (1990) 12 EHRR 161.

40 See, for example, *Lawrence David v Ashton* [1988] IRLR 60, *Sadler v Imperial Life Assurance Co* [1988] IRLR 388, *Office Angels Ltd v Rainer-Thomas* [1991] IRLR 214.

41 Including duties of confidentiality to third parties, for example to NHS patients – discussed by Vickers, below.

42 See also L Vickers, "Freedom of Speech in the National Health Service, (1999) 21 *Journal of Social Welfare and Family Law* 120, and G Pink, *Whistleblowing: For Whom the Truth Hurts* (1992).

43 The Ponting case was discussed by Tam Dayell MP, to whom Ponting (anonymously) blew the whistle on the Belgrano affair, during the Second Reading of the 1996 Public Interest Disclosure Bill: H C Debs, 1 March 1996, col. 1135. It is also reported at [1985] Crim LR 318.

44 Tisdall is reported in *The Times*, 26 March 1984.

45 [1964] AC 763. The decision is less than clear, part of Lord Reid's speech being relied upon by the defence in *Ponting* to argue that the 'State' should be understood as the 'organised community', part being relied upon by the prosecution to argue that the government of the day should be the final arbiter of the State's interests. The judge directed the jury on the basis of the latter argument.

46 See discussion in A W Bradley & K D Ewing, *Constitutional and Administrative Law* (12th ed, 1997), pp 652-655.

47 *The Guardian,* 21 November 1998.

48 See also J Gobert and M Punch, "Whistleblowers and the Public Interest" (2000) 63 MLR 25, pp 35-37.

49 To these examples Public Concern at Work (http://www.pcaw.demon.co.uk/) adds the BCCI collapse, the Frank Beck child abuse affair and the Lyme Regis canoe disaster.

50 Save in the cases – see D Lewis, "Whistleblowing and Job Security" (1995) 58 MLR 208 – where the whistleblowing was protected under statutory victimisation provisions.

51 "Whistleblowing: Freedom of Expression in the Workplace", above.

52 See new Employment Rights Act 1996, s.43K. The definition does not, however, extend to the police.

53 And, where the worker's employer is 'an individual appointed under any enactment by a Minister of the Crown', or 'a body any of whose members are so appointed', to a Minister of the Crown.

54 Gobert and Punch, note 48 above, pp 31-37.

55 These are listed in the Public Interest Disclosure (Prescribed Persons) Order 1999, SI 1999/1549.

56 This the subject of much dispute, the question whether the normal caps should apply being left open by the Public Interest Disclosure Act 1998 and resolved by the Public Interest Disclosure (Compensation) Regulations 1999 SI 1999/1548.

57 Citing *Vaughan v Weighpack Ltd* [1974] IRLR 105 in which the court stated that the fact of dismissal, however distressing, did not give rise to compensation, although in rare cases in which the manner of the dismissal caused financial loss this could be compensated.

58 Gobert and Punch, *op cit*, note 67.

59 Cited by Gobert and Punch, *ibid,* at note 69.

60 [1989] 2 All ER 248.

61 [1977] 1 WLR 760.

62 Arguably less generous than the most generous common law approaches – *Woodward v Hutchins op cit,* though wider than the narrowest approaches – *Beloff v Pressdram Ltd* [1973] 1 All ER 241.

63 See *Initial Services v Putterill* [1967] 3 All ER 145, *Lion Laboratories Ltd v Evans* [1984] 2 All ER 41, and *British Steel v Granada Television* [1981] AC 1097 on the types of disclosures regarded as being 'in the public interest'.

64 Adopting Lord Donaldson MR's suggestion, in the Court of Appeal, that Wright's concerns over alleged MI5 misdeeds could have been brought, inter alia, to the Director-General, the Home Secretary, the Prime Minister, the Leader of the Opposition or to previous holders of the office of Home Secretary outside the government.

65 The Public Interest Disclosure Act 1998 has been welcomed as 'The most far-reaching whistleblower protection law in the world' (Public Concern at Work, comment available on their website, above). See also C Camp, "Openness and Accountability in the Workplace" (1999) NLJ 46.

66 (1999) 5 BHRC 654.

67 See also *Granada v British Steel*, above, for a contrasting House of Lords decision on very similar facts.

68 See also *Fuentes Bobo v Spain,* above.

69 Application 4818/89, 4 Dec. 1989, unreported.

70 Or, in Scotland, the Scottish Criminal Cases Review Commission.

71 Definitions of 'damaging' are included within ss.1-4.

72 (1982) 14 EHRR 153, citing *Handyside v United Kingdom* (1980) 1 EHRR
737, *Sunday Times v United Kingdom* (1980) 2 EHRR 245 and *Lingens v
Austria* (1986) 8 EHRR 103.

73 (1993) 16 EHRR 219.

74 (1996) 22 EHRR 123

75 (1992) 14 EHRR 229.

76 [1988] 3 WLR 776.

77 F Klug and K Starmer remark somewhat tartly, in "Incorporation Through
the Back Door?" [1997] PL 223, at p 227, that 'the claim that the common
law and the Convention "march arm in arm" is usually a prelude to ignoring
the latter, or, at best, paying lip service to it'.

78 *Sunday Times v United Kingdom op cit.*

79 [1991] 1 AC 1.

80 [1999] QB 124.

81 This proviso being Mummery LJ's.

82 See note 77 above. Such was the concern about judicial approaches to
freedom of expression under the Human Rights Act that the Bill was
amended during its passage to incorporate s.12, which restricts the use of *ex
parte* hearings in cases in which 'a court is considering whether to grant any
relief which, if granted, might affect the exercise of the Convention right to
freedom of expression'; provides that such relief may not be granted 'so as to
restrain publication before trial unless the court is satisfied that the applicant
is likely to establish that publication should not be allowed' and which
requires courts in these cases to 'have particular regard to the importance of
the Convention right to freedom of expression and, where the proceeding
relate to material which the respondent claims, or which appears to the court,
to be journalistic, literary or artistic material (or to conduct connected with
such material), to – (a) the extent to which – (i) the material has, or is about
to, become available to the public; or (ii) it is, or would be, in the public
interest for the material; to be published...'

83 Whether this is irrebutably presumed in the case of disclosure by intelligence
or secret service personnel or those notified as to their coverage by the
Official Secrets Act 1989, s.1, or established within the terms of the Act in
other cases.

Chapter 4

Article 11 and the right to freedom of association

K D Ewing

ONE of the articles of the Convention which might be thought most likely to affect employment law is article 11. This provides a guarantee of freedom of association, including specifically a right of individuals to form and join trade unions for the protection of their interests[1]. But as in the case of other Convention rights, article 11 is qualified by paragraph 2 which allows restrictions to be imposed on the right to freedom of association on a number of permitted grounds. The full text of article 11 is as follows:

Freedom of assembly and association

1 Everyone has the right to freedom of peaceful assembly and to freedom of association with others, including the right to form and to join trade unions for the protection of his interests.

2 No restrictions shall be placed on the exercise of these rights other than such as are prescribed by law and are necessary in a democratic society in the interests of national security or public safety, for the prevention of disorder or crime, for the protection of health or morals or for the protection of the rights and freedoms of others. This article shall not prevent the imposition of lawful restrictions on the exercise of these rights by members of the armed forces, of the police or of the administration of the State.

The aim of this chapter is to consider how these provisions can be used to promote trade union rights in British law. Although it would be a mistake to be too optimistic, even the human rights sceptics must learn to make bricks out of straw.

Article 11 gives rise to a number of possibilities in terms of developing a litigation strategy for the removal of the restrictions on freedom of association which were introduced by the Thatcher and Major administrations and which have been retained by the present government. These restrictions fall broadly into three quite different categories. First, there is the right of the worker to be in association with others for the protection of his or her interests without suffering discrimination as a result. Secondly, there is the right of workers to be free in their association, in the sense that they should be able to develop their own constitutions and rules without State interference. And thirdly, there is the right of workers to act freely in association with others to promote their collective interests. In each of these different dimensions, British law and practice has been found to violate the freedom of association guarantees in international human rights instruments such as ILO Convention 87[2], and the European Social Charter of 1961, articles 5 and 6[3]. How far can the Human Rights Act 1998 be used to challenge these restraints, and deliver a blow for trade union freedom to which the government would be compelled to respond?

Before we proceed to consider that question, it may be helpful to remind ourselves of the type of restrictions on trade union right that we have in mind. So far as the freedom to be in association with others is concerned, the main issue here is the decision of the House of Lords in *Associated Newspapers plc v Wilson*[4], and the Ullswater amendment which is a product of that litigation[5]. Together the decision and the amendment separately permit discrimination against trade unionists on matters relating to pay, and otherwise. So far as the right of the association to organise its internal affairs is concerned, there are a number of issues here: the restrictions on trade union admission and expulsion rules to comply with the TUC Disputes Principles and Procedures[6]; the restrictions on the right of trade unions to discipline and expel strikebreakers and others[7]; and the detailed requirements relating to the election of officials[8]. And so far as the right of workers to act freely in association is concerned, there are questions about the fact that the trade union recognition rights are very highly qualified and exclude large sections of the British workforce[9], as well as the restrictions on the right to strike (said by the Court of Appeal to be a 'fundamental human right')[10] which are considered in the following chapter[11]. Here we concentrate on the first two of these three issues.

Article 11 and the European Court of Human Rights

ARTICLE 11 has been considered by both the European Commission of Human Rights and the European Court of Human Rights on a number of occasions. It will be helpful to begin with these cases and the principles which they establish: for although the British courts are not bound by these decisions, they are nevertheless bound by the Human Rights Act to take these cases into account[12]. Some of the earliest cases of the Commission and the Court are in fact concerned with article 11, and some of the cases have been concerned with the labour law and industrial relations practices of this country. In one case the Court found that closed shop practices violated the Convention[13], but in another the Commission found that the trade union ban at GCHQ did not constitute a breach[14]. It is also the case that although a number of applications have been made to the Strasbourg Court alleging a breach of article 11, in none of these has a trade union applicant succeeded. These may not have been strong applications, and it is perhaps unfortunate that the early complaints were brought against countries (Belgium and Sweden) with high levels of protection for trade union activities[15]. Nevertheless there is a great deal of value in some of these judgments, which could be relied upon in litigation under the Human Rights Act.

Freedom of association

The first case is *National Union of Belgian Police v Belgium*[16] where the union complained that it was not recognised by the government 'as one of the most representative organisations that the Ministry of Interior is required to consult under [legislation of] 1961 on matters relating to terms and conditions of employment'. The union complained not only that it was put at a disadvantage compared to other unions which were considered representative and were therefore consulted, but that municipal police officers were obliged as a result to join one of these other bodies, despite the fact that they had a 'political' character incompatible with the 'special vocation' of the police. The argument was rejected by the European Court of Human Rights which held that there was no breach of article 11, pointing out that the union had other means available to it to represent the views of its members. In dismissing the application, the Court nevertheless made some important observations about the scope and content of article 11. In particular it emphasised that the wording of the article was such as to demonstrate that the Convention 'safeguards freedom to protect the occupational interests of trade union members by trade union action, the conduct and development of which the Contracting parties must both permit and make possible'[17].

The Court continued by saying that 'it follows that the members of a trade union have a right, in order to protect their interests, that the trade union should be heard', though article 11(1) 'leaves each State a free choice of the means to be used towards this end'[18]. This begs many questions which may be revisited in the future. In particular what is 'trade union action' which the State must permit and make possible for this purpose? And to what extent must the State intervene to make such action possible, when, say, there is resistance from an employer? These are questions which wait to be answered, bones for the English courts to chew on in future cases. For the present we may note that the Court found in the *National Union of Belgian Police* case that the union had sufficient opportunities to represent its members for the purposes of article 11, observing in particular that it was undisputed that 'the applicant union can engage in various kinds of activity vis-a-vis the Government'[19]. This case was followed and applied in the two subsequent applications in 1975[20]. In the *Swedish Engine Drivers' Union* case[21] it was held that article 11 did not create a right for a public sector union to engage in collective bargaining, though on the other hand it was not disputed that the union could 'engage in various kinds of activity vis-a-vis the government'[22].

Freedom of non association

Although article 11 has thus been narrowly construed so as not to imply any protection for any particular form of trade union action, it has on the other hand been widely construed to include an individual right not to associate. The effect of this of course was to undermine pre-entry and post-entry closed shop arrangements whereby workers could be required as a condition of employment to be or become a member of one or more specified trade unions[23]. This is not to say that closed shop practices in Britain were attacked simply because of the ECHR: the Thatcher government had the closed shop in its sights long before the decision of the Strasbourg Court in the leading case, *Young, James and Webster v United Kingdom*[24] in 1981. But there is no doubt that the decision added a measure of legitimacy to the then Government's strategy (if it felt the need for such legitimacy), and there is no doubt also that the Strasbourg jurisprudence has contributed to the ending of a practice which had operated not without cause or reason since the earliest days of trade unionism[25]. This is not a plea for the restoration of the closed shop[26]: but there is now a serious question about the extent to which the ECHR as interpreted by the Strasbourg Court has helped to remove forever other forms of union security arrangements from the political agenda[27].

It is no doubt paradoxical that the most important cases on article 11 include those which have been concerned not to promote trade union freedom, but to undermine it. While adopting a narrow and cautious approach to the content of the positive right to associate, the court has taken a bold and adventurous approach to the question of the negative right not to associate. The latter position was all the bolder and adventurous for the fact that those drafting the Convention had deliberately excluded the negative right[28]. Nevertheless in *Young, James and Webster*, the Court held that employees could not be compelled to associate where (i) membership of a trade union was introduced as a new condition of continuing employment, rather than as a condition of initial employment; (ii) there was no choice of the union which the employee could be required to join; and (iii) where membership of the union would violate other Convention rights such as articles 9 (on freedom of conscience and religion) and 10 (on freedom of expression)[29]. This was taken a logical step further in *Sigurjonsson v Iceland*[30] (not a trade union case but a case about the compulsory membership of a taxi drivers' association as a condition of a taxi licence) where drawing on a dominant European tradition in which compulsory membership of an organisation is prohibited, the Court said that

'the Convention is a living instrument which must be interpreted in the light of present – day conditions. Accordingly, Article 11 must be viewed as encompassing a negative right of association. It is not necessary for the Court to determine in this instance whether this right is to be considered on an equal footing with the positive right'[31].

Discrimination against trade unionists

SO how will the Human Rights Act help? The first and most fundamental aspect of freedom of association is the right of the worker to join a trade union for the protection of his or her interests without suffering any discrimination as a result. It would make a mockery of the limited protection provided by article 11 if workers were free to form and join trade unions for the protection of their interests, but if employers were then free to discriminate against or dismiss workers who exercised this right. Yet British law goes a long way towards making a mockery of the protection by permitting employers to discriminate against trade union members who wish to have their interests represented by their trade union. The issue arises partly because of the decision of the *House of Lords in Wilson v Associated Newspapers plc*[32], partly because of the Trade Union Reform and Employment Rights Act 1993, s.13 (the Ullswater amendment) which was passed in response to the Court of Appeal decision in *Wilson*), and partly because of the present government's failure fully to address these shortcomings. At the time of writing the matter is before the European Court of Human Rights in Strasbourg. The decision in that case is likely to determine important questions about the scope of article 11, while the long shadow cast by the affair is likely to give rise to a number of questions for the Human Rights Act.

The *Wilson and Palmer* case

The facts of this *cause celebre* are now well known[33]. A member of the NUJ and members of RMT refused to agree to have their terms and conditions of employment determined by personal contracts rather than by collective agreement. The employers responded by withholding pay rises and other inducements which were duly paid to employees who agreed to the new arrangements. In both cases the industrial tribunals held that the applicants had been the subject of discrimination on account of their trade union membership, contrary to what is now Trade Union and Labour Relations (Consolidation) Act 1992, s.146[34]. In both cases the EAT reversed, only to be overturned by the Court of Appeal which endorsed the position adopted by the EAT in an earlier case[35], where it was said that there was 'no genuine distinction between membership of a union on the one hand, and making use of the essential services of a union on another'[36]. But in upholding an appeal by the employers, the House of Lords disagreed: the legislation applied only to 'action' short of dismissal: it did not apply to an omission, or failure to act, as in this case[37]. In any event, said a majority of the Lords, the statutory protection was designed only to protect trade union membership as such: it was not intended to protect employees from discrimination for using the services of the union or because they insisted on being paid under a collective agreement rather than enter into a personal contract.

The House of Lords decision in *Wilson and Palmer* was addressed by the Employment Relations Act 1999. So far as the first limb of the decision is concerned, the Act amended s.146 of the 1992 Act to make it clear that the protection applies to acts and omissions[38], thereby reinstating the decision of the Court of Appeal in *NCB v Ridgway*[39], which had been overturned by the House of Lords. So far as the second limb of the decision is concerned, this is addressed by s.17 of the 1999 Act which empowers the Secretary of State to make regulations to deal with cases where a worker is subjected to a detriment by his or her employer or is dismissed 'on the grounds that he [or she] refuses to enter into a contract which includes terms which differ from the terms of a collective agreement which applies to him [or her]'. But not only is there 'no indication that such regulations have been made or are in the process of being drafted'[40], the value of any such regulations (if they are made) will be greatly diminished by s.17(4), the so called Millar amendment, after the Tory peer who tabled it[41]. This provides that the payment of higher wages to someone is not to be treated as falling within s.17 provided that (a) there is no inhibition in the contract of employment of the worker receiving the same from being the member of a trade union, and (b) the payments 'reasonably relate to services provided by the worker' under his or her contract of employment.

The Ullswater Amendment

As already suggested, the House of Lords decision is only one threat to freedom of association arising as a result of the *Wilson and Palmer* affair. It will be recalled that the Court of Appeal decided in favour of the victims in this case, holding that they had been unlawfully discriminated against. This was not to the liking of the then government which, without having seen a copy of the Court of Appeal's decision and without waiting to find out if it would be appealed, introduced an amendment to the Trade Union Reform and Employment Rights Bill which conveniently was at a late stage in its parliamentary journey[42]. Becoming section 13 of the 1993 Act (amending the Trade Union and Labour Relations (Consolidation) Act 1992, s.148), the Ullswater amendment (after the hapless junior minister who tabled and defended it) permits an employer to discriminate against an employee on the grounds of trade union membership or activities where there is evidence that the 'employer's purpose was to further a change in his [or her] relationship with all or any class of his [or her] employees', and there is also evidence that his or her purpose was one falling within section 146. In such a case, the tribunal is to disregard the latter purpose, 'unless it considers that the action was such that no reasonable employer would take'.

Paradoxically in 1995 the House of Lords reversed the Court of Appeal decision which had given rise to the Ullswater amendment[43]. So as a result of that decision, there were now two sources of authority for an employer proposing to discriminate against trade unionists. As we have seen the House of Lords decision was partially addressed by the Employment Relations Act 1999: one limb but not two. But even this is more than can be said for the Ullswater amendment which has been neither amended nor repealed, with the result that it remains possible for an employer to discriminate against trade unionists not only (as in *Wilson and Palmer*) because they refuse to enter into a personal contract following derecognition, but more generally for any reason provided that the employer's purpose is to 'further a change in his [or her] relationship with all or any class of his [or her] employees', and it is 'such that no reasonable employer would take'. Predictably this is a provision which has been roundly condemned by both the Committee of Experts of the ILO, and the Committee of Independent Experts of the Council of Europe.[44] The government nevertheless claims that the Ullswater amendment 'serves a useful purpose and ought to be retained'[45].

Discrimination against trade unionists: the Human Rights Act

THIS is an area where it might be thought that the Human Rights Act would have some bearing. But so far as any legal challenge under the Act is concerned, it is important to keep in mind the fact that there two separate legal instruments permitting discrimination here, however inter-related they may be: the first is TULRCA 1992, s.146 as construed by the House of Lords in a decision which after the 1999 Act remains substantially in force; and the second is the Ullswater amendment or what is now TULRCA 1992, s.148. So far as the first of these is concerned, as already suggested the position is under consideration by the European Court of Human Rights in *Wilson and Palmer v United Kingdom*[46], and at the time of writing a date for a hearing is awaited. That decision is likely to determine whether the discrimination of the kind in these cases violates article 11 of the Convention, and if so whether s.146 of the 1992 Act as construed by the House of Lords is consistent with the Convention. So far as the second issue is concerned, as already suggested and as will be explained, the outcome of the decision in the *Wilson and Palmer* case may not necessarily mean that the amendment will be immune from challenge as a result of the Human Rights Act (if the application is unsuccessful), or that it will have to be repealed (if the application is successful).

Wilson and Palmer and the ECHR

Addressing the first of the two legal questions raised by these affairs, it is obviously unclear at this stage whether the *Wilson and Palmer* application will succeed. Although the European Court of Human Rights has taken a narrow approach to the interpretation of article 11 (so far as the positive aspect of freedom of association is concerned), it has nevertheless provided enough material for a cogent and convincing argument to be presented that there has been a breach of the Convention in this case. The case is strengthened by the fact that article 11 provides protection not for the right to freedom of association generally, but also specifically for the right of the individual to form and join trade unions for the protection of his interests, said to be 'a special aspect of freedom of association'[47]. The specific protection is presumably designed to add value to the general, and indeed in the cases discussed and referred to above the Strasbourg Court has taken the view that these specific protections for trade union activities were not 'redundant' as had been suggested by the European Commission of Human Rights[48]. As we have seen, the Court has gone further to suggest that article 11 means that States must both permit and make possible trade union action, without prescribing what that action should be and without requiring trade unions to be permitted to engage in any particular form of trade union action[49].

It is thus important to emphasise that the Convention does not provide simply a right to form and join trade unions, but a right to form and join trade unions for the protection of one's interests. As a result, the protection in article 11 is wider than the protection in s.146 of the TULRCA 1992 which narrowly construed applies only to trade union membership and activities (at an appropriate time) but not otherwise. The distinction between the Convention and domestic legislation is a particularly important distinction in the present case where the applicants were not discriminated against because they were trade union members, but because they wished to continue to have their interests protected by their trade union, the interests being their terms and conditions of employment which the union had negotiated on their behalf. This is not to say that they had a right to have their union recognised for the purposes of collective bargaining. But it is to say that where the union was recognised, and where their terms and conditions had been negotiated by the union, they were entitled to rely on the benefits which the union had secured, and were entitled to do so without discrimination.

The Ullswater Amendment and the Human Rights Act

Turning to the second of the two legal issues raised by the *Wilson and Palmer* affairs, the Ullswater amendment may not be directly affected by the decision of the Court in the *Wilson and Palmer* application, whichever way the decision goes. Obviously if the application is unsuccessful, there will be no need to change anything to comply with the decision: employers will have a green light to continue to discriminate under s.146, and TULRCA 1992, s.148 will not be prejudiced by it. At this point, however, there will be a role for the Human Rights Act. Although an unsuccessful application by *Wilson and Palmer* would give employers considerable licence to discriminate, it may still be necessary for employers to rely on Ullswater where they wish to discriminate in circumstances which *are* unlawful under s.146, exceptional though such cases are likely to be in such circumstances (and there are no reported cases to date involving a matter of this kind). In these cases, the employer would be permitted to discriminate provided the requirements of s.148(3) are met, including the requirement that what the employer has done is such that no 'reasonable' employer would not do. At this point the Human Rights Act takes centre stage: presumably it would not be 'reasonable' to do anything which conflicts with article 11, so that any defence based on the Ullswater amendment would be sustained only if the employer could show that his or her conduct was consistent with the Convention rights of the applicants.

But what if the *Wilson and Palmer* application succeeds? At this point the role of the Human Rights Act would be much more interesting. Although it is difficult to be certain at this stage, it may be that a successful application would not require a repeal of the amendment. A successful application perhaps could be met by beefing up s.146, possibly by regulations under s.17 of the 1999 Act, provided of course that the Millar amendment was removed to allow the necessary regulations to be made. In these circumstances the government may choose not to repeal the Ullswater amendment, in view of its apparent value[50]. So we may be faced with the situation where an employer discriminates against a trade unionist on a matter relating to pay, which he or she would again have to show was reasonable under s.148(3), which again he or she would have to show was compatible with Convention rights. But if as a result of the *Wilson and Palmer* decision such conduct is a breach of article 11(1), the employer would have great difficulty in making out the defence that his or her conduct was reasonable. In order to do so the employer would be forced back on article 11(2), and would have to show that the discrimination was 'necessary in a democratic society' for 'the protection of the rights and freedoms of others'. So although a successful application in *Wilson and Palmer* might not require the removal of the Ullswater amendment, the Human Rights Act could be fatal to its continued operation.

Trade union autonomy and the TUC Disputes Principles

A SECOND area of concern in the specific context of article 11 relates to State control of the way in which trade unions are organised. For a hundred years (1871-1971), the British State treated trade unions with a light regulatory touch, with the role of the law being confined to ensuring that the trade union's own rules were complied with[51]. But with the exception of the legislation relating to political funds and amalgamations, it was left to trade unions themselves to determine the content of their own rules[52]. In this way British law reflected the principle in article 3 of ILO Convention 87 that

> 'Workers' and employers' organisations shall have the right to draw up their constitutions and rules, to elect their representatives in full freedom, to organise their administration and activities and to formulate their programmes.'[53]

But the position was gradually to change from the 1970s, with a number of controls on trade union admission and expulsion rules being introduced by the Industrial Relations Act 1971. These were substantially removed by the Trade Union and Labour Relations Act 1974 (as amended in 1976), but this was to prove to be simply a prelude for more wide ranging and far reaching controls on internal trade union government introduced from 1980 onwards. One of the most contentious areas of intervention relates to the right of trade unions to control membership of their organisations, particularly to give effect to a ruling of a Disputes Committee under the TUC Disputes Principles and Procedures[54].

The TUC Disputes Principles and Procedures

The TUC Disputes Principles and Procedures were adopted initially at the Bridlington Congress of the TUC in 1939[55], and are 'designed to minimise disputes between unions over membership questions'[56]. In the words of the TUC the principles were drawn up

> because trade unionists recognised that, in situations where more than one union was capable of representing a particular grade of worker, it was necessary to prevent the indiscriminate proliferation of unions if stable and rational trade union structures and collective bargaining machinery were to be developed. Their existence has also prevented the instability that would occur if breakaway unions were formed, or if groups of workers were able to move from one union to another without agreed regulation and procedure[57].

To these ends, the principles provided that no one who was or had recently been a member of any affiliated union would be accepted

---

into membership in another without enquiry of the present or former union. If the latter union objected to the transfer, and the former union believed the objection to be unreasonable, the matter could be referred to the TUC for adjudication if the two unions were unable to reach an agreement. This was designed to stop the poaching by one union of the members of another. The other main principle in contrast was designed to stop one union from organising in a workplace where another was already established, and provided that

> 'No union shall commence organising activities at any establishment or undertaking in respect of any grade or grades of workers in which another union has the majority of workers employed and negotiates wages and conditions, unless by arrangement with that union'.

Membership disputes between trade unions were (and are) dealt with under the Procedures accompanying the TUC Disputes Principles. If the dispute is not capable of resolution by agreement or conciliation, it would be necessary to establish a Disputes Committee of three senior trade unionists to resolve the matter. The Committee is empowered to make an Award, which previously could require one union to terminate the membership of a member or members who had wrongly been taken into membership. The courts were unwilling to imply such a power of termination into trade union rule books[58], so individual unions adopted a model rule which provided that the union in question could terminate a membership by giving 6 weeks' notice in order to comply with a decision of the TUC Disputes Committee[59]. This gave rise to a number of difficulties in practice, the courts never at ease with the Bridlington Principles[60]. In one case it was held that the rule did not authorise a termination of membership where the Disputes Committee had acted *ultra vires*, and in another that it did not authorise a termination of membership where the member had been recruited in breach of the Principles though no Award had yet been made by a Disputes Committee[62]. But in the leading case, to which we return below, the House of Lords overturned a Court of Appeal ruling that the model rule was invalid[63].

The Trade Union Reform and Employment Rights Act 1993, s.14

It was perfectly predictable that the Conservative governments of 1980 to 1997 would have something to say about the Disputes Principles and Procedures. And so they had, with the Major government taking a particularly strong exception to them[64]. According to Gillian Shephard, the responsible minister at the time, the TUC Disputes Principles and Procedures imposed another 'outdated and undemocratic' restriction on workers' 'freedom of choice'. In her view

People should be free to take jobs regardless of whether they are union members and they should have the freedom to choose which union they join.

Recognising that the Disputes Principles and Procedures were introduced as a means of resolving conflicts between unions over membership rights, they nevertheless 'always had a fundamental flaw', in that they made 'no provision for union members to be consulted or for their wishes to be taken into account'[66]. In the same vein, Michael Forsyth thought that the 'unions people choose to join should be a matter for them and should not be decided in smoke-filled rooms'[67]. Those who thought otherwise were accused of 'advancing the age old argument which has been put by dictators and collectivists over the years, which is that it is more efficient for two or three people to decide what is good for the rest'[68].

These concerns found legislative expression in the Trade Union Reform and Employment Rights Act 1993, s.14[69], which imposes wide ranging restrictions on trade union admission and expulsion rules[70], reflecting the general principle that trade unions should accept into membership anyone who wants to join, rather than anyone they would like to join. Yet despite the expansive drafting of what became TULRCA 1992, s.174, the main purpose of the change is to prevent trade unions from excluding or expelling members to comply with a TUC Disputes Committee ruling, though the section is not confined to such exclusions or expulsions[71]. Section 174 provides that

1 An individual shall not be excluded or expelled from a trade union unless the exclusion or expulsion is permitted by this section.

2 The exclusion or expulsion of an individual from a trade union is permitted by this section if (and only if) –

   a he does not satisfy, or no longer satisfies, an enforceable membership requirement contained in the rules of the union,

   b he does not qualify, or no longer qualifies, for membership of the union by reason of the union operating only in a particular part or particular parts of Great Britain,

   c in the case of a union whose purpose is the regulation of relations between its members and one particular employer or a number of particular employers who are associated, he is not, or is no longer, employed by that employer or one of those employers, or d the exclusion or expulsion is entirely attributable to his conduct.

3 A requirement in relation to membership of a union is 'enforceable' for the purposes of subsection (2)(a) if it restricts membership solely by reference to one or more of the following criteria –

    a employment in a specified trade, industry or profession,

    b occupational description (including grade, level or category of appointment), and

    c possession of specified trade, industrial or professional qualifications or work experience.

4 For the purposes of subsection (2)(d) 'conduct', in relation to an individual, does not include –

    a his being or ceasing to be, or having been or ceased to be –

      i a member of another trade union,

      ii employed by a particular employer at a particular place, or

      iii a member of a political party, or

    b conduct to which section 65 (conduct for which an individual may not be disciplined by a trade union) applies or would apply if the references in that section to the trade union which is relevant for the purposes of that section were references to any trade union.

The effect of the legislation was to require a major revision of the TUC Disputes Principles and Procedures. The basic principles remain in force, though in an amended form[72]. But membership of a trade union can no longer be refused because someone is already a member of another union, and membership of a trade union can no longer be terminated to comply with a Disputes Committee Award. Under the new procedure, a union which has recruited or organised in breach of the Principles may be required to provide financial compensation to the other union which lodged the complaint[73].

Trade union autonomy and the TUC Disputes Principles: The Human Rights Act

THIS is also an area where the Human Rights Act could have a bearing. Here it is important to recall that the principle of freedom of association is a multi-dimensional principle. It includes the right of the individual to be a member of an association and the right as such not to be discriminated against because of membership, for sure. But it also includes the right of individuals to be free in their association, in the sense that they should be able to develop their own constitutions and rules without State interference. This important second dimension to the principle is fully recognised in ILO Convention 87, which as we have seen provides that workers' organisations have 'the right to draw up their constitutions and rules... in full freedom'. An important aspect of this second dimension is the freedom of the association not only to determine its own government, procedures and rules, but also to determine its own membership. If people are to be free in association it can only be in association with people of their choice. An association which is compelled to take individuals into membership is no more free than the individual who is compelled into membership of an association. In suggesting that this is a worm on which the Human Rights Act might bite, there are a number of helpful developments on which it may now be possible to draw.

Cheall v APEX

The starting point of our consideration whether s.174 violates Convention rights is the particularly helpful decision of the House of Lords in *Cheall v APEX*[74]. Cheall had joined APEX without the consent of his union ACTSS, and was subsequently expelled following a TUC Disputes Committee ruling. He argued that his expulsion was unlawful for a number of reasons: these included the claim that the rule authorising the expulsion (the model rule) was contrary to public policy because it was in breach of article 11 of the ECHR. The point was dismissed at first instance, but taken and accepted by Lord Denning in the Court of Appeal which by a majority upheld Cheall's appeal[75]. According to Lord Denning, the English courts should give effect to the principle in article 11 which he read to mean 'the right of every man to join a trade union of his choice for the protection of his interests'. If a man has a right to join a trade union for the protection of his interests, he continued, he has the right not to be expelled from it without good cause and without a hearing, requirements which were not met in this case[76]. The effect was to transform article 11 which now gave workers a right to join a union of their choice and imposed a duty on the part of the union to accept them into membership and to retain them as members.

But there was an obvious flaw in this argument which was spotted by the House of Lords in upholding the union's appeal. In the words of Lord Diplock

> "*freedom of association can only be mutual; there can be no right of an individual to associate with other individuals who are not willing to associate with him.* The body of the membership of APEX, represented by its executive council and whose best interest it was the

---

duty of the executive council to promote, were not willing to continue to accept Cheall as a fellow-member. No doubt this was because if they continued to accept him, they ran the risk of attracting the sanction of suspension or expulsion of APEX from the TUC and all the attendant disadvantages to themselves as members of APEX that such suspension or expulsion would entail. But I know of no existing rule of public policy that would prevent trade unions from entering into arrangements with one another which they consider to be in the interests of their members in promoting order in industrial relations and enhancing their members' bargaining power with their employers... Different considerations might apply if the effect of Cheall's expulsion from APEX were to have put his job in jeopardy, either because of the existence of a closed shop or for some other reason." (Emphasis added)[77]

This is a passage of great significance, which reveals that the right to freedom of association is based on a principle of mutuality: there may be a right of an individual to associate with others, but there is no duty on the part of these others to associate with him or her. What Lord Diplock highlights and what Lord Denning ignored or overlooked is that the existing members of a trade union also have rights under the Convention: they too have a right to freedom of association, including a freedom to associate with people of their choice.

The European Commission of Human Rights

The House of Lords judgment in the *Cheall* case contains powerful support for the view that the provisions of TULRCA 1992, s.174 constitute a breach of article 11 of the ECHR and that they are thus vulnerable to challenge under the Human Rights Act. This is a view which is reinforced by the decision of the European Commission of Human Rights in Cheall's unsuccessful application to Strasbourg[78]. The application was ruled inadmissible, and although the English courts may not pay a lot of attention to the rulings of the Commission, they are required by the Human Rights Act to take them into account[79]. This one is particularly important, with the Commission accepting that for the purposes of article 11 of the ECHR, the right to freedom of association includes the right of the individual to be free in his or her association:

In the Commission's view the right to form trade unions involves, for example, the right of trade unions to draw up their own rules, to administer their own affairs and to establish and join trade union federations. Such trade union rights are explicitly recognised in Arts 3 and 5 of ILO Convention No 87 which must be taken into account in the present context.

In an equally important passage, the Commission went on specifically to say that

> The right to join a union for the protection of his interests cannot be interpreted as conferring a general right to join the union of one's choice irrespective of the rules of the union. In the exercise of their rights under Art 11(1), unions must remain free to decide, in accordance with union rules, questions concerning admission to and expulsion from the union[80].

It might be thought that these observations strengthen immeasurably the approach taken by the House of Lords in the same case. Still, we should not overdo it, and should keep in mind what these cases were ultimately concerned with. They were concerned with the question whether the individual has a right to membership of an association. They were not concerned directly with the question whether the association has the right not to take individuals into membership. It is of course the case that the two questions may be the two sides of the same coin, and that it would be indefensible sophistry to say that an individual has no right to join an association but that an association has no right to refuse an individual into membership. It would be all the more indefensible not only in view of Lord Diplock's acknowledgement that the right to freedom of association must be mutual (which must mean freedom for both parties) but also in light of the fact that the European Court of Human Rights has unequivocally held that the right to freedom of association includes a negative right not to associate[81]. If individuals cannot be compelled by the State to join associations, then presumably the members of the association (also the bearers of the negative right) cannot be compelled to take individuals into membership[82].

The importance of the Social Charter

SO there are perhaps two different areas where article 11 may be useful for trade unions and their members in litigation under the Human Rights Act. In both of these cases, an important dimension to any possible litigation under the Human Rights Act will be the role of other international treaties, most notably ILO Convention 87 and the Social Charter of the Council of Europe. Indeed as we have seen the European Commission of Human Rights directed that the former 'must be taken into account' in the construction of article 11[83]. Both of these treaties also protect the right to freedom of association, in different ways and in much greater detail than the ECHR, and both of these treaties have been found to have been breached by the United Kingdom in many of the areas discussed in this chapter. The question which arises is whether and to what extent the jurisprudence of the supervisory bodies under both of these treaties can be relied upon in the English courts in any application based based on a submission that domestic law or practice is in breach of article 11. To date the courts in this country have shown little willingness to have regard to either ILO Conventions or the Social Charter of 1961, even in cases where they have been cited in argument[84], and in which they may have been helpful in resolving the issue which the court was dealing with[85].

The Social Charter and Freedom of Association

Freedom of association is protected by the Social Charter of 1961, article 5, a provision which has been accepted by the United Kingdom. Dealing specifically with the Right to Organise, this provides that

> With a view to ensuring or promoting the freedom of workers and employers to form local, national or international organisations for the protection of their economic and social interests and to join those organisations, the Contracting Parties undertake that national law shall not be such as to impair, nor shall it be so applied as to impair this freedom. The extent to which the guarantees provided for in this Article shall apply to the police shall be determined by national laws or regulations. The principle governing the application to the members of the armed forces of these guarantees and the extent to which they shall apply to persons in this category shall equally be determined by national laws or regulations[86].

Unlike the ECHR, the Social Charter is not enforced by the European Court of Human Rights but by a body which is now referred to as the Social Rights Committee. The Committee reviews the law and practice of parties which have ratified the Social Charter and makes Observations based on its review. There is also a procedure now under the Collective Complaints Protocol of 1995 whereby non governmental organisations can make a complaint to the Social Rights Committee alleging that a government is in breach of one or more of its obligations under the Charter. This is in addition to the regular process of supervision which the Committee undertakes. But the United Kingdom has not ratified the Collective Complaints Protocol. So this is not a course of action open to trade unions in the United Kingdom, as it is in a number of other countries.

The United Kingdom in fact has one of the poorest records of compliance with the Social Charter. We have accepted to be bound by fewer of the 72 obligations than most of the other 23 countries which have ratified the Social Charter and we have accepted fewer than all but one (Denmark) of the member states of the EC[87]. We are, moreover, in breach of more of the core articles of the Social Charter than any other country and we can claim to be in full and acknowledged compliance with only one half of the 46 provisions which were the subject of scrutiny during the 14th and most recent cycle of supervision by the Social Rights Committee[88]. One area of difficulty is article 5 which we have been found to have breached in the 12th, 13th and 14th cycles of supervision. On the last occasion the breach was said to arise on five grounds, including 'a possibility for employers to take certain measures such as awarding preferential remuneration to employees in order to persuade them to relinquish trade union activities and collective bargaining'; as well as 'a limitation of the right of trade unions to exclude or expulse (sic) an individual'[89]. But it is not only the Social Rights Committee which has drawn negative conclusions about the United Kingdom's compliance with article 5. The Committee of Ministers have also issued a Recommendation addressed to the United Kingdom because of a number of failings, which include article 5 because of the Ullswater amendment in particular[90].

The Social Charter and the Human Rights Act

The relationship between the ECHR and the Social Charter was considered by the Strasbourg Court in the 'article 11 trilogy' in the mid 1970s. In these early cases, the Social Charter was used to narrow the definition of article 11. For although article 6(2) of the Social Charter binds Contracting States 'to promote joint consultation between workers and employers', this is not 'a real right to consultation'[91]. Besides, said the Court, 'Article 20 [of the Social Charter] permits a ratifying State not to accept the undertaking in Article 6(1)'. This led the Court to decline to accept the submission that article 11 included a right on the part of the complainant union to be consulted. To have accepted this argument, 'would amount to admitting that the 1961 Charter took a retrograde step in this direction'[92]. But although the same views were expressed almost verbatim in the other cases which form the 'article 11 trilogy'[93], a different tone was struck in *Sigurjonsson v Iceland*[94] where it was held by the Court that the Social Charter could be used as an aid to the construction of article 11 of the Convention, taking into account also for this purpose the jurisprudence of the Committee of Independent Experts (as the Social Rights Committee was then called).

In taking this view the Court appears to have overcome its concerns that not all the provisions of the Social Charter were binding even on those States which had ratified it. But even if this were a concern, it is not one which need trouble the British courts which are free to have regard at least to those numbered paragraphs of the Social Charter which we have accepted. It would be extremely useful if the British courts could be persuaded to follow the example of the Strasbourg Court and have regard to the Social Charter and the jurisprudence relating thereto when construing article 11[95]. If they were to do so, it would conclusively resolve any uncertainty about whether the two measures discussed in this chapter constitute a breach of article 11. It would reinforce the arguments that the Ullswater amendment and the issues surrounding it violates article 11, and it would do the same for arguments alleging a breach in relation to the current restrictions on trade union autonomy about the admission and expulsion of members. It would also clear a path for ILO Conventions in domestic law, not only because ILO jurisprudence strongly influences the Social Rights Committee of the Council of Europe, but also because ILO Conventions are another source relied upon directly by the Strasbourg Court (and the Commission when it existed) in the construction of article 11[96].

Conclusion

THE Human Rights Act is likely to be anxiously debated in the press, form the basis of many different legal challenges on a wide range of different issues, and have political implications and repercussions which at this stage probably could not be imagined[97]. So far as trade unions are concerned, the experience of rights based adjudication in our courts, in the European Court of Human Rights and in the courts of other countries in the common law tradition has not been a happy one. There are few trade union victories at the trough of adjudication: it is tempting to think that the best that can be hoped for is the Canadian approach which has been one of constitutional *laissez-faire*: the Supreme Court of Canada has generally stood back and been reluctant to intervene in trade union matters[98]. So it has been unwilling on the one hand to challenge restrictions on trade union bargaining rights or on the right to strike[99], and on the other to challenge attempts to restrict union shops or trade union political activities[100]. The constitutional right to freedom of association has been neither given nor taken away, though guarantees of free speech have operated to restrain the remedies which might be granted by the Labour Relations Boards when dealing with anti-union conduct by employers[101].

But the Canadians are starting from a higher base of legal protection for trade unions than we are in this country, with the result that it would be reasonable to look to the Human Rights Act to address some of the more vicious attacks on freedom of association which were made during the Thatcher/Major years and which have yet fully to be addressed by the Labour government. This chapter has focussed on two areas, both of which give rise to strong and compelling arguments that article 11 has been breached, one relating to the statutory power of employers under the Ullswater amendment to discriminate against trade unionists, and the second to the statutory restrictions on trade unions to control their own membership. The judgement that these measures may violate article 11 is based on the jurisprudence of the Strasbourg Court which has emphasised that the express protection of trade union rights in article 11 is of substantive value, and that in interpreting article 11 it is permissible to have regard to the Social Charter and the rich jurisprudence relating thereto, as well as appropriate ILO Conventions. But in view of the fact that important aspects of the first of the two issues considered in this chapter is already in the Strasbourg system, the real opportunity presented for trade unions in practice may relate mainly to the issues surrounding the Trade Union Reform and Employment Rights Act 1993, s.14[102].

The focus in this chapter on two discrete issues has been deliberate. The aim is to reinforce the suggestion made in the introduction to the chapter that there is a need to think strategically about how to use the Act. This means developing a positive and co-ordinated litigation strategy, which means in turn picking issues which are ripe for challenge. The two issues discussed in this chapter appear at this stage to provide the most fertile ground for the application of article 11 in domestic legal proceedings, though it is important not to lose sight of the fact that there may be others, most notably the current restrictions in TULRCA 1992, s.65 restricting the power of trade unions to take disciplinary action against members who act in breach of the rules. First introduced in 1988 these measures in particular restrain trade unions from disciplining members who refuse to support industrial action, even when properly called under the rules of the union and the legislation currently in force[104]. Although this is not a major issue at the time of writing, nevertheless many of the arguments which could be deployed against TULRCA 1992, s.174 would apply here too[105]. But even this may not exhaust the potential of the Act: it remains to be seen, for example, how far the Human Rights Act may be used in litigation under the new trade union recognition procedure. And it remains to be seen too how the Act might be used by trade union members against their unions –

for example the effect of the article 6 right to a fair trial on trade union disciplinary procedures.

Notes

1 The best general account of article 11 is still M Forde, "The European Convention on Human Rights and Labor Law" (1983) 31 *American Journal of Comparative Law* 301.

2 See K D Ewing, *Britain and the ILO* (2nd ed, 1994).

3 See K D Ewing, "Social Rights and Human Rights: Britain and the Social Charter – the Conservative Legacy" [2000] EHRLR 91.

4 [1995] 2 All ER 100.

5 Trade Union Reform and Employment Rights Act 1992, s.13, amending Trade Union and Labour Relations (Consolidation) Act 1992, s.148(3).

6 Trade Union Reform and Employment Rights Act 1992, s.14, amending Trade Union and Labour Relations (Consolidation) Act 1992, s.174.

7 Trade Union and Labour Relations (Consolidation) Act 1992, ss 64-67. For an elegant argument that these provisions breach article 11, see S Leader, "The European Convention on Human Rights, The Employment Act 1988 and the Right to Refuse to Strike" (1991) 20 ILJ 39.

8 Trade Union and Labour Relations (Consolidation) Act 1992, ss.46-59.

9 Employment Relations Act 1999 s.1 and Sch 1, introducing new Trade Union and Labour Relations (Consolidation) Act 1992, Sch A1. It would be premature to contemplate the Human Rights Act being used to help with this, and the point is not pursued, though it may be necessary to return to it depending on how the jurisprudence develops.

10 *London Underground Ltd v NUR* [1996] ICR 170, at p 181.

11 See also J Hendy, 'The Human Rights Act, Article 11, and the Right to Strike' [1998] EHRLR 582.

12 Human Rights Act 1998, s.2.

13 *Young, James and Webster v United Kingdom* (1982) 4 EHRR 28.

14 *Council of Civil Service Unions v United Kingdom* (1988) 10 EHRR 269.

15 See *National Union of Belgian Police v Belgium* (1975) 1 EHRR 578, *Swedish Engine Drivers' Union v Sweden* (1975) 1 EHRR 617, and *Schmidt and Dahlstrom v Sweden* (1975) 1 EHRR 637.

16 (1975) 1 EHRR 578.

17 *ibid*, p 591.

18 *ibid*.

19 *ibid*. The steps in question included the presenting of claims and the making of representations, there being no suggestion that the steps taken by the union were 'ignored by the Government'.

20 *Swedish Engine Drivers' Union v Sweden, op cit*, and *Schmidt and Dahlstrom v Sweden, op cit*.

21 (1975) 1 EHRR 617.

22 *ibid*, at pp 628-629.

23 The practice prevailed in the United Kingdom until the 1980s, and was facilitated by legislation in the 1970s which permitted (but did not require) employers and trade unions to enter into union membership agreements whereby employees were required to be or become members of one or more specified trade unions as a condition of employment. Any employee who refused to join a trade union or who was denied membership of or expelled from a trade union could be dismissed, and would have no remedy for unfair dismissal, save in exceptional circumstances (for religious objections).

24 (1982) 4 EHRR 28.

25 On the incidence of the closed shop today, see N Millward, A Bryson and J Forth, *All Change at Work?* (2000), p 89.

26 Its death warrant was signed at European level by the Community Charter of the Fundamental Social Rights of Workers 1989, art 11 which provides that 'Every employer and every worker shall have the freedom to join or not to join [professional organisations or trade unions] without any personal or occupational damage being thereby suffered...'.

27 Such as operate in Canada and the United States where agency shop arrangements allow agreements to be made whereby employees must be members of a trade union or pay an agency fee in lieu of membership. These arrangements have survived constitutional challenge in the United States, though the Supreme Court has held that agency fee payers should not be required to make a contribution to the political activities of the union. Agency fee payers also have legally enforceable rights against the union which owes all members of a bargaining unit a duty of fair representation. Such arrangements are expressly forbidden in this country, which allows some workers to take a free ride on the backs of their colleagues, to the extent that they enjoy the benefits of collective bargaining without having to help meet the costs, either as members of the union or otherwise.

28 See *Young, James and Webster, op cit*, at p 53.

29 See M Forde, 'The Closed Shop case' (1982) 11 ILJ 1.

30 *Sigurjonsson v Iceland* (1993) 16 EHRR 462.

31 *ibid*, at p 479.

32 [1995] 2 All ER 100. This is the so-called *Wilson and Palmer* case.

33 For a full account, see K D Ewing, 'Dancing with the Daffodils' (2000) 50 *Federation News* 1.

34 The position was then governed by the Employment Protection (Consolidation) Act 1978, s.23.

35 *Discount Tobacco and Confectionery Ltd v Armitage* [1990] IRLR 15.

36 *Wilson v Associated Newspapers Ltd/Palmer v Associated British Ports* [1993] IRLR 336.

37 In so holding it was also openly acknowledged by Lord Browne-Wilkinson that their Lordships' decision 'leaves an undesirable lacuna in the legislation protecting employees against victimisation' (p 112).

38 Employment Relations Act 1999, Sch 2.

39 [1987] 3 All ER 100.

40 ILO, Report of the Committee of Experts on the Application of Conventions and Recommendations (2000), p 261.

41 See K D Ewing, 'Freedom of Association and the Employment Relations Act 1999' (1999) 28 ILJ 283.

42 For fuller treatment, see K D Ewing, 'Dancing with the Daffodils' (2000) 50 *Federation News* 1.

43 *Associated Newspapers plc v Wilson, op cit.*

44 Ewing, 'Dancing with the Daffodils', *op cit.*

45 This is because there 'will continue to be circumstances in which employers seek, quite legitimately, to change their bargaining arrangements, for example following voluntary or statutory derecognition or where the bargaining unit has changed'. But apart from begging the question of how employers

managed before now without any apparent difficulty, it is also the case that this is not a reason for retaining Ullswater which goes some way beyond permitting the parties to agree more or less than a collective agreement prescribes: it also expressly allows for discrimination against trade unionists, provided that a court is satisfied that the discrimination is not unreasonable. See Ewing, *ibid.*

46 Application Nos 30668/96, 30671/96, and 30678/96.

47 *Cheall v United Kingdom* (1986) 8 EHRR 74.

48 *National Union of Belgian Police v Belgium, op cit.*

49 *ibid,* p 591.

50 See note 45 above.

51 The Trade Union Act 1871, s.4 sought unsuccessfully to exclude the courts from trade union membership disputes.

52 For a good account, see C Grunfeld, *Modern Trade Union Law* (1966).

53 Article 3(2) then provides that 'The public authorities shall refrain from any interference which would restrict this right or impede the lawful exercise thereof'. Article 11 is also relevant: 'Each member of the International Labour Organisation for which this Convention is in force undertakes to take all necessary and appropriate measures to ensure that workers and employers may exercise freely the right to organise'. The British government had no diffculty in ratifying the Convention (though in relation to Great Britain only): see International Labour Conference, Proposed action by His Majesty's Government in the United Kingdom and Northern Ireland on the Convention concerning Freedom of Association and Protection of the Right to Organise (Cmd 7704, 1948 - 49).

54 For analysis (now somewhat dated), see P Kalis, "The Adjudication of Inter-union Membership Disputes: The TUC Disputes Committee Revisited" (1977) 6 ILJ 19, and P Kalis, "The Effectiveness and Utility of the Disputes Committee of the Trades Union Congress" (1978) 16 BJIR 41. See also C Ball, "The Resolution of Inter-union Conflict: The TUC's Reaction to Legal Intervention" (1980) 9 ILJ 323.

55 They have been amended on a number of occasions subsequently, most recently in 1993. For a good account of the history, see *TUC Disputes Principles and Procedures* (1993), pp 6-9.

56 *TUC Disputes Principles and Procedures, ibid,* p 6.

57 *Ibid.*

58 *Spring v NASDS* [1956] 1 WLR 585.

59 See for example FBU Rules, Rule 8(3)(e), GMB Rules, Rule 5(4), NURMTW Rules, Rule 2(21), TGWU Rules, Rule 20(19), and UNISON Rules, Rule C7.6.

60 See P Davies and M Freedland, *Labour Law Text and Materials* (2nd ed, 1984), pp 611-617.

61 *Rothwell v APEX* [1976] ICR 211.

62 *Walsh v AUEW, The Times,* 15 July 1977.

63 *Cheall v APEX* [1983] ICR 398. See also *EMA v ACAS* [1980] ICR 215.

64 See Employment Department, *Industrial Relations in the 1990s. Proposals for Further Reform of Industrial Relations and Trade Union Law,* (Cm 1602, 1991).

65 H C Debs, 17 November 1992, col 171. See also Employment Department, *op cit,* para 6.10, where reference was made to difficulties encountered by

USDAW members who wanted to join the GMB because thay objected to the USDAW's position on Sunday Trading, but who were prevented because of Bridlington. According to the government these people were 'locked to a union with whose policy on an important issue of conscience they fundamentally disagreed' (para 6.10). The government's view was that 'just as no one should be obliged to become a union member or a non-member as a price of obtaining a job, so no-one should be obliged to choose between joining a union to which he does not wish to belong and joining no union at all' (para 6.13).

66 H C Debs, *ibid.* See also Employment Department, *ibid*, para 6.8.

67 Official Report, Standing Committee F, 8 December 1992, col 122.

68 *ibid.*

69 See now Trade Union and Labour Relations (Consolidation) Act 1992, s.174.

70 For a good account of the changes, see B Simpson, 'Individualism versus Collectivism: An Evaluation of Section 14 of the Trade Union Reform and Employment Rights Act 1993' (1993) 22 ILJ 181.

71 See *Gluchowski v NACODS* [1996] IRLR 252.

72 They are set out in TUC Disputes Principles and Procedures, *op cit.*

73 *Ibid*, p 24. The amount of compensation is not to exceed two years loss of contributions to the complainant union. See *UNISON and TGWU: Middlesbrough Borough Council* (TUC Disputes Committee Award, 1999).

74 [1983] ICR 398.

75 [1982] ICR 543.

76 *ibid*, pp 554-5.

77 [1983] ICR 398, at p 405.

78 *Cheall v United Kingdom* (1986) 8 EHRR 74.

79 Human Rights Act 1998, s.2. See C A Gearty, chapter 1 above.

80 But it was also accepted that there may be circumstances where the State may interfere to 'protect the individual against any abuse of a dominant position by trade unions'. Here the Commission had in mind the situation where 'exclusion or expulsion was not in accordance with union rules, or where the rules were wholly unreasonable or arbitrary or where the consequences of exclusion or expulsion resulted in exceptional hardship such as job loss because of a closed shop'. None of these considerations applied here. The Commission noted in particular that the expulsion was carried out in accordance withe the rules of the union (the model rule) which could not be considered to be 'unreasonable' (p 75).

81 See section 2 above.

82 For further treatment of this issue by the European Court of Human Rights, see *Gustafsson v Sweden* (1996) 22 EHRR 409.

83 *Cheall v United Kingdom, op cit.*

84 See *Associated Newspapers plc v Wilson* [1995] 2 All ER 100.

85 There does not appear to be a single reference to the Social Charter in a reported judgment of an English court, and on one famous occasion ILO Convention 87 was dismissed as a 'minor matter': *Council of Civil Service Unions v Minister for the Civil Service* [1985] AC 374 (the GCHQ case). There is a reference to the importance of the Social Charter by the European Court of Justice in *Defrenne v SABENA* [1976] 2 CMLR 98. It is also referred to in the EC Treaty and in the EU Treaty, as well as in many EC Directives on employment law.

86 Article 6 of the Social Charter deals separately with collective bargaining and the right to strike.

87 For a full account, see Ewing, 'Social Rights and Human Rights: Britain and the Social Charter – the Conservative Legacy', *op cit*.

88 *ibid.*

89 Council of Europe, Committee of Independent Experts, Conclusions XIV-1, vol 2, pp 799-800.

90 Council of Europe, Committee of Ministers, Recommendation No R ChS (97)3 on the application of the European Social Charter by the United Kingdom during the period 1992-93.

91 *National Union of Belgian Police v Belgium, op cit.*

92 *ibid*, p 591.

93 *Swedish Engine Drivers' Union v Sweden, op cit*, and *Schmidt and Dahlstrom v Sweden, op cit.*

94 (1993) 16 EHRR 462.

95 As already pointed out above, the British courts are required to have regard to this jurisprudence. They will have to have good reasons for saying that the Social Charter (and ILO Convention 87) have no bearing on the construction of Convention rights.

96 *Sigurjonsson v Iceland, op cit*, at p 479. See also *Cheall v United Kingdom, op cit.*

97 A currently controversial issue is whether road side speeding cameras produce circumstances which cause a breach of article 6. Who would have thought it? How many people must die or be injured in the interests of the human rights of the speeding motorist?

98 See the valuable contribution by Judy Fudge in chapter 7 of this volume.

99 *Reference re Public Service Employee Relations Act* (1987) 38 DLR (4th) 161; *Public Service Alliance of Canada v The Queen* (1987) 38 DLR (4th) 249; *Government of Saskatchewan v Retail, Wholesale and Department Store Union, Locals 544, 496, 635, and 955* (1987) 38 DLR (4th) 277.

100 *Lavigne v Ontario Public Service Employees Union* (1991) 81 DLR (4th) 545.

101 *Re National Bank of Canada and Retail Clerks' International Union* (1984) 9 DLR (4th) 10. In that case the Bank was found to have violated freedom of association rights and was instructed by the Labour Relations Board to send a letter to employees stating that it had violated the Labour Code and that it was committed to the objectives of the Code. This was said by Beetz J in the Supreme Court of Canada to be 'totalitarian and as such alien to the tradition of free nations such as Canada, even for the repression of the most serious crimes' (p 31). It seems that the violation of internationally protected rights to organise is not also 'totalitarian'.

102 Now Trade Union and Labour Relations (Consolidation) Act 1992, s.174.

103 See Human Rights Act 1998, s.3.

104 See now Trade Union and Labour Relations (Consolidation) Act 1992, ss.64-67.

105 These measures have also been found in breach of international labour standards.

Chapter 5

Article 11 and the right to strike

John Hendy QC

THE question to be addressed in this chapter is whether the Human Rights Act which brings article 11 of the European Convention for the Protection of Human Rights into United Kingdom law, will introduce with it a right to strike. There is not, and never has been a right to strike in this country and it would be a surprise to many if the introduction of the Convention gave British trade unionists a new and fundamental right of this kind. Watchers of the European Court of Human Rights have noted its apparent lack of sympathy for the collective rights of trade unionism (ditto our own courts). But there is a formidable logic to the argument that a right to strike can be found in the Convention, though it is most certainly not expressly stated. If so, then the Human Rights Act will permit the courts here to express that right in United Kingdom law.

This chapter considers the impact of the Convention on the common law, the unlawfulness of strikes at common law, the extent to which article 11 guarantees a right to strike, and the possible effect of article 11 on the law of strikes[1].

Article 11: Freedom of assembly and association

ARTICLE 11 of the Convention makes no mention of the right to strike. It reads as follows:

"1. Everyone has the right to freedom of peaceful assembly and to freedom of association with others, including the right to form and to join trade unions for the protection of his interests.

"2. No restrictions shall be placed on the exercise of these rights other than such as are prescribed by law and are necessary in a democratic society in the interests of national security or public safety, for the prevention of disorder or crime, for the protection of health or morals or for the protection of the rights and freedoms of others. This article shall not prevent the imposition of lawful restrictions on the exercise of these rights by members of the armed forces, of the police or of the administration of the State".

The principal jurisprudence on article 11 is, of course, the case law of the European Court of Human Rights. But freedom of association provisions are familiar and are found, in a format of varying similarity, in other international instruments, in particular: the United Nations Declaration of Human Rights 1948, article 3(4); the International Covenant on Economic Social and Cultural Rights 1966 article 8(1); the International Covenant on Civil and Political Rights 1966, article 22; ILO Convention 87 (in a very different format); and the Social Charter of 1961 of the Council of Europe, articles 5 and 6 (also in markedly different form). These instruments have some impact on the European Court of Human Rights and consequently may be the subject of consideration by United Kingdom courts faced with the application of the Human Rights Act. Most recently the first Draft Charter of Fundamental Rights of the European Union has been published with the intention that it should be adopted by the Inter-Governmental Conference in Nice in December 2000 (as amended by negotiation, no doubt)[2]. This draft too provides for a right of collective action. These instruments, their associated jurisprudence, and their relevance to the Convention and its likely application in the United Kingdom will be considered in the author's chapter "Industrial Action and International Standards" in the forthcoming book by the Institute of Employment Rights on the Employment Relations Act.

The Convention and the common law

IT will be recalled that under the Human Rights Act, legislation which is held by the courts to be incompatible with the Convention will nonetheless remain effective (s.3(2)(b) and (c)) though it will be declared incompatible (s.4) so leading later to amending legislation (s.10 and 11). And primary and secondary legislation, whether pre- or post- the Act, "must be read and given effect in a way which is compatible with the Convention rights" (s.3(1)). But the common law is subject to no such protective machinery to soften the effect of the Convention .

The Act makes no express provision for the Convention's effect on the common law, so that it is assumed that the Convention must take precedence over incompatible common law rules and rights. Courts and tribunals (s.6(3)(a)), (as well as certain public authorities[3]) are bound not "to act in a way which is incompatible with one or more of the Convention rights" (s.6(1))[4]. Consequently there is no bar in the Act to prevent the common law being subjected by the courts to the full force of the Convention[5].

Article 11 is not only intended to protect against interference with the rights contained within it but the European Court of Human Rights has held, in a trade union rights case, that "there may be positive obligations to secure the effective enjoyment of these rights"[6]. In this the United Kingdom courts, as organs of the State, must presumably play their part. One means at their disposal is adaptation of the common law.

This is highly significant to the subject of this chapter because, notwithstanding the mass of trade union legislation of the 1980s and early 1990s (and indeed that of the last century and more), it is the common law and not statute which renders strikes unlawful and hence precludes the existence of any right to strike in the United Kingdom.

Consequently if a right to strike were found by British judges to be nestling within the Convention, the common law could be immediately adapted to give effect to it. The extent to which the common law would be so adapted by the courts were such a right to be held to be found in the Convention remains to be seen, of course. Recent judicial enthusiasm for human rights and, indeed, a certain detectable distaste for the extent of the curtailment of trade union freedom by the legislation of the 1980s and early 1990s[7], may not be matched by a corresponding fervour for the establishment of a broad right to strike[8].

The absence of the right to strike in the United Kingdom – from the worker's perspective

THE absence of the right to strike in the United Kingdom is characterised by the fact that a strike[9] is unlawful at common law. Consequently, as the United Kingdom government pointed out in its 1998 Report to the ILO[10]:

Under United Kingdom law, individuals are almost invariably breaking their contracts under which they work when they take any form of industrial action, irrespective of whether the action is

official or unofficial, or whether the action is lawfully or unlawfully organised. They can therefore be sued on an individual basis by
employers for damages.

The taking of strike action is a breach of the employee's contract of
employment in virtually every case. This applies even where the
worker's trade union has fulfilled the onerous obligations imposed
by Part V of the Trade Union and Labour Relations (Consolidation)
Act 1992 to secure protection for the union.

A strike will be in breach of the contract of employment for two
reasons. Firstly, the striker is failing to perform the obligations of
work in the contract. Secondly, by seeking to cause disruption to the
employer's business, the striker is breaching the "implied term to
serve the employer faithfully within the requirements of the contract"[11].

It is not merely a "strike"[12] which is in breach of the contract of
employment. Because of the inevitable breach of the duty of faithful
service, virtually all other forms of industrial action will breach the
contract of employment[13]. Consequently in this chapter, references
to "strike" and "striker" may usually be taken to apply to industrial
action short of a strike.

The consequence of industrial action being in breach of contract
is severe for the worker. "Any form of industrial action by a worker
is a breach of contract which entitles the employer at common law
to dismiss the worker..."[14], or to refuse to pay wages[15], or to sue for
damages[16]. The employer's power to impose these penalties is not
diminished to any extent whatever by the fulfilment of the union's
statutory obligations under Part V of the 1992 Act.

Independent of the contract of employment but to some degree
protecting it, there is, of course, a right to claim reinstatement
and/or compensation for unfair dismissal by virtue of Part X of the
Employment Rights Act 1996. However this right is subject to a
number of limitations amongst which are that such right is denied to
any worker dismissed whilst participating in a strike which is not
"official", ie. supported by his or her union[17]. Where a strike is
denied protection by reason of a failure by the union to comply with
the requirements of the 1992 Act, the consequences of the union
making the strike official would be unlawful and restrainable by
injunction and render the union liable in damages if sued. Consequently, such a union will not make such a strike official or, if the
strike commences, the union will be obliged to repudiate it in writing through the burdensome machinery of sections 20-21 of the
1992 Act. Any person thereafter striking in pursuit of the dispute
would therefore be denied the right to complain of unfair dismissal

if dismissed. The only remedy for non-compliance with an order for reinstatement or re-engagement is an award of further compensation. Whilst in relation to dismissals on trade union grounds this used to be at a greatly enhanced rate[18], it now (since 1999) is the same formula as for other unfair dismissals, namely an additional award of between 26 and 52 weeks' pay[19].

Section 16 and Schedule 5 of the Employment Relations Act 1999 enlarge the rights of strikers to claim unfair dismissal by inserting a new s.238A into the 1992 Act. The 1999 provisions limit the right to claim unfair dismissal to those engaged in industrial action which is protected. The new provision guarantees an automatic finding of unfair dismissal and consequential compensation. It does not guarantee reinstatement or re-engagement.

Were the law to recognise a right to strike, the question is whether it would relieve in some way the consequence that a strike is in breach of the contract of employment, so preventing dismissal. The acknowledgement of the right to strike would not appear to impinge on the statutory scheme of unfair dismissal so far as it affects those on strike unless the right to strike was held to prevent the dismissal (in which case the unfair dismissal provisions would not be relevant), or unless it was held that the unfair dismissal protection was sufficient protection of the right to strike, ie. that the limitations of the unfair dismissal provisions were within the United Kingdom's "margin of appreciation" (see below).

A recent example of the impact of the absence of a right to strike on workers is illustrated in *University College London NHS Trust v UNISON*[20]. There the absence of the right to strike combined with a desire on the part of the workers (and the union) to remain within the law, resulted in the workers and the union being denied the right to take strike action in circumstances where it would be thought, in probably every other country in western Europe, that there was no valid reason for the law to intervene to deny the right to strike. The facts were that the union sought from the current employers a guarantee that terms and conditions would be maintained when, in the near future, staff were transferred from the existing to a new employer. This industrial dispute was found (after the statutory ballot) not to be within the statutory definition of "a trade dispute". Because, as Judge LJ put it in the judgment of the Court of Appeal,

> In reality, the understandable concern of the union is to secure the protection of all these workers by achieving satisfactory terms and conditions, not with their present but with their future employers.

Hence the union lost its statutory protection and, if the workers had taken industrial action, they would have been at risk of dismissal for breach of contract and outside the benefit of the new unfair dismissal regime (though in fact the latter was not in force at the time).

The absence of the right to strike in the United Kingdom – from the trade union's perspective

THERE are judicial dicta recognising that the right to strike as an aspect of collective bargaining, the very purpose of trade unionism. Lord Wright said in *Crofter Hand Woven Tweed v Harris*[21]:

> Where the rights of labour are concerned, the rights of the employer are conditioned by the rights of the men to give or withhold their services. The right of workmen to strike is an essential element in the principle of collective bargaining.

It is the case that, notwithstanding the provenance of this explicit recognition of the right to strike, the cases show that there is no right to strike in the United Kingdom whether on the part of the workers or the union.

Trade union organisation of or support for a strike in United Kingdom law is governed by the central feature that the calling or supporting of a strike by a trade union (or other person) will be prima facie unlawful because it will constitute an inducement of breach[22] of the contracts of employment of the workers called on strike. It may also constitute breach or interference with the performance of other contracts by reason of the breaches of contracts of employment[23]. It can also amount to any one of a wide variety of "industrial torts" developed by the common law. All these depend on proof of an element of unlawfulness as a preliminary element in the establishment of the tort. This element of unlawfulness is usually, but not invariably[24], fulfilled by demonstrating the inevitable breach of the contract of employment by the worker[25].

In consequence of the unlimited liability of trade unions for calling strikes which breached the workers' contracts of employment[26], freedom for unions to organise and support strike action was procured in 1906 by the grant of protection from legal action for certain acts done "in contemplation or furtherance of a trade dispute"[27]. This phrase ("the golden formula"[28]) has remained unchanged over the years. But the protection it has given has been subject to expansion and diminution in response to judicial innovations and parliamentary reaction at various times over the years. The detail of the changes is not relevant here.

It is to be noted that the need for reliance on the statutory protection of trade unions (and others) for the organisation and support of industrial action would be significantly diminished if the right to strike was held, in some way, to overcome the unlawfulness which flows from the pivotal thesis that inducing a strike is tortious because, at the least, it induces a breach of contract by the worker[29]. This unlawfulness could be overcome by altering the common law to hold that it was not unlawful to induce a strike; it would not be necessary to make the more fundamental finding that the strike was not a breach of the contract of employment.

The Convention and its jurisprudence

ON the face of it article 11 appears to confer no rights in relation to trade union membership other than the right, in effect, merely to hold a union card in association with others. There is no express inclusion of any other right (or freedom) derived from that right. However, a right of union membership so constrained would be *"legalistic, ungenerous and vapid"* (as the Chief Justice of Canada put it[30]) and is inconsistent with the jurisprudence of the European Court of Human Rights.

Though the Court has not so far been noted for its enthusiasm for trade union rights over those of other litigants, it has nonetheless declined to adopt a literal approach to article 11 and has recognised implied rights within the express right to trade union membership[31].

More relevantly in the present context, the Court has rejected a narrow construction of the words of article 11 and held that from the express positive right of union membership other positive rights are to be derived[32]. These include the right to draw up and enforce union constitutions: *Cheall v United Kingdom*[33]; *Johansson v Sweden*[34]. Most importantly, the Court has also held that the article 11 right to trade union membership implies a positive right to be heard and a positive right to trade union action.

Two cases are of particular relevance. In *Swedish Engine Drivers' Union v Sweden*[35] the issue was whether article 11 meant that a union could require a State employer to reach a collective agreement with it. The Court held that article 11 did not extend so far, certainly where the union, on the facts of the case, had the right to represent its members vis-à-vis the employer, negotiated with the employer, and where the employer extended to the members of the union the benefits of a collective agreement concluded with other unions which satisfied representativity criteria designed to promote an orderly system of collective bargaining in the relevant sectors[36]. The Strasbourg Court observed (of the applicant union):

It is open to it, for instance, to present claims, to make representations for the protection of the interests of its members or certain of them, and to negotiate with the employer. Nor does the applicant union in any way allege that the steps it takes are ignored by the [employer]. In these circumstances and in the light of the two foregoing paragraphs, the fact alone that the [employer] has in principle refused during the past few years to enter into collective agreements with the applicant union does not constitute a breach of article 11(1) considered on its own.

But the Court was emphatic that from article 11 there was to be derived a positive inferred right on the part of a union in order to protect the interests of members:

The Court does not, however, accept the view expressed by the minority in the Commission who describe the phrase 'for the protection of his interests' as redundant. These words, clearly denoting purpose, show that the Convention safeguards freedom to protect the occupational interests of trade union members by trade union action, the conduct and development of which the Contracting States must both permit and make possible. In the opinion of the court, it follows that the members of a trade union have a right, in order to protect their interests, that the trade union should be heard. Article 11(1) certainly leaves each State a free choice of the means to be used towards this end. Whilst the concluding of collective agreements is one of these means, there are others. What the Convention requires is that under national law trade unions should be enabled, in conditions not at variance with article 11, to strive for the protection of their members' interests.

In the other case, *National Union of Belgian Police v Belgium*[37] the issue was whether the union could insist on being consulted on behalf of its members by the authorities. The European Court of Human Rights held that it could not, in particular because it was in any event in practice consulted. In the same language as that of the previous case it reiterated the rights to trade union action and to be heard and stated:

No-one disputes the fact that the applicant union can engage in various kinds of activity vis-à-vis the [employer]. It is open to it, for instance, to present claims and to make representations for the protection of the interests of its members or certain of them. Nor does the applicant union in any way allege that the steps it takes are ignored by the [employer]. In these circumstances, the fact alone that the [employer] does not consult with the applicant under the Act of 27 July 1961 does not constitute a breach of article 11(1) considered on its own.

Chapter 5 : Article 11 and the right to strike

But in the United Kingdom there will be many cases where, precisely because of the limitations of the freedom to take strike action, employers will refuse to entertain claims and representations by trade unions, or refuse to negotiate, or adopt a position of intransigence. It is in such cases that the need for a right to take strike action arises most visibly in order that the members' interests may be protected. Without that right there may be no other means available for doing so.

The European Court of Human Rights has held that strike action is one way of exercising the right to be heard at work. In *Schmidt and Dahlstrom v Sweden* the Court:

recall[ed] that the Convention safeguards freedom to protect the occupational interests of trade union members by trade union action, the conduct and development of which the Contracting States must both permit and make possible. Article 11(1) nevertheless leaves each State a free choice of the means to be used towards this end. The grant of a right to strike represents without any doubt one of the most important of these means, but there are others. Such a right, which is not expressly enshrined in article 11, may be subject under national law to regulation of a kind that limits its exercise in certain instances. The Social Charter of 18 October 1961 only guarantees the right to strike subject to such regulation, as well as to 'further restrictions' compatible with its article 31, while at the same time recognising for employers too the right to resort to collective action (article 6(4) and App.). For its part, the 1950 Convention requires that under national law trade unionists should be enabled, in conditions not at variance with article 11, to strive through the medium of their organisations for the protection of their occupational interests. Examination of the file in this case does not disclose that the applicants have been deprived of this capacity[38].

Though the strike may not be the only means of the union being heard so as to protect its members interests, the right to strike within the restrictions permitted by the Convention is held to be "indispensable for the effective enjoyment of trade union freedom" and is an "element necessarily inherent in [that] right guaranteed by the Convention"[39].

This proposition derives some support from a decision of the former European Commission of Human Rights which held in 1998[40] that the obligation in United Kingdom statute requiring a union to disclose the names of voters in a strike ballot (and subsequently the names of strikers) was not "a significant limitation on the right to take collective action". It appears to follow that the Commission took the view that had there been a requirement which did impose a *significant limitation* on the right to take collective action, it would have infringed article 11.

On the other hand, there must be limits on the right to strike, and all countries with that express right have limitations upon it. There is obviously, therefore, much variation between States as to the presence of which factors or circumstances will have the effect of removing legitimacy from strike action. Not surprisingly the European Court of Human Rights has emphasised (as in the passage cited from *Schmidt and Dahlstrom* above) that in this area of law there is a broad "margin of appreciation" (ie. the margin by which, because of its particular circumstances, a member State may diverge from the standards laid down in the Convention). The United Kingdom courts will most certainly look to the breadth of that margin as a means of support for the preservation of the existing legal structure in relation to industrial action. In *Gustafsson v Sweden*[41] the European Court of Human Rights explained that:

> In view of the sensitive character of the social and political issues involved in achieving a proper balance between competing interests and, in particular, in assessing the appropriateness of State intervention to restrict union action aimed at extending a system of collective bargaining, and the wide degree of divergence between the domestic systems in the particular area under consideration, the Contracting States should enjoy a wide margin of appreciation in their choice of means to be employed.

Notwithstanding the extent of the margin of appreciation in this field, it must be arguable that the margin is not so wide as to extinguish the right to take trade union action in the form of a strike in circumstances where (i) there is no particular policy justification for the denial of the right (such as a legal structure intended to promote orderly collective bargaining for the benefit of workers generally), and (ii) other member States do not deny the right to strike in those circumstances.

So whilst it might conceivably be justifiable to render the organisation and support for industrial action unlawful by reason of a failure to hold a statutory pre-strike ballot required so as to ensure industrial democracy, the *UNISON* case exemplifies a denial of the right to strike based on no industrial relations or rationale other than the gratuitous grant to employers of a blanket immunity from industrial pressure where they threaten to downgrade contractual terms and conditions of employment and collective agreements on a transfer of business from one employer to another. This, it is suggested, does not amount to a legitimate reason to restrict union action

Chapter 5 : Article 11 and the right to strike

under article 11. Furthermore such an immunity is not one which Parliament has ever sought to impose by legislation, nor is it one on which the Court of Appeal sought to rely. Thus it can not be said that the United Kingdom regards such a restriction as "*necessary in a democratic society*" (see below). This must necessarily "*seriously qualify*" any arguments based on the margin of appreciation[42].

The divergence between the domestic systems of the Contracting States is not as great as may be imagined in relation to the right to strike (see below).

Convention restrictions

THERE are other grounds for restricting Convention rights contained within the Convention itself. The right of trade union membership in article 11(1) is subject to the restrictions of article 11(2)[43]. The European Court of Human Rights has held that these restrictions are to be construed strictly[44].

The first characteristic of a permitted restriction is that it be "prescribed by law". This requirement will be fulfilled in almost every case in the United Kingdom since the law on industrial action is not in doubt[45].

The scope of the restrictions which may be justified by the "interests of national security[46] or public safety, for the prevention of disorder[47] or crime, for the protection of health[48] or morals or for the protection of the rights and freedoms of others" are far exceeded by the unlawfulness imposed by the breach of contract rule in United Kingdom law. The law in the United Kingdom does not differentiate, in relation to the right to strike, between workers generally[49] and public servants with the exception of the police[50], prison officers[51], the military and the security services[52].

In relation to the protection of the rights and freedoms of others, it is of course arguable that trade union rights, and specifically the right to strike, will necessarily infringe the rights and freedoms of employers[53], in particular the latter's rights under contracts of employment with their employees. But if that argument had substance there would be no basis for the acknowledgement of the right to strike in *Schmidt and Dahlstrom*, nor in the European Social Charter, nor in the constitutions and laws of so many States. The justification for the superiority of the right to strike over the employer's contractual rights may be that of "*proportionality*". This is a fundamental principle of the jurisprudence of the European Court of Human Rights. It involves a fair balance between the protection of individual rights and the interests of the community at large which, it has been consistently held, can be achieved only if restrictions on individual rights are strictly *proportionate* to the legitimate aim they pursue[54].

The blanket unlawfulness imposed by the breach of contract characteristic of United Kingdom strike law would appear to be disproportionate to the aim of protecting employers' contracts save in particular factual situations.

Under the doctrine of proportionality, the justification for the abridgement of the Convention right must also be both "relevant and sufficient"[55]. It would be hard to demonstrate any "pressing social need" which must be "convincingly established"[56] for the protection of employers' contracts from industrial action based on an acceptable assessment of the relevant facts in the circumstances prevailing in the United Kingdom on the occasions when Parliament has considered the tortious nature of inducing industrial action and has legislated in relation to it.

Furthermore, the abridgement itself "must not restrict or reduce the right in such a way or to such an extent that the very essence of the right is impaired"[57]. The universality of the breach of contract consequence of United Kingdom strikes might be thought to render the equally universal object of protection of employers' contracts insufficient as a justification. The breach of contract consequence would appear to fall foul of the requirement that the abridgement of a Convention right must not impair the right, except to the extent that it could be argued that the statutory protections against tort liability for unions and statutory protection against unfair dismissal for workers leave the right to strike in the United Kingdom unimpaired. For the reasons already touched on, this does not seem a strong argument.

In any event all the article 11(2) restrictions are subject to the overriding criterion that they must be "necessary in a democratic society." The absence of prohibitions equivalent to those in the United Kingdom in the other democratic societies in Europe (and the instruments they and the civilised countries of the world have concluded and ratified) demonstrate that this qualification for restriction may not be fulfilled.

Other democratic societies – European jurisdictions

IN "the European countries which are like minded and have a common heritage of political traditions, ideals, freedom and the rule of law"[59] there appears to be associated with the right to form and join trade unions, an almost universal recognition of the right to strike, subject to varying degrees of regulation. Space does not permit more than a selective summary of the status of the law on strikes in member States of the recently expanded Council of Europe within which the European Court of Human Rights applies[60]. In their consideration of whether article 11 has an impact on the United Kingdom law of strikes, the United Kingdom courts are likely to have regard to the law on strikes of these countries, just as regard will be paid to the approach of other common law jurisdictions to similar questions.

Where there is a constitution, it is normally the first source for inspection for a state's distinctive labour law system[61]. The British constitution, if such there be, provides little help in arranging the labour law system in any clear order of principle[62]. In Italy, the constitution affords rights: of association, of peaceful assembly, to form and join trade unions and conduct union activity (at the workplace and generally) as well as a right to strike[63]. It is noteworthy that courts in Europe tend to insist that each freedom must be given its proper ambit, including trade union rights of organisation. Although some constitutions state that subsequent laws may regulate some of the rights set out (for instance, in respect of the ambit or modalities of strike action), this happens comparatively rarely. Examples are the Italian law 146/90 on strikes and constitutionally protected rights and performance of which is "indispensable"[64] and the French law of 1963 on strikes in "public services"[65].

Some constitutions expressly provide for the right to strike, others grant only trade union freedom of association from which a right to strike has been inferred by the relevant courts.

So, for example, the 1958 Constitution of France[66] recognises an individual right of employees to resort to strikes. In Sweden a constitutionally guaranteed right to strike is given only to trade unions. Andorra, the Czech Republic, Georgia, Greece, Iceland, Lithuania, Moldova, Poland, Portugal, Romania, San Marino and Slovenia all have constitutional rights to strike[67].

There is no express right to strike in the Spanish constitution but the right has been derived from the provision guaranteeing trade union freedom of association, and the Spanish Constitutional Court has given a wide meaning to constitutional trade union action[68] saying:

> it is not necessary for the interests defended in a strike to be those of the strikers themselves, but only the interests of a 'category' of workers...the claim that *l'interêt professionel* must have a direct link with the strike, is unconstitutional, and secondary action is lawful[69].

In Germany the constitution guarantees persons the right to form

---

and join associations generally and "the right to form associations to safeguard and improve working and economic conditions is guaranteed to everyone and to all trades, occupations and professions"[70]. This simple formula, together with the Collective Agreements Act, has been used by the German courts as the basis of wide areas of labour law including the right to form and join trade unions and engage in union activity including strikes and collective bargaining (much taking place within works councils). The right to strike is limited by such doctrines as "parity of arms", proportionality, the *ultima ratio* rule (the last recourse in a deadlock in bargaining), a new category of lawful short "warning strikes," and other rules such that the obligee employer must be an entity that can make a collective agreement)[71].

In Switzerland too the constitutional right to strike is specifically derived from the right to freedom of association[72].

In Ireland, the right to strike also does not derive from the Constitutional "right of the citizens to form associations and unions"[73]. But instead:

> The right to dispose of one's labour and to withdraw it seem to me a fundamental personal right which, though not specifically mentioned in the Constitution as being guaranteed, is a right of a nature which I cannot conceive to have been adversely affected by anything within the intendment of the Constitution[74].

In other Contracting States, the right to strike is established by legislation or (as in the Netherlands[75]) by the courts. In Finland, certain forms of industrial action are expressly prohibited by the Collective Agreements Act of 1946. However, based on the principle that what is not forbidden is allowed, other forms of industrial action are permitted. This principle is also applicable in Norway[76] and in Austria. In Denmark most forms of industrial action are lawful.

By contrast, the courts in the Netherlands had no constitutional or even legislative assistance in making their fundamental labour law, leading them to adopt the Council of Europe's Social Charter 1961 as their basic norm (even before the Charter was ratified in that country) and after 1976 they varied old principles judicially in the light of it (for example, on "blockade" of the employer, traditionally common in the Netherlands as in the Nordic countries for non-payment of wages).

The United Kingdom's breach of contract common law rule for strikes, is not found to be a problem in other European jurisdictions. Many provide that a legitimate strike does not breach but instead suspends the employment contract. So, notably, in France since 1950 the *Code du Travail* provides that a strike does not break the contract of employment except where the employee is guilty of serious and extraneous misconduct[77]. Suspension of the contract of employment during industrial action is not universal, however, in Europe. That is the rule in Norway but not (surprisingly) in Denmark where industrial action terminates contracts of employment[78]. But even some common law jurisdictions (see below) have rendered the common law consistent with the right to strike by holding that the effect of an otherwise lawful strike is not to break but merely to suspend the contract of employment. In Canada legislation at Federal level (and in different ways in most Provinces) has provided that employees do not lose their employment status and their contracts are not terminated by reason of taking part in a lawful strike but their contracts are suspended[79]. In Ireland the Supreme Court[80] reached the same conclusion as a matter of common law. The consequences of the doctrine of suspension do vary, as expected, among different States. The suspension doctrine once had support in the United Kingdom but is now regarded as having been decisively rejected[81].

Most of the European systems referred to above accept the legality of some kind of sympathetic or "secondary" action, none without limitations. In Germany such a right is very narrow as where the second employer is an "ally" of the employer in primary dispute (some say so narrow as to be theoretical). In Italy it is very wide indeed (necessarily in a system which permits "protest strikes"). France distinguishes lawful action *externe*, where the interests of a large number of workers are touched (even nationally) from solidarity action *interne* where legality involves a more direct interest of the workers in the dispute inside the enterprise[82]. Spain, as noted above, makes no such demand.

For completeness it should be added that it is also true that even in jurisdictions as liberal as France and Italy there is a principle which renders illegal stop-start stoppages or continuous defective work done in order to ruin the enterprise completely ("malevolently" to disorganise its very existence, said a French court in 1958). In Italy the same principle outlaws damage to *la produttività* rather than *la produzione* of the enterprise, the former arising when strikers deliberately act in order to ruin the employer's economic unit. But in recent decades courts have rarely relied upon such principles[83]. German labour courts, however, operate a rule that strikes must not aim at the destruction of the enterprises attacked, either because of their length, quality or intensity[84].

There is a thread, however, which links those European systems across their intense diversities (most of which derive from their several social and trade union histories, as well as general cultural features[85]). That common thread is adherence to freedom of association and its attendant rights, whether implemented by law or collective bargaining.

By contrast that notion has no firm hold in Britain where the common law's influence was, and is still, based largely on a belief in the reality of an individual 'freedom to contract' in the labour market[86]. That common law tradition and the appearance of a labour-orientated political party only after the growth of strong autonomous trade unions, encouraged the individual worker to seek relief from the inequalities of the employment relationship through autonomous collective channels (in those areas where there was no statutory protection[87]). An examination of these systems cannot fail to reveal the underlying vulnerability of the United Kingdom system, through the absence of a right to strike and its lack of security for freedom of association. The weakness of the United Kingdom system in this area is also consequential on the open texture of English law which creates opportunities for the application of common law rules more appropriate to the law of 'master and servant', or interpretations of statutes which weaken the countervailing influence of workers' unions.

Other democratic societies – the common law heritage

IN assessing the United Kingdom courts' attitude to the application of the Human Rights Act to strikes, regard must be had to recent jurisprudence in the United Kingdom and other common law jurisdictions.

In contrast to other states which have derived a right to strike from a constitutional trade union freedom of association, the English courts have, even where statute provides protections for the right to be a member of a trade union, denied that any incidental rights may be derived from it. In effect statutory protection of the right to be a trade union member in the United Kingdom means no more than the right to hold a trade union card. This is the effect of the House of Lords decision in the case of *Associated Newspapers Ltd. v Wilson* and *Associated British Ports plc v Palmer*[88]. This judgment is currently the subject of challenge in the European Court of Human Rights[89].

It may be safely assumed that without the influence of the jurisprudence of the European Court of Human Rights, or perhaps its ruling, the United Kingdom courts would be unlikely to find that article 11 of the European Convention imported a right to strike into United Kingdom law.

This common law approach with its distaste for trade union rights, is a reflection of earlier cases[90] in other common law jurisdictions where there was a constitutional freedom of association which the courts held did not encompass derivative rights and certainly not a right to strike. These decisions thereby reduced freedom of association to a level equivalent merely to freedom of assembly. However, it must be stressed that these other cases were interpretations of constitutions guaranteeing freedom of association without mention of the objectives in action of such association, as in article 11 of the Convention where freedom of association includes "the right to form and join trade unions for the protection of his interests"[91].

A Canadian case epitomises the approach. There a Supreme Court decision[92] held by a majority of 3 to 2 that the right to strike was not a necessary incident of the freedom of association guaranteed by the Canadian constitution[93]. Though collective exercise of the right was made lawful in many circumstances by various statutes, striking remained unlawful for the individual as a breach of the contract of employment[94]. Accordingly a statute abridging the right to strike for public servants was not unconstitutional[95].

In the Canadian case (and its equivalents[96]) the purposive and adjectival phrase "for the protection of his interests" in article 11(1) of the Convention (or any equivalent) was missing from the constitutional or statutory freedom of association provision under consideration. This phrase, as the Strasbourg court has emphasised, has the effect of protecting not merely membership but also trade union action (see below). The court has unambiguously held that there are implied rights concealed within the express words referred to.

But the common law jurisdictions do not all take this approach. In the Republic of Ireland the right to strike was, as appears above, the creation of the common law independent of the Constitution.

In South Africa the right to strike (as well as to join a trade union and to participate in its activities) is expressly guaranteed by the Bill of Rights in the Constitution[97], and the right is detailed in the Labour Relations Act 1995 where it is subject to the restrictions[98] imposed by a highly regulated system. There the Constitutional Court derived a right to exercise economic power (in that case the right to lock-out) from the right to collectively bargain:

"Once a right to collective bargaining is recognised implicit within it will be the right to exercise some economic power against partners in collective bargaining."[99]

In Australia, with its unique (though endangered) system of labour law, the right to strike in furtherance of an "industrial dispute" is (at

Commonwealth level – the States have differing provisions) specifically protected subject to certain constraints[100].

The European Union

THE law of the European Union ("Community law") must be mentioned. It is, of course, a different system of law applying to a different (though largely overlapping) grouping of European states. On the other hand great respect is not surprisingly shown by the panels of Judges to the jurisprudence (where relevant) of their opposite numbers in the respective courts at the apex of each system of law, the European Court of Human Rights and the European Court of Justice. Overlapping jurisdiction has not so far occurred. Indeed, whilst human rights issues do not often arise in the European Court of Justice, issues of Community law (which is the extent of the jurisdiction of the European Court of Justice) may be said virtually never to arise in the European Court of Human Rights. However, in the field of trade union rights there is a little jurisprudence of the European Court of Justice to which the European Court of Human Rights may have regard.

Issues of pay, freedom of association, and the right to strike and to lock out have so far been specifically excluded from the ambit of European Union law-making by the European Community Treaty[101]. Thus at present the European Court of Justice has no jurisdiction over trade union rights save in one respect. That one respect is a special jurisdiction restricted to certain issues relating to the employment of European Union employees[102].

In the exercise of this jurisdiction the European Court of Justice has confronted the principle of freedom of association (though not the right to strike) which, in this connection, did not derive directly from the Convention or other international instruments, but from the European Union Staff Regulations. Article 24(a) of the Staff Regulations provided that European Union officials: "shall be entitled to exercise the right of association; they may in particular be members of trade unions...".

The European Court of Justice, like the European Court of Human Rights, has held that there are implied rights to be derived from the right of trade union membership. The European Court of Justice has held that the right to be a trade union member is not restricted to the mere right to be a member in association with others and to hold a membership card; instead it involves the right to participate in legitimate trade union activities; such exercise of the right of such participation may involve the surrender of certain rights of the employer; and the employer may not prohibit exercise of the right of such participation nor may the employer discriminate against the participants.

This logic would appear to lead to acknowledgement of the right to strike, plainly subject to certain, as yet undefined, limits.

In *Union Syndicale, Massa and Kortner v European Communities Council*[103] the issue was whether a union which organises European Union officials and staff had a right to bring legal proceedings in the European Court of Justice. In holding that it did, the European Court of Justice concluded that:

> Under the general principles of labour law, the freedom of trade union activity recognised under Article 24a of the Staff Regulations means not only that officials and servants have the right without hindrance to form associations of their own choosing, but also that these associations are free to do anything lawful to protect the interests of their members as employees. The right of [legal] action is one of the means available for use by these associations.

The same words were reiterated in the similar case of *Syndicat General du Personnel des Organismes Européens v Commission*[104]. In *Maurissen and European Public Service Union v Court of Auditors of the European Communities*[105], a union representing European Union employees applied to overturn a temporary ban imposed by the European Commission on use of the messenger service to distribute union circulars, and on permitting time off work for union representatives to attend consultative meetings with the employer, the Commission. The European Court of Justice held that, following the two earlier cases[106]:

> It thus follows, in the first place, that the Community institutions and bodies may not prohibit their officials and servants from joining a trade union or staff association or from participating in trade union activities, or impose any penalty whatsoever on them by reason of such membership activities.
>
> It also follows that the Community institutions and bodies must allow trade unions and staff associations to fulfil their proper role, inter alia by keeping officials and servants informed, representing them vis-à-vis the institutions and other bodies and participating in consultations with those institutions and bodies on all matters affecting staff, and may not treat them differently without justification.

One further aspect of Community law needs mention, especially for the future. In 1989 the European Union adopted a Social Charter of the Fundamental Social Rights of Workers which was purely declaratory and not enforceable (of itself) by the European Court of

---

Justice or by the member States. It nonetheless illustrated the ostensible policy aspirations of the European Union and the inter-relationship between the right to trade union membership, to collective bargaining and to strike. It provides:

11. Employers and workers of the European Community shall have the right of association in order to constitute professional organisations or trade unions of their choice for the defence of their economic and social interests.

12. Employers or employers' organisations, on the one hand, and workers' organisations, on the other, shall have the right to negotiate and conclude collective agreements under the conditions laid down by national legislation and practice.

The right to resort to collective action in the event of a conflict of interests shall include the right to strike subject to the obligations arising under national regulations and collective agreements.

In order to facilitate the settlement of industrial disputes the establishment and utilisation at the appropriate levels of conciliation, mediation and arbitration procedures should be encouraged in accordance with national practice.

Since the Charter of 1989, and particularly since 1995[107], momentum has grown to embellish the social dimension of the European Union with an equivalent to the European Court of Human Rights but which is more detailed in its social and economic provisions than the European Court of Human Rights. Consequently, following an initial draft proposed by a group of experts in 1999[108], a first Draft Charter of Fundamental Rights of the European Union has been published[109] with the intention that it should be adopted by the Inter-Governmental Conference in Nice in December 2000 (as amended by negotiation, no doubt). This draft provides for a right to strike and take industrial action.

Article 12 of the Draft Charter is entitled "Freedom of Assembly and Association." The first (relevant) part of it provides:

Everyone has the right to freedom of peaceful assembly and to freedom of association, in particular in political, trade union and civic matters. ·

Article 26 of the Draft Charter reads:

Right of Collective Bargaining and Action

Employers and workers have the right to negotiate and conclude collective agreements and, in cases of conflicts of interest, to take collective action to defend their interests, in accordance with Community law and national laws and practices.

The Draft Charter is desired by the European Parliament to be made legally binding. However, it is said by the United Kingdom government to be intended to be declaratory only, merely "a show-case of existing rights"[110]. The preamble to the Draft Charter in its current form states:

5. This Charter reaffirms... the rights as they result, in particular, from the constitutional traditions common to the Member States, the Treaty on the European Union... the European Convention on Human Rights and Fundamental Freedoms, the Social Charters adopted by the Community and by the Council of Europe and the case law of the Court of Justice of the European Community and of the European Court of Human Rights.

6. ...

7. Each person is therefore guaranteed the rights and freedoms set out hereafter.

If the terms of the preamble remain unamended, it is hard to see why these rights might be regarded as merely declaratory. In order to negate the express guarantee in paragraph 7, it would be necessary to construe paragraph 5 very narrowly so as to mean that the paragraph 7 guarantee is limited to those rights found within the Charter only to the extent that they can be said to "result" from the named instruments. The phrase "the rights as they result from" would then need to be constrained to mean those rights which are enforceable and found in the named instruments. However, though this seems an unlikely restriction on the apparent clarity of paragraph 7, it remains the case that the forum for the *enforcement* of the Draft Charter rights is not stated, and unless and until the Draft Charter is put into effect by one of the legal mechanisms of Community law it will, in fact, be no more than declaratory, certainly in the United Kingdom. In the European Court of Justice, if the Draft Charter is not given effect by Community law it will offer the Court no more than guidance in the exercise of their very limited and specific jurisdiction, a jurisdiction which does not extend, as noted above, to the law of labour disputes. The European Trade Union Confederation and the Platform of European Social NGOs are pressing for the Draft Charter to become incorporated into the European Union Treaty. That would make it enforceable in national courts and in the European Court of Justice. The final compromise in December 2000 will reveal whether the Draft Charter provisions on the right to strike will be, in the United Kingdom, no more than an empty declaration of non-existing rights (as are the equivalent provisions of the 1989 Charter) or whether they represent a further forum in which the absence of the right to strike in the United Kingdom may be challenged.

Other international instruments

THE other international instruments, many of which bind the United Kingdom, may be brought to bear on courts considering the impact of article 11 on industrial action. As mentioned they are dealt with fully in the chapter on "Industrial Action and International Standards" in the forthcoming book on the Employment Relations Act by the Institute of Employment Rights.

Taken as a whole they support the thesis that the right to strike is an essential incident of trade union freedom of association. Taken with the ECHR embellishment that this freedom of association is "for the protection of [the worker's] interests", the argument is powerful indeed that a consequence of the Human Rights Act is that there must be a right to strike in the United Kingdom.

Implications

IF the above analysis is correct there is a forceful case to be made that under the Human Rights Act, by reason of the introduction of article 11 into United Kingdom law, the absence of the right to strike may be challenged. But what, if anything flows from that?

Assuming it is possible to persuade a United Kingdom court that article 11 does involve a right to strike, the sequential argument will be raised that all the restrictions on the right's lawful exercise in the United Kingdom fall into the margin of appreciation given to the United Kingdom (and the other member States). The answer must be that some do but others may not. Restrictions to the point of extinguishing the right altogether in circumstances where the other democratic societies of western Europe (and elsewhere) have not found it necessary to do so, may well be held to be outside that margin. The necessary conditions for so persuading a court would seem to be that in the given circumstances of the case, the strike weapon is a necessary means by which the union can make itself heard on behalf of its members and that the freedom to organise or support industrial action is restricted by law in circumstances which other democratic societies do not regard as justifying such restriction.

A case has yet to come before the United Kingdom courts on this issue but the UNISON case is currently before the European Court of Human Rights[111], as is the case of *The Federation of Oil Workers' Trade Unions v Norway*[112]. In the latter challenge is made to a "provisional ordinance" which banned a proposed strike on certain offshore platforms and imposed compulsory state arbitration. The

UNISON case has also been referred to the European Social Charter and ILO supervisory bodies which may be anticipated to express views in the relatively near future.

Implications for trade unions

IN the United Kingdom reliance on article 11 might be sought even where the strike action attracted the statutory protection against tort liability. In such a case the union would challenge the allegation that inducement of breach of contract (or other "industrial tort" alleged to make the strike or its support unlawful) was unlawful in a strike situation, ie. at "stage 1" of the legal analysis[113], before invoking statutory protection against that unlawfulness[114]. If successful, application of stage 2 (to consider if the immunities applied) and stage 3 (to consider whether *prima facie* immunities were removed by the statutory restrictions thereon) would be otiose. But if the statutory protection would otherwise ensue, the challenge would be likely to be regarded as academic. The real issue would arise where the strike was outside the scope of statutory protection and where the union claimed that the lack of protection was not paralleled in international covenant or in other countries. Such situations lie in the area outside statutory protection but within a constructed consensus of what ought to be legitimate based on the laws and practices of other member States and the pronouncements of the international supervisory bodies. This is not, of course such a wide territory as might appear at first blush. But challenge might well arise in cases such as *UNISON* where the dispute and hence the strike would be regarded as entirely normal and legitimate outside the United Kingdom.

For a court minded to hold that article 11 legitimated the right to strike in appropriate circumstances, the simplest mechanism of achieving that result would be to conclude that the primary tortious act on the part of the union was rendered lawful by virtue of article 11. Thus, for example, the interference in the breach of contract of the employee could be deemed to be legitimated by article 11. This would not necessarily have the consequence of rendering the employee's strike action no longer in breach of contract, so discriminating between the consequences of article 11 for the union and the worker (see below).

Should the courts be persuaded that article 11 required the legitimation of otherwise unprotected industrial action in certain circumstances, an alternative approach would be to hold that certain of the statutory limitations on the immunities were incompatible with article 11. For example, a challenge could be mounted (along the lines of the ILO condemnation) on the exclusion (at stage 3) of secondary action from the statutory immunity for organising industrial action[115]. On the other hand union breach of the statutory balloting requirements would not be so easily susceptible since even the ILO has generally accepted the legitimacy of a balloting requirement[116].

Whilst overriding the primary liability in tort would instantly render the strike lawful, a declaration of incompatibility of a statutory restriction would not make lawful the strike in question but merely start the process of parliamentary consideration of the statute. The right would thus remain violated in the instant case, which might be critically disadvantageous for a union in interlocutory injunction proceedings[117].

The use in strike cases of interlocutory injunctions with their standard of proof set at showing only "a serious issue to be tried" and the order being granted on a "balance of convenience"[118] so disfavouring trade unions, might be susceptible of challenge as they have been under the ECHR in other spheres[119].

Implications for workers

A CHALLENGE under article 11 might arise in relation to individual workers in three situations. Firstly a worker may seek relief where he or she was denied effective protection against unfair dismissal because the strike is unprotected so making the benefit of unfair dismissal unavailable. An individual worker might also make the challenge where the strike is protected but the remedy of reinstatement is denied perhaps on the ground of impracticability because strike breakers have been hired. Challenge might also be raised where reinstatement is ordered but the employer declines to comply with it, perhaps because they do not want union loyalists back. Since the employment tribunal jurisdiction is fixed by statute, the challenge would have to be by way of injunction and declaration that the dismissal was ineffective in consequence of article 11, to terminate the contract of employment at common law.

The first of these three situations would parallel the arguments of the union in relation to unprotected industrial action and would appear arguable at the least. However the argument on behalf of the individual worker is not without difficulties in spite of the strong pronouncements of the various international bodies above. The right to automatic reinstatement after lawful industrial action is not universal even in Europe[120] and therefore may be arguable as a matter within the national margin of appreciation, though the denial of all legal protection to the worker on what would be legitimate strike action elsewhere may fall outside the margin in all countries which fail to provide any such protection. As suggested above the court could distinguish between the union and the worker by making the inducement to breach of contract lawful for these purposes without changing the unlawful nature of the breach of contract. Under the 1999 amendments to the unfair dismissal legislation this is arguably not sufficient to bring the worker within the scope of the protection since the protection only applies to inducements rendered not actionable in tort by s.219 of the Trade Union and Labour Relations (Consolidation) Act 1992, a section which would have no application if there was no tort to be rendered not actionable.

The second and third situations each rank more weakly since it might be said that where national law does provide protection of the right to strike of the individual striker, its scope is properly within the margin of appreciation and subject to variation between States.

If the breach of contract rule of common law was found to violate a right to strike on the part of the worker pursuant to article 11, the rule would have to give way to that right. The basis on which and the circumstances within which the breach of contract rule would be set aside would be novel territory indeed[121]. Space does not permit investigation here but, though there are technical problems[122], one possibility[123] could be the reactivation of the "bold if misconceived"[124] concept that in appropriate circumstances a strike may not break but merely suspend the contract of employment[125]. This approach has been adopted in Ireland by the Supreme Court[126], and has been applied on one occasion in Australia[127]. It is the norm in France and Norway but not in Denmark (see above). But though it retains the authority of the Court of Appeal, the suspension doctrine has not been followed in the United Kingdom[128].

The consequences of finding that in an appropriate case a strike did not breach the contract of employment are, of course, profound. And unless there was judicial enthusiasm to restore the suspension doctrine it is likely that the United Kingdom courts will shy away from interfering with the law of contract particularly where Parliament has so recently legislated.

Means by which a union may be heard on behalf of its members

SINCE the right to strike has been held only one of the ways in which a union may be heard on behalf of its members as required by article 11, it remains to consider whether it could be said that sufficient means exist in the general case in the United Kingdom, to justify the absence of the right to strike generally.

It seems unlikely that such a justification can be sustained even after the implementation of the recognition machinery of Schedule A1 of Trade Union and Labour Relations (Consolidation) Act 1992. The effective denial of a right to be heard (save where the employer cares to permit it) is one of the most distinctive characteristics of United Kingdom industrial relations law up to 1999. In consequence, "Britain has, in a relatively short time, become exceptional within Europe in its low (and diminishing) coverage of collective agreements"[129].

Throughout the 1980s and 1990s trade unions have been "disempowered"[130] and employers correspondingly empowered by a barrage of legal changes[131]. From 1890 until 1980 there was established by statute some (limited) machinery by which collective bargaining would be promoted and collective agreements would be extended. These and virtually all legal props to collective bargaining have been swept away[132]. The sole vestige of legislative protection for collective bargaining until the advent of the recognition machinery was the right to information for collective bargaining[133]. There is, even after the recognition provisions, no principle of "inderogability"[134] in the United Kingdom so as to preclude individual contracts of employment giving less favourable terms than relevant collective agreements.

The autonomy of unions to regulate their internal affairs has been reduced[135], "disassociation" has been facilitated[136], and limitations on trade union freedom to organise industrial action have been imposed[137]. For the most part there has been no reversal of these changes, the government party having made clear that "[t]he key elements of trade union legislation of the 1980s – on ballots, picketing and industrial action – will stay"[138]. So the Prime Minister wrote before the election which brought him to office: "The changes that we do propose would leave British law the most restrictive on trade unions in the Western World"[139].

The law, in addition to removing the legal machinery to support, encourage and extend collective bargaining has been changed so as to positively discourage it and to disable union capability to seek it[140].

Consultation rights for workers via their unions are very limited[141] principally in respect of health and safety representation, collective dismissals, business transfers, and occupational pension schemes. These have been the subject of amendments to accommodate condemnation by the European Court of Justice[142] of dependency on voluntary recognition[143]. The amendments do not guarantee trade union representation rights[144]. Existing rights to consultation in the limited circumstances specified in United Kingdom law do not seem a sufficient satisfaction of the obligation to ensure a right to be heard. Those consultation rights, especially those derived from EU Directives, are usually exercisable by all workers whether or not exercising their right to be a union member. The circumstances in which consultation law permits workers to have a voice are surely too limited in subject matter to come near the universality of the "interests" referred to in article 11 which workers may wish to seek to protect by being heard via their unions. If the industrial action concerned subject matter outside the specified issues, the right to be heard would remain demonstrably denied.

Most fundamentally there is, even after the introduction of Schedule A1 of the Trade Union and Labour Relations (Consolidation) Act 1992, no right to be represented by a union at work on any subject matter whatever[145].

It is necessary to consider whether the introduction of the recognition machinery of Schedule A1 might provide sufficient "means" to satisfy the requirement of article 11 "that the trade union should be heard". The argument would be that a right to recognition would be a means of being heard which justified the United Kingdom (within its margin of appreciation) in maintaining its restrictions on the freedom to strike and to organise strikes. To that it could be answered that the existence of available recognition machinery is not enough to justify removal of the right to strike, where it was felt that machinery was not sufficient to protect the interests of the workers and a strike was necessary. But even assuming that the existence of recognition (whether via the statutory route or voluntarily) was capable of justifying the absence of the right to strike, the question arises as to whether the possibility of recognition would justify the absence by law of the right to strike in every case.

Of course, Schedule A1 does not itself impose any restriction on the right to strike, the situation envisaged is where the pre-existing legal obstacles have rendered a strike unlawful, article 11 is relied upon to remove them and the argument is put forward that with the advent of Schedule A1, unions in the United Kingdom now have the right to be heard so that the requirements of article 11 are fulfilled without need to remove the obstacles.

A worker whose union is denied recognition by the employer or who is unable to secure recognition by the legislative machinery[146] may be regarded as being denied his or her right to be heard, whether or not other workers have the benefit of recognition or the means of establishing it. The right in article 11 is an individual right of "everyone" (though unions may seek to enforce it or exercise it, as in the *Swedish Engine Drivers* and *Belgian Police*). It seems unsustainable to hold that the margin of appreciation is so large that the mere existence of a legal mechanism for recognition is sufficient fulfilment of the article 11 requirement that unions have the right to be heard even though workers may be unable to avail themselves of it. This is not to say that the Convention provision is such as to extend to a single worker or to a minority union the power to enforce representation regardless of Schedule A1; that is plainly not the case[147]. The nature and reasons for the non-availability of the legislative machinery will have to be examined and weighed against the denial of the right to be heard[148].

There may also be situations where it could be argued that, even where an employer purports to recognise a union (whether voluntarily or under the statutory machinery), its employee members are denied the right to be heard. This might occur where an employer conducts discussions but remains immovable, or does not "bargain in good faith"[149]. The argument might be mounted that the recognition legislation does not provide effective machinery[150] to compel an intransigent employer to hear the views expressed, "thereafter considering those views properly and genuinely"[151], "with a view to reaching an agreement"[152]. In such case too it would appear difficult to justify an absence of the right to strike on the ground that the union had the right to be heard.

Conclusion

IT appears that in a limited range of situations article 11 may be prayed in aid to extend the freedom of unions and workers to take strike action.

Notes

1   This Chapter should be read with the author's chapter "Industrial Action and International Standards" in the forthcoming book by the Institute of Employment Rights on the Employment Relations Act. Together they are a revised, updated and much expanded version of the author's earlier article: "The Human Rights Act, Article 11 and the Right to Strike" [1998] EHRLR 582.

2   Draft as proposed by the Praesidium, 28 July 2000.

3   Excluding the Houses of Parliament but including bodies "certain of whose functions are functions of a public nature" (s.6(3)(b)) except where the act challenged is of a private nature (s.6(5)). Employment matters are held to be of a private nature, at least so far as administrative law in the United Kingdom is concerned (*R v Berkshire Health Authority, ex parte Walsh* [1984] ICR 743, *McLaren v Home Office* [1990] ICR 824, though there are exceptions: *CCSU v Minister for the Civil Service* [1985] AC 374). But public employees are likely to be able to enforce Convention rights against their public employers: *Halford v United Kingdom* [1997] IRLR 471; *Leander v Sweden* (1987) EHRR 433; *Ahmed v United Kingdom* (1982) 4 EHRR 126.

4   This is consistent with the view of the European Court of Human Rights that the Convention may have horizontal effect: *X and Y v Netherlands* (1986) 8 EHRR 235.

5   In Canada the Supreme Court in *Hill v Church of Scientology* [1995] 2 SCR 1130 has held that though the Canadian Charter of Rights does not apply directly to private action, it can be used to influence the development of the common law so that common law rules should evolve in a manner consistent with Charter values: "it is up to the party challenging the common law to bear the burden of proving not only that the common law is inconsistent with Charter values but also that its provisions cannot be justified" (Cory J, at pp 1171-2). See also *UFCW v K Mart Canada Ltd.* [1999] 2 SCR 1083 and *Allsco Building Products Ltd v UFCW Local 1288P* [1999] 2 SCR 1136 (freedom of expression legitimates consumer boycott but not picket in labour dispute – for a discussion see P Macklem, "Secondary Picketing, Consumer Boycotts and the Charter" (2000) 8 CLELJ 1; M MacNeil, "Labour Picketing and Consumer Boycotts: Judicial Ideology in *K Mart and Allsco*", *ibid.* p 80). In the United Kingdom the courts have already developed the common law in the light of the Convention: see for an "audit" of the position as at 1996: M Beloff and H Mountfield, "Unconventional Behaviour: Judicial uses of the European Convention in England and Wales" [1996] EHRLR 467.

6   *Gustafsson v Sweden* (1996) 22 EHRR 408, para 45.

7   In *Intercity West Coast Ltd. v RMT* [1996] IRLR 583; *London Underground v RMT* [1995] IRLR 636.

8   *University College London NHS Trust v UNISON* [1999] ICR 204. Nor an enthusiasm for fundamental trade union rights more generally: *Associated Newspapers Ltd v Wilson; Associated British Ports plc v Palmer* [1995] 2 AC 454.

9   The notion of a strike is defined in s.246 of the Trade Union and Labour Relations (Consolidation) Act 1992: "'strike' means any concerted stoppage of work." There is a further definition found in s.235(5) Employment Rights Act 1996 for other and different statutory purposes:

"'strike' means – (a) the cessation of work by a body of employed persons acting in combination, or (b) a concerted refusal, or a refusal under a common understanding, of any number of employed persons to continue to work for an employer in consequence of a dispute, done as a means of compelling their employer or any employed person or body of employed persons, or to aid other employees in compelling their employer or any employed person or body of employed persons, to accept or not to accept terms or conditions of or affecting employment."

10 United Kingdom Government's Reply to the Committee of Experts' Observations (1996), para 6.

11 Per Ralph Gibson LJ giving the judgment of the Court of Appeal in *British Telecommunications plc v Ticehurst* [1992] ICR 383, at pp 398-399.

12 See note 9 above.

13 Including working strictly according to contract (*Secretary of State v ASLEF (No.2)* [1972] 2 QB 455), or refusing to carry out some aspects only of contractual duties (*Ticehurst, op cit*). The only exceptions might be where industrial action followed notice to terminate the contract of employment (*Boxfoldia v NGA* [1988] ICR 752), or where the strike consisted in not renewing contracts of employment (*Allen v Flood* [1898] AC 1), or where the contract of employment expressly provided a right to strike.

14 *Miles v Wakefield MDC* [1987] ICR 368, at p 389 (Lord Templeman).

15 *Wiluszynski v Tower Hamlets LBC* [1989] IRLR 259.

16 *NCB v Galley* [1958] 1 WLR 16.

17 Schedule 5 of the Employment Relations Act 1999 and s.238(2A) of the 1992 Act provide rights to strikers to complain of unfair dismissal in limited circumstances but do not give any such rights where the strike is unofficial: s.237 of the 1992 Act.

18 Trade Union and Labour Relations (Consolidation) Act 1992, s.125.

19 In consequence of Employment Relations Act 1999, s.33.

20 [1999] ICR 204.

21 [1942] AC 435, at p 463.

22 Or, in more sophisticated form, interference in the performance of a primary obligation: *Merkur Island Corp. v Laughton* [1983] ICR 490, at pp 505-506.

23 *Thomson (DC) & Co. Ltd. v Deakin* [1952] Ch 646, *Torquay Hotel Ltd v Cousins* [1969] 2 Ch 106.

24 Eg. "breach of an unenforceable statutory duty" will constitute unlawful means where the union has shown an "intention to harm": *Associated British Ports v TGWU* [1989] ICR 557; so will "economic duress": *Dimskal Shipping Co. v ITWF* [1992] 2 AC 152.

25 *Rookes v Barnard* [1963] 1 QB 623, *Stratford (JT) & Son Ltd. v Lindley* [1965] AC 269.

26 *TaffVale Railway Co Ltd v Amalgamated Society of Railway Servants* [1901] AC 426. There is in this principle deep in the heart of English trade union law, a special contrast with the way that French law handles trade union vicarious liability with its very different rules. See Lord Wedderburn, *Labour Law and Freedom* (1995), ch 4.

27 Trade Disputes Act 1906, s.3.

28 Lord Wedderburn, *The Worker and the Law* (1st ed, 1965), p 236.

29 Save in the rare circumstances where notice to terminate the contract is given.

30 Dickson CJC in a dissenting judgment in *Reference re Public Service Employee Relations Act* (1987) 38 DLR (4th) 161, at p 195.

31 The court held, for example, that (contrary to the trade union interest in collectivity) there is an implied negative right to dissociate in article 11. The ground was laid in *Young, James and Webster v United Kingdom* [1981] IRLR 408, and decisively confirmed in *Sigurjonsson v Iceland* (1993) 16 EHRR 462.

32 The academic view (and that of other courts and international bodies – see below) is that the right to strike is an essential element of trade union freedom of association: R Ben-Israel, *International Labour Standards: the case of Freedom to Strike* (1988).

33 (1985) 42 DR 178, at p 185.

34 (1990) 65 DR 202, at p 205.

35 (1976) 1 EHRR 617.

36 This was also the legitimate purpose behind a refusal to permit a union to be recognised so as to conclude a collective bargain and participate in collective bargaining in App. No. 9792/82 *v Germany*, and App. No. 7361/76 *v Belgium*. Consequently, since the unions in those cases did have the opportunity to be heard nonetheless, the Commission held that they were inadmissible.

37 (1975) 1 EHRR 578.

38 (1976) 1 EHRR 632 at p 644. In that case individual applicants had complained that a collective agreement entered into after a strike in which they did not participate discouraged them from thenceforth availing themselves of their right to strike because the collective agreement gave certain benefits to non-unionists who had not struck denied to them as members of unions which had participated in the strike. It is unsurprising that the court found that the applicants had been deprived of the capacity as trade unionist to strive through the medium of their organisations for the protection of their occupational interests.

39 *Schmidt and Dahlström, op cit,* and other cases.

40 *National Association of Teachers in Further and Higher Education v United Kingdom* (case No. 28910/95), effectively an appeal from *Blackpool and Fylde College v NATFHE* [1994] ICR 648.

41 (1996) EHRR 408.

42 According to the Commission: *Silver v United Kingdom* (1981) ECHRR (series B) 43, para 121.

43 And the parallel restrictions in the other instruments need consideration: see, on article 22(2) of the ICCPR, see Nowak, *UN Covenant on Civil and Political Rights: CCPR Commentary* (1993) at p 393 *et seq*; on article 8(1)c ICESCR, "The Limburg Principles of the International Covenant on Economic, Social and Cultural Rights", 1987 9 HRQ 122 at 128-130; Alston and Quinn, "The Nature and Scope of States Parties' Obligations under the International Covenant on Economic, Social and Cultural Rights", (1987) 9 HRQ 156; and, on article 31 of the Charter, Gomien, Harris and Zwaak, *Law and Practice of the European Convention on Human Rights and the European Social Charter,* 1996, at 431 *et seq*.

44 See *Sunday Times v United Kingdom* (1977) 28 ECHR (series B) 64, at paras 194-5.

45 Following *Malone v United Kingdom* (1985) 7 EHRR 14; *Huvig v France* (1990) 12 EHRR 528: *Halford v United Kingdom* (1997) 24 EHRR;

Kokkinakis v Greece (1993) 17 EHRR 397, it might be said of the *UNISON* case, prior to the court's decision, the legislation was unintelligible to the extent that no citizen could reasonably have known (even with the assistance of lawyers) that the law had the effect of depriving workers of the freedom to take strike action in the situation exemplified.

46 Such as the ban on union membership at GCHQ (*CCSU v United Kingdom* (1987) 10 EHRR 269), though "administration of the state" was sufficient for the Commission.

47 Under the ICCPR this would not justify a general prohibition on strikes by. public employees: *Alberta Union v Canada* No. 118/1982 UN Human Rights Committee, at least in the view of Nowak *op cit*, at p 395 by reason of proportionality and the wide restrictions which are reserved for the armed services and police in article 22 ICCPR. (Art 11(2) of the Convention is wider in that reservation, including those in the administration of the State).

48 There is, in United Kingdom law, a virtually unused criminal offence of (in short) wilfully breaking a contract of employment so as to endanger human life or destroy or injure property: Trade Union and Labour Relations (Consolidation) Act 1992, s.240. The equivalent for merchant seafarers is Merchant Shipping Act 1995, ss.58, 59, 119.

49 There are restrictions in relation to certain classes of worker most of whom were in the public sector but who are now found in the public sector, eg. telecommunications workers – Telegraph Act 1863, s.45, Telecommunications Act 1985, s.1 (mentioned in *Mercury Communications Ltd. v Scott-Garner* [1984] ICR 74); Post Office Act 1953, ss.58, 68 (mentioned in *Gouriet v Union of Post Office Workers* [1978] AC 435).

50 By virtue of Police Act 1996, s.1.

51 By virtue of Criminal Justice and Public Order Act 1994, s.127.

52 The settlement reached by the present government in relation to GCHQ was to agree that the workers may now be union members but that strikes remain impermissible.

53 Article 1 of the First Protocol in Schedule 1 of the Human Rights Act provides the right to peaceful enjoyment of property.

54 See *Dudgeon v United Kingdom* (1982) 4 EHRR 149; *F v Switzerland* (1988) 10 EHRR 411; *Soering v United Kingdom* (1989) 11 EHRR 439; *Powell and Rayner v United Kingdom* (1990) 12 EHRR 355: *Open Door Counselling and Well Woman v Ireland* (1993) 15 EHRR 411;

55 *Jersild v Denmark* (1995) 19 EHRR 1; *Vogt v Germany* (1996) 21 EHRR 205; *Buckley v United Kingdom* (1997) 23 EHRR 101.

56 See in a non-industrial context: *Autronic AG v Switzerland* (1990) ECHRR (series A) 178; *Weber v Switzerland* (1990) ECHRR (series A) 177; *Barthold v FDR* (1985) ECHRR (series A) 90. *Sunday Times v United Kingdom op cit*; *Olsson v Sweden* (1988) 11 EHRR 259; *Observer and Guardian v United Kingdom* (1991) ECHRR (series A) 216; *Lingens v Austria* (1986) ECHRR (series A) 103; *Ezelin v France* (1991) ECHRR (series A) 202; *Oberschlick v Austria* (1991) ECHRR (series A) 204.

57 *Rees v United Kingdom* (1987) 9 EHRR 56; *F v Switzerland* (1987) 10 EHRR 411.

58 See *Young, James and Webster v United Kingdom* [1981] IRLR 408.

59 European Convention on Human Rights, Preamble.

60 For which I am indebted to Professor Lord Wedderburn of Charlton QC, FBA, joint author with me of the application to the European Court of Human Rights in the case of *UNISON v United Kingdom* Case no.5357499. I am solely to blame for the errors in this summary. The full text of the *UNISON* application is available (with the kind permission of *UNISON*) on our chambers' website: www.oldsquarechambers.co.uk. A strike which conforms to the following requirements would appear to be lawful in most western European countries:

• the strike may not be in breach of a peace obligation of a collective agreement, contract or award;

• the strike must be called after exhaustion of available procedures for resolution;

• the strike must be the last resort;

• the strike may not be in breach of statutorily required conciliation or arbitration process;

• the strike must be in furtherance of an occupational and economic demand(s);

• the dispute must be a conflict of interests rather than of rights;

• the demand may not be to alter or challenge the validity or interpretation of an existing collective agreement nor to demand a new agreement before the existing one has expired;

• the strike must be called by a union;

• the union calling the strike must have status to represent the strikers;

• the union calling the strike must be representative or most representative;

• the demand must be made of an employer;

• the demand must be made on the employer of the workers;

• the employer must be capable of satisfying the demand;

• the employer must have refused the demand;

• the demand if met must be capable of being put in the form of a collective agreement;

• the strike must be conducted without unlawful accompanying measures;

• the strikers must not be within a prohibited class of worker e.g. military, police, state security service, certain categories of other public servant;

• the strike must not threaten life or health;

• the strike must not be "gravely unreasonable" (eg. because the dispute could be resolved by legal process);

• the strike must not be a disproportionate measure;

• strike notice must have been given to a specified state official or to the employer in the case of certain classes of worker;

• the strike may not be for the purpose of supporting an unlawful strike by another union, nor to support workers employed by an employer who is not an ally of the strikers' employer, nor to support other workers where the secondary strikers have no interest of their own to protect (France), nor to support other workers where the secondary strikers do not have the interest required, ie. that laid down by a collective agreement or the test of "life, honour, or welfare" (Denmark);

• the strike must conform to laws which impose legitimate restrictions on strike action, eg. a statutory requirement to have a pre-strike ballot;

• the strike must not constitute an abuse in the form of an attack on the whole nature of the enterprise.

61 The constitution of a state gives also a flavour of its social context: the commentary of Sir Otto Kahn-Freund on the relationship between constitutions and labour laws is well known: O Kahn-Freund, "The Impact of Constitutions on Labour Law" (1976) CLJ 240.

62 For a general and comparative survey, see Lord Wedderburn, "Laws about strikes", in W McCarthy (ed.), *Legal Intervention in Industrial Relations* (1992), ch 4.

63 The most relevant articles of the constitution are: 17, 18 (rights of association and peaceful assembly), 39, 40 (guarantee of trade union freedom and activity at local and higher levels, and right to strike "within the limits of later laws"), 41 (guarantee for private economic initiative, within the limits of social benefit, of safety of society, liberty and human dignity); see too the "Workers' Statute" Law 300/1970 (rights at the workplace for trade unions – "rappresentanze aziendali sindacali" – and penalties for anti-union behaviour). For an introduction for Italian readers: Lord Wedderburn, "Il diritto del lavoro inglesi: un' introduzione comparata" in S Sciarra (ed.), *I Diritti del Lavoro*, (1998). There is no overarching "duty" to bargain, but many statutes elsewhere place an "onus to bargain" on employers: this telling phrase is from S Sciarra, *Contratto Collettivo e Contrattazione in Azienda* (1985), p 144.

64 Law 146/90, and its Comitato di Garanzia (commonly cited as the law on "essential services", though the law goes much wider, including teachers, attendants in museums, banking employment and garbage collection). See M Rusciano and G Pantoro Passarelli, *Lo Sciopero ne Servizi Essenziali* (1991); G Giugni, *Diritto Sindicale* (10th ed. 1996) chap 13. Italian law goes furthest in permitting strikes "di imposizone economico-politica", strikes against policies of public bodies and political "protest strikes", provided they do not aim to "subvert constitutional order" or obstruct the machinery through which "popular sovereignty is expressed": Cass. no.165/1983. See G Ghezzi and U Romagnoli, *Il diritto sindicale* (3rd ed, 1993) pp 223-4; and Wedderburn (1983) 12 ILJ pp 253-8.

65 Prohibition of strikes except after five days notice by a "representative" union (during which period parties should negotiate) and of "rolling" strikes (*Code du Travail*, article L-521-3ff.). On other administrative sanctions and powers even of conscription to uphold l'ordre public or in emergencies: see J-C Javillier Manuel, *Droit du Travail* (6th ed, 1998), pp 662-9. (The last may challenge the ILO concepts of "freedom of association": see ILO, *Freedom of Association* (3rd ed,1985), cases cited pp 31, 32, 41).

66 The right to strike was in the preamble of the 1946 Constitution and subsequently incorporated in the 4 October 1958 Constitution as a fundamental right.

67 So too do other many non-European countries with modern constitutions, including South Africa (see below), Mexico, Brazil, Argentina, Burkina Faso, and Rwanda.

68 The main provisions are: Constitution articles 6, 7, 14, 28; also: the Workers' Statute, 10 March 1980, (as later amended), Decree-Law 1977 (in part repealed), and Law 11/85 with Law 4/86 (on trade union rights and liberties): see T Sala Franco, *Derecho del Trabajo* (5th ed, 1990), pp 99-118. The Constitutional Court has from the outset interpreted the rights of

workers and unions very broadly: see decisions 11/81, 23/83, 98/85: and M Rodriguez-Pinero, *Le Tribunal Constitutionel Espagnol in Les Transformations du Droit du Travail* (1989), pp 104-122.

69 Sentenza 11/81 interpreting the Constitution, article 28 and Law 11/85, and declaring unconstitutional that part of the Decree-Law 1977 which purported to render solidarity (sympathy) strikes unlawful.

70 Article 9 (3), Basic Law.

71 *Op. cit*; see M. Weiss, *Labour Law and Industrial Relations in Germany* (1990) pp 33, 105-9 on constitutional freedom of association, "positive" and "negative".

72 Which right is guaranteed, respectively, by article 56 of the Swiss Federal Constitution and by article 9(3) of the Basic Law (Constitution of the Federal Republic of Germany). In Germany, the Federal Labour Court and the Federal Constitutional Court have played a fundamental role in interpreting the Basic Law and inferring a right to strike.

73 Article 40.6 of Bunreacht na hIireann.

74 *Education Co. v Fitzpatrick (No.2)* [1961] IR 345, per Kingsmill Moore J at p 397. As an unenumerated right, this right would derive its protection from article 40.3 and accordingly would be subject to considerations of practicability and justice (see J Casey, *Constitutional Law in Ireland* (1992), pp 491-2) which would have to be constitutionally justifiable and for the common good: *Ryan v A-G* [1965] IR 294, at pp 312-3.

75 The Netherlands Supreme Court directly applied article 6(4) into domestic law to found a right to strike: Hoge Raad, Nederlands, *Jurisprudentie* 1986, p 688.

76 See the useful analysis of the right to strike in *Federation of Offshore Workers' Trade Unions v The Norwegian State* represented by the Ministry of Local Government and Labour, Case no.24/1997, 10 April 1997, Norwegian Supreme Court, (English translation made by the Ministry of Local Government and Labour).

77 Article L521-1 *Code du Travail*, which has provided since 1985 that any dismissal inconsistent with this is null and void.

78 See O Hasselbach, "Lawful Industrial Action and the Employment Relationship in Denmark," (2000) 16 *Int. Jo. of Comp. Lab. Law and IR,* p 143. Where the workers are unionised and there is a collective agreement there is no contract of employment to terminate, it seems.

79 See the extensive review of the statutory provisions by McIntyre J in *Reference re Public Service Employee Relations Act* (1987) 38 DLR (4th) 161, at p 230; and, more up to date, H Arthurs et al *Labour Law and Industrial Relations,* (4th ed, 1993), pp 276-277.

80 *Bates v Model Bakery Ltd.* [1993] 1 IR 359, and see *Becton Dickinson & Co. Ltd. v Lee* [1973] IR1.

81 *Simmons v Hoover Ltd* [1977] ICR 61, declining to follow Lord Denning M.R. in *J. T. Stratford & Son Ltd. v Lindley* [1965] AC 269, at p 285 and *Morgan v Fry* [1968] 2 QB 710, at p 727, where Lord Denning was supported by Davies LJ at p 733. (Lord Denning was followed by the Irish Supreme Court in the cases cited above). Several English academics have supported the approach: P O'Higgins (1973) 2 ILJ 145; Wedderburn, *The Worker and the Law* (2nd ed, 1971), pp 109-111, 195-6; S Foster (1971) 34

MLR 275; and, more recently, G Pitt, *The Limits of Industrial Action* (Institute of Employment Rights, 1995), pp 8-9; G Pitt, "The Right to Strike: a Shift in Focus" in A McColgan (ed.) *The Future of Labour Law* (1996), pp 115-6. See also K D Ewing, "The Right to Strike" (1986) 15 ILJ 143, at pp 149-151.

82 See Lord Wedderburn *Employment Rights in Britain and Europe* (1991), 276 at pp 293-6, 304; and for comparative assessments of sympathy action, Lord Wedderburn, "Laws about strikes" *op cit.*

83 Some scholars doubt the validity of the distinction: "It is in fact difficult to distinguish damage to produttività from damage to produzione." G Giugni *Diritto Sindicale op.cit,* 252-4; G Lyon-Caen, J Pélissier and A Supiot, *Droit du Travail, op.cit* pp 934-5 (this difficult distinction in principle means: désorganiser l'enterprise elle-même rather than désorganiser la production).

84 See M.Weiss, *Labour Law and Industrial Relations in Germany* (1990), p 136.

85 See Lord Wedderburn "Industrial Relations and the Courts" (1980) 9 ILJ 65-86; and see generally B Hepple (ed.) *The Making of Labour Law in Europe: Nine Countries to 1945* (1986).

86 On the eventual categorisation of the United Kingdom as a system of "collective laisser faire" and relative absence of legal machinery in collective labour relations, see O Kahn-Freund "Labour Law", in M Ginsberg (ed.) *Law and Opinion in England in the 20th Century* (1959) 215. Compare P Davies and M Freedland *Labour Legislation and Public Policy* (1993), pp 11-37.

87 In areas like occupational health and safety there was from 1833 a gradual coverage by statutory provision. See the summary by J Hendy and M Ford in *Munkman on Employers' Liability,* (12th ed, 1995), ch 1. But statutory provision is not by itself always a safe shield against the assertion of liability by the courts: see *Associated British Ports v TGWU* [1989] ICR 557, where the Court of Appeal held that a statutory provision in the Dock Work scheme relieving dockworkers from actual work, but giving the employers no right of action as such, was nevertheless actionable by the employers in tort because of the union's "intention to injure" them. The Dock Work Scheme was shortly after revoked.

88 [1995] 2 AC 454.

89 Applications of *Wilson, National Union of Journalists and others v the United Kingdom,* Cases no. 30668/96, 30671/96, 30678/96.

90 *Collymore v Attorney-General* [1970] AC 538 on the constitution of Trinidad and Tobago; *Banton v Alcoa Minerals of Jamaica Inc.* (1971) 17 WIR 275; *All India Bank Employees Association v National Industrial Tribunal* (1962) 49 AIR 171.

91 Though see the decision of the Human Rights Committee of the United Nations in *Alberta Union of Provincial Employees v Canada,* discussed later.

92 *Reference re Public Service Employee Relations Act* (1987) 38 DLR (4th) 161. See also *Public Service Alliance v The Queen* (1987) 38 DLR (4th) 249, and *Government of Saskatchewan v Retail, Wholesale and Department Store Union, Locals 544, 496, 635 and 955* (1987) 38 DLR (4th) 277. The principle was recently reiterated in *Delisle v Canada* [1999] 2 SCR 989.

93 Via s.2(d) of the Canadian Charter of Rights and Freedoms.

94 *Reference re Public Service Employees Relations Act, op cit,* per McIntyre J at p 229.

Chapter 5 : Article 11 and the right to strike

95 The majority overruled the opinion of the Chief Justice, Dickson CJC at 195 that: "If freedom of association only protects the joining together of persons for common purposes, but not the pursuit of the very activities for which the association was formed, then the freedom is indeed legalistic, ungenerous, indeed vapid." Likewise they overruled the conclusion in an earlier case that: "freedom of association if it is to be a meaningful freedom must include freedom to engage in conduct which is reasonably consonant with the lawful objects of an association. And I think a lawful object is any object which is not prohibited by law." (Galligan J in *Re Service Employees International Union, Local 204 and Broadway Manor Nursing Home* (1983) 4 DLR (4th) 231, at p 248, and see Smith J at 302. This is the European Court of Justice's approach, see *Union Syndicale*, below).

96 See note 91 above.

97 Now article 23(2) of the Bill of Rights of the Constitution of the Republic of South Africa, as amended on 11 October 1996. The Bill of Rights in the Interim Constitution, article 27, restricted the right to strike to the pursuit of collective bargaining. The 1996 Bill of Rights does not.

98 Those restrictions which do not breach the Constitution: *Cape Local Authorities Employers Organisation v Independent Municipal and Allied Trade Union* 1997 (1) SA 656; *Mbelu v MEC for Health and Welfare, Eastern Cape* 1997 (2) SA 823 (Tk), which held that statutory restrictions on the right to strike of public servants did not breach the constitutional guarantee.

99 *In re Certification of the Constitution of the Republic of South Africa* 1996 (4) SA 744, at p 795.

100 Workplace Relations Act 1996, s.170ML-MP, s.170WC-WE.

101 C Barnard, "The United Kingdom, the Social Chapter and the Amsterdam Treaty," (1997) 26 ILJ 275.

102 Pursuant to EEC Treaty article 179.

103 [1974] ECR 917.

104 [1974] ECR 933, at p 944.

105 [1990] ECR 95.

106 The European Court of Justice concluded, however, that freedom of association did not impose a duty to provide assistance (such as distribution of circulars) to facilitate trade union activity where such assistance was not required to be given by any other principle, regulation or agreement. Furthermore it held that the absence of that assistance did not impede the exercise of trade union activity (since there was no bar on circulation of material in other ways). Freedom of association did, however, extend to require time off work to be given to representatives to enable them to attend the consultative meetings.

107 In consequence of the Comité des Sages report: *For a Europe of Civic and Social Rights* (European Commission, 1995). See also the Comité des Sages report: *Leading by Example: A Human Rights Agenda for the European Union for the Year 2000* (European University Institute, 1998).

108 S Simitis, *et al, Affirming Fundamental Rights in the European Union, Time to Act,* Report of the Expert Group on Fundamental Rights, February 1999, European Commission. This draft contains forerunners to articles 12 and 26 (and other articles) in the First Draft.

109 Draft as proposed by the Praesidium, 28 July 2000.

110 See Keith Vaz MP, Minister for Europe in evidence to the House of Lords Select Committee on the European Union, summarised in Part 3, 8th Report, 16 May 2000; Lord Goldsmith, United Kingdom Government negotiator on the Draft Charter, in an interview in *The Guardian*, 1 August 2000.

111 Application no.5357499, dated October 1999.

112 Application no. 38190/97, dated September 1997.

113 *Merkur Island Corp. v Laughton* [1983] 2 AC 570, per Lord Diplock at pp 604-5.

114 Trade Union and Labour Relations (Consolidation) Act 1992, s.219.

115 Trade Union and Labour Relations (Consolidation) Act 1992, ss.242 and 244(5). In Spain secondary action was declared illegal by the Royal Decree Law of 1997 but rendered permissible in accordance with the constitution by the Constitutional Tribunal ruling of 8.4.81.

116 So has the Committee of Experts under the Charter: CII 187. However, aspects of the United Kingdom requirements are plainly challengeable, note the application to the European Court of Human Rights by NATFHE arising out of *Blackpool and Fylde College v NATFHE* [1994] ICR 648 (identification by name of potential strikers).

117 See Lord Diplock in *NWL v Woods* [1979] ICR 867, at p 879.

118 *American Cyanimid Co. v Ethicon Ltd.* [1975] AC 396.

119 *Sunday Times v United Kingdom (No.2)* (1991) 14 EHRR 229. And note the observations of the European Court of Human Rights in relation to the requirements of fairness in various forms of court order in *Chappell v United Kingdom* (1987) 12 EHRR 1; *AGOSI v United Kingdom* (1987) 9 EHRR 1; *Air Canada v United Kingdom* (1995) 20 EHRR 150.

120 See O Hasselbach, *op cit*, from which it appears that the refusal of reinstatement in Danish Labour Court case 98.342 on the ground that lawful industrial action terminated the contract of employment came as a surprise to many labour law specialists.

121 Perhaps "the socialisation of the common law" as Ewing reflects in "The Charter and Labour: The Limits of Constitutional Rights", in G Anderson (ed.), *The Canadian Charter of Rights: The Implications of Incorporation of the European Convention on Human Rights* (1998).

122 Noted in *Simmons v Hoover Ltd op cit;* and see Royal Commission on Trade Unions and Employers Associations Cmnd. 3623, 1968, para. 943.

123 Which Pitt considers realistic: G Pitt, *The Limits of Industrial Action, op cit*, pp 8-9; and "The Right to Strike: a Shift in Focus" *op cit*, pp 115-6. See also K D Ewing, "The Right to Strike" (1986) 15 ILJ 143, at pp 149-151.

124 Lord Wedderburn, *The Worker and the Law*, (3rd ed, 1986) at p 192.

125 Developed by Denning MR in *J T Stratford & Son Ltd. v Lindley* [1965] AC 269, at p 285 and *Morgan v Fry* [1968] 2 QB 710, at p 727, and supported by Davies LJ at p 733. See note 81 above.

126 in *Beckton Dickinson & Co. Ltd. v Lee* [1973] IR 1 which T Kerr and G Whyte, *Irish Trade Union Law* (1985) at p 209) consider satisfactorily answers all but one of the technical problems referred to above.

127 *Latham v Singleton* [1981] 2 NSWLR 843.

128 *Simmons v Hoover Ltd, op cit*. In Canada the doctrine takes statutory form: McIntyre J in *Re Public Employee etc, op cit* at p 230.

129 W Brown, S Deakin and J Ryan, "The Effects of British Industrial Relations Legislation 1979-97" (1997) 161 *National Institute Economic Review* N69, at p 75. This diminution of collective bargaining coverage continues: N Millward, A Bryson and J Forth, *All Change at Work?* (2000) at p 159 *et seq.*

130 P Davies and M Freedland, *Labour Legislation and Public Policy* (1993), p 467.

131 P Smith and G Morton, "Union Exclusion and Decollectivisation of Industrial Relations in Britain" (1993) 31 BJIR 97, and "Union Exclusion – Next Steps" (1994), 25 IRJ 3. See also J Hendy, *A Law unto Themselves; A National and International Assessment of the Conservative Employment Laws* (Institute of Employment Rights,1994); Davies and Freedland, *op cit,* especially chapters 9 and 10.

132 Employment Protection Act 1975, Schedule 11 (extension of collective bargains to other employers) and s.11 of the same Act (compulsory union recognition machinery) repealed by Employment Act 1980. Wages Councils (save for Agricultural Wages Board): abolished (after earlier pruning of their powers and application in 1986) by Trade Union Reform and Employment Rights Act 1993, s.35. Even the duty of the Advisory, Conciliation and Arbitration Service (ACAS) to "encourage the extension of collective bargaining and the development and, where necessary, reform of collective bargaining machinery", was removed by s.43(1) of the 1993 Act. The modest duties of publicly owned industries to erect consultation machinery (such as Coal Industry Nationalisation Act 1946, s.46; Electricity Act 1947, s.53; Gas Act 1948, s.57; Iron and Steel Act 1949, s.39) were all repealed prior to privatisation. Those changes were undertaken against a background of 8 Acts of Parliament weakening trade unions in a host of other ways (eg. ban on industrial action in support of union recognition clauses in commercial contracts: see below), as well as rising unemployment, privatisations and ceaseless anti-union propaganda.

133 Trade Union and Labour Relations (Consolidation) Act 1992, s.181.

134 See Lord Wedderburn and S Sciarra, *Collective Bargaining as Agreement and as Law: Neo-Contractualist and Neo-Corporative Tendencies of our Age,* in Pizoruss, (ed.) *Law in the Making* (1988), especially at pp 187-196; Lord Wedderburn, "Inderogability, Collective Agreements and Community Law" (1992), 21 ILJ 245; Lord Wedderburn, *Labour Law and Freedom* (1995), at pp 85-6 and 212-236.

135 Executive committee elections (by postal ballot): Trade Union and Labour Relation (Consolidation) Act 1992, ss.46, 49; membership registers, scrutineers: ss.24, 24A, 49, 75, 100A; election addresses: s.48; rules on amalgamations etc: ss.99, 100; candidature in elections: s.47; injunctions and receivers in relation to union funds: s.16; no indemnification of members' fines: s.15; accounting records and annual returns: ss.29,32, 32A; authorisation for check-off: s.68; political fund restrictions: ss.71-77A.

136 "Unreasonable" exclusion: s.174; "unjustifiable" discipline: ss.64-5; grievances: s.63.

137 Restriction of the immunities: ss.219, 244; prohibition of secondary industrial action: s.224; or in support of a closed shop: s.222; or to urge employment of union labour: s.225; or to urge reinstatement of sacked

strikers: s.223; limitations on pickets: ss.220, 224; imposition of complex
pre strike balloting requirements; ss.226, 226A, 226B, 226C, 228, 229,
231, 234, 234A; loss of protection if unofficial action not repudiated: ss.20,
21; restriction of unfair dismissal protection for strikers; ss. 237, 238; State
official to fund legal action against unions: ss.235B.

138 In, for example, *New Labour, New Life for Britain* (1996), p 5, and
    elsewhere.

139 *The Times,* 31 March 1997.

140 Ban on industrial action aimed at getting a contractor to include a clause in
    a subcontract requiring union-only labour or that unions should be
    recognised or consulted: s.225; clauses in commercial contracts providing
    for union-only labour declared void: s.144; likewise such clauses providing
    for union recognition: s.186; unlawful to refuse to deal with a contractor on
    union membership grounds: s.145; or on union recognition grounds: s.187;
    public bodies prohibiting from taking into account terms and conditions of
    contractors' employees in selecting contractor: Local Government Act,
    1988, s.17.

141 See J Hendy, *Every Worker...*, *op cit*, at p 24.

142 In *EC Commission v United Kingdom, Cases C-382/92, C-383/92* [1994] ICR
    664.

143 Amongst the rights dependent on prior recognition are: time off with pay
    for union duties: s.168; time off for union activities: s.170.

144 See M Hall, "Beyond Recognition? Employee Representation and EU
    Law" (1996) 25 ILJ 15. The amendments (Collective Redundancies and
    Transfer of Undertakings (Amendment) Regulations 1995) were subject to
    a predictably unsuccessful challenge in the British courts: *R v Secretary of
    State for Trade and Industry ex p. UNISON, GMB, and NASUWT* [1996]
    ICR 1003. Further amendments are proposed but still trade union
    representation rights will not be guaranteed in all circumstances. The
    present government have blocked further rights to information and
    consultation proposed by the European Commission: *Guardian,* 17 March
    1998

145 J Hendy, *Every Worker...*, *op cit*, pp 16-21. *Associated Newspapers Ltd. v
    Wilson* and *Associated British Port plc v Palmer* [1995] 2 AC 454, at p 487;
    that case effectively overruling *Discount Tobacco v Armitage* [1990] IRLR 15,
    (notwithstanding the valiant *Speciality Care plc v Pachela* [1996] IRLR 248).

146 Perhaps because the necessary majority has not been won; or because the
    legislation requires a threshold for demanding a ballot which has not been
    reached; or because of an exemption for small firms; or because a ballot has
    been lost, and though a majority is subsequently attainable, there is a bar in
    the legislation to re-balloting for the next three years; or because some
    other exception in the legislation applies.

147 Legislation intended to achieve majority unionism and orderly industrial
    relations which may nevertheless have the effect of denying minority rights
    is permissible and those in the minority will not necessarily have a
    legitimate complaint under the Convention, as the *Swedish Engine Drivers*
    and *Belgian Police* cases show, at paras 42 and 41, respectively.

148 It seems logical to suppose that non-availability of recognition because of a
    limitation in the legislation to firms employing more than a specified

number of employees might be held to be insufficient justification for abridgement of the individual right in small firms to be heard. On the other hand, failure to obtain the necessary majority in a ballot might be prima facie within the margin of appreciation on the basis that a means of representation was at least within grasp, though arguably it might not be sufficient to outweigh (in the hypothesised case) the absence of all other means of being heard via the union.

149 As required in the US legislation: s.8(d) National Labor Relations Act.

150 On this (and on the recognition machinery generally) see Lord Wedderburn, "Collective Bargaining or Legal Enactment: the 1999 Act and Union Recognition" (2000) 29 ILJ 1 at pp 38-41.

151 Part of Glidewell LJ's analysis of the nature of consultation in *British Coal Corporation ex parte Price* [1994] IRLR 72, at p 75, following *R v Gwent CC ex parte Bryant* [1988] COD 19; followed by *Rowell v Hubbard Group Services Ltd* [1995] IRLR 19, and *King v Eaton Ltd* [1996] IRLR 199; see also *R v Warwickshire DC, ex parte Bailey* [1991] COD 284.

152 Words imposed on the United Kingdom (in relation to certain statutory consultation obligations) by European Directive (in consequence of *European Commission v United Kingdom* [1994] ICR 664) and found now (for business transfers) in reg. 10(5) Transfer of Undertakings (Protection of Employment) Regulations 1981 and (for collective dismissals) in s.188(2) Trade Union and Labour Relations (Consolidation) Act 1992.

Chapter 6

Article 14 and the prohibition of discrimination: the nature of the protection

Tess Gill

Article 14 – Prohibition of discrimination

"THE enjoyment of the rights and freedoms set forth in this Convention shall be secured without discrimination on any ground such as sex, race, colour, language, religion, political or other opinion, national or social origin, association with a national minority, property, birth or other status."

International standards

PROMOTING equality and prohibiting discrimination have formed an important part of a number of international instruments and a focus of concern on the international human rights agenda. Article 1(3) of the Charter of the United Nations Organisation which promotes economic, social and cultural rights as well as civil and political rights, calls for international co-operation

"in promoting and encouraging respect for human rights and for fundamental freedoms for all without distinction as to race, sex, language or religion".

The international covenants adopted by the UN General Assembly have provisions for dealing with non-discrimination and equality. Article 2 of the Universal Declaration of Human Rights, 1948 declares that:

"Everyone is entitled to all the rights and freedoms set forth in this declaration without distinction of any kind, such as race, colour, sex, language, religion, political or other opinion, national or social origin, property, birth or other status."

Also important is article 7: this provides that:

"All are equal before the law and are entitled without discrimination to equal protection of the law."

The International Covenant on Civil and Political Rights (ICCPR) goes considerably further than article 14 of the European Convention. Article 26 provides comprehensive protection against discrimination in all matters of legal regulation. It provides:

"All persons are equal before the law and are entitled without any discrimination to equal protection of the law. In this respect the law shall prohibit any discrimination and guarantee to all persons equal and effective protection against discrimination on any ground such as race, colour, sex, language, religion, political or other opinion, national or social origin, property, birth or other status."

It would be a breach of article 26 for the State to enact legislation which discriminates and equally to fail to enact effective laws against discrimination.

In contrast to article 26 of the ICCPR article 14 of the ECHR provides protection against discrimination only in so far as the discrimination relates to the rights and freedoms set out elsewhere in the Convention. It is known as a 'parasitic' article which can only be relied upon in conjunction with an alleged breach of another article. On the positive side and unlike domestic law[1], the grounds upon which discrimination is prohibited is open ended. The list of grounds in article 14 which itself is comparatively comprehensive is not exhaustive. The grounds on the list are examples as indicated by the words 'on any ground such as' and 'all other status'. Certain categories of 'other status' have been identified, but as the basis of discrimination is not closed any other form of differential treatment may be found to be discriminatory if not justified. Other grounds of discrimination which have been identified include sexual orientation[2], marital status, illegitimacy[3], status as a trade union, military status, conscientious objection and professional status.

This chapter surveys how far article 14 affords protection against discrimination by comparing it with the protection afforded in domestic and EC law. The concept of discrimination is discussed with reference to indirect discrimination and positive or affirmative action. The extent to which article 14 may be usefully utilised under the Human Rights Act is examined and finally the draft Protocol 12 which significantly broadens the scope of discrimination protection is discussed.

Article 14: scope and content

ARTICLE 14 only provides protection against discrimination when the right being claimed is one that falls under the Convention, though the grounds on which discrimination is forbidden are widely drawn[4]. Many employment and trade union rights are excluded. The Convention does not guarantee the right to a job, the right to trade union recognition, the right to minimum pay or safe working conditions; though it may be argued that where there are grave hazards at work there is an infringement of article 2; but this would only be the case where there was a life-threatening hazard[5].

Article 14 is only binding on public bodies or private bodies with public functions. In this respect its application is more restricted than that of article 26 of the ICCPR which covers 'any field regulated and protected by public authorities'[6]. The relationship between the substantive articles and article 14 is not entirely straightforward. It is not the case that an article 14 claim can only succeed if the substantive article has been breached. Indeed it is possible for the applicant to have a claim of discrimination alone provided the substantive article is engaged[7].

The protection afforded by article 14 extends beyond those rights that a State is required by the Convention to guarantee: it also applies to those measures which the State chooses to guarantee although not obliged to do so[8]. This point is illustrated in *Abdulaziz, Cabales and Balkandali v United Kingdom*[9]. The Court held there was no obligation on the United Kingdom to allow resident alien husbands, who had a right to remain, to be joined by their wives. As the United Kingdom did allow wives to join their husbands, the question of whether the failure to allow wives in similar circumstances to be joined by their husbands fell within the ambit of the right to respect for family life, and article 14 could be engaged in so far as it could be shown that there was differential treatment[10].

What is discrimination?

THE European Court of Human Rights has viewed the equality principle as requiring that equal situations are treated equally and unequal situations differently. Failure to do so will amount to discrimination unless an objective and reasonable justification exists. The draft explanatory report accompanying the draft Protocol 12 is the latest official exposition of this view. In certain circumstances the principle may allow positive discrimination but this is not required. The concept of indirect discrimination is barely formulated. In these respects discrimination under the Convention is a less sophisticated and effective weapon to achieve equality of results than other international and national instruments[11].

There are two stages in establishing discrimination. First, the applicant has to show that he or she has been treated differently from others in the same or analogous situation. The reason for the different treatment may be one of the grounds identified in article 14; a ground which although not identified in the article has already been recognised in case law; or any other reason which the Court accepts is discriminatory. If the Court does not accept that there is less favourable treatment of the applicant compared to others in a comparative situation the claim will be rejected.

The facts of the case may make proof of discrimination an easy matter. In *Dudgeon v United Kingdom* it was the law in Northern Ireland which criminalised Dudgeon's homosexual activities unlike the law in England or Wales. In fact the Court dealt with the claim under article 8 and found that the law was disproportionate in that the justifications were outweighed by the detrimental effects on homosexuals. It did not deal with the article 14 point that the law discriminated against homosexuals. In other cases the chosen comparison is rejected by the court. So in *Stubbings v United Kingdom* the applicants, who were children who had suffered sexual abuse and were complaining about the limitation period which prevented them bringing a claim, compared themselves with victims of negligent acts who had more generous limitation periods. The comparison was rejected by the Court as 'artificial'.

Justification

If the applicant succeeds in establishing differential treatment in a comparable situation it will only be held to be in violation of article 14 if there is no objective and reasonable justification. This is so although the terms of article 14 are expressed absolutely and without qualification unlike many of the substantive articles which provide for exceptions. It is only unjustified differential treatment which is held to be discrimination[12]. Allowing such a defence in all circumstances where differential treatment has been made out is in contrast to domestic law on race and sex discrimination where direct discrimination cannot generally be justified. A narrow list of genuine occupational qualifications and some specified exceptions are the only defences allowed.

The test of justification is similar to that adopted by the European Court of Justice (ECJ) in claims of indirect discrimination, but so far the ECJ has not permitted justification of direct discrimination[13]. In order to prove justification, the State must show that the difference in treatment pursues a 'legitimate aim', and that there is a 'reasonable relationship of proportionality between the means employed and the aim sought to be realised'. The first stage of justification is the State to satisfy the Court that the matter complained of has a rational aim. There may be a dispute of fact as to what is the aim. For example, in the *Abdulaziz* case the State asserted that the aim was to protect the labour market and to protect public order. The applicants claimed that the immigration laws were racially motivated. That was rejected by the Court.

Legitimate aims have included protecting the labour market and public order (*Abdulaziz*), developing linguistic unity, (*Belgian Linguistics Case No. 2*) supporting and encouraging the traditional family (*McMichael v United Kingdom*[14]). It is virtually unheard of for the State not to succeed at this stage. Almost the only exception to this is in *Darby v Sweden*[15], a case concerning taxation in which the State failed to put forward a legitimate aim. Once a legitimate aim has been established the next stage is to consider whether the impact of the means employed to achieve the legitimate aim is proportionate to the aim and objective. This brings in the test of proportionality. The State must satisfy the Court that there is a fair balance between the protection of the interests of the community and respect of the rights and freedoms safeguarded by the Convention[16]. In *National Union of Belgian Police v Belgium*[17] the denial of consultation rights to a trade union because of its small size, compared to other unions who were given consultation rights, was justified. It was held that it did strike a reasonable balance between the rights of the union and the interests of the employers in ensuring a coherent and balanced staff policy.

Where the State seeks to justify the differential treatment by generalisations unsupported by evidence it may well fail[18]. It will assist the applicant in showing that the means adopted are not proportionate to the ends if an alternative means for achieving the same ends which has lesser discriminatory impact is identified[19].

The margin of appreciation

The Court allows the state a margin of appreciation when considering whether the difference in treatment is proportionate to the legitimate aim[20]. It is strongly arguable though, that the concept of a margin of appreciation is not appropriate when it comes to domestic implementation[21]. The extent of the margin of appreciation is linked to the grounds of the difference in treatment. Certain grounds are considered more serious than others[22].

Discrimination on grounds of sex falls into such a category, similarly illegitimacy. One element in assessing whether the State has acted within the margin of appreciation is whether its treatment falls within or departs from a common standard adopted by Convention states. Again, whether this would be appropriate when the national court is considering whether there has been a violation may be questionable. However, if the applicants are able to point to a common standard whether by way of practice or international agreement which prohibits discrimination on a particular ground, that should be a powerful argument against a State's action being proportionate[23].

Hidden discrimination and indirect discrimination

Where there is a dispute as to the reason for the treatment, with the applicant asserting that it is on a discriminatory ground and the State putting forward another non-discriminatory reason, the European Court has almost universally accepted the State's explanation[24]. However, domestic judges should be in a better position to assess the evidence and come to a conclusion as to whether or not there is a discriminatory ground. The tests adopted under the domestic legislation for asserting whether or not a prohibited ground comes into play should equally be adopted in respect of article 14 claims. This would require the application of the objective 'but for' test[25]. Once the focus shifts from the aim or intention of the State to the impact on the applicant it becomes more likely that such disputes will be resolved in the applicant's favour.

Indirect discrimination

There is so far no clear ruling from the European Court of Human Rights on whether article 14 prohibits indirect discrimination. There are indications that it does in the *Belgian Linguistics* case. In the context of justification the court stated that: 'The existence of such a justification must be assessed in relation to the *aims and effects* (emphasis added) of the measure under consideration, regard being had to the principles which normally prevail in democratic societies'[26]. However, in other cases such as *Abdulaziz*, the Court has declined to make a finding of indirect discrimination.

There is no Convention definition of indirect discrimination as is found in domestic statutes which prohibit discrimination on grounds of sex and race[27]. The position is also to be contrasted to EC jurisprudence. The European Court of Justice has ruled that discrimination on grounds of nationality (EC Treaty, article 39, ex article 48), covers not only overt discrimination but also all covert forms of discrimination which, by the application of other criteria of differentiation, lead in fact to the same result[28]. Indirect discrimination is explicitly recognised in Regulation 1612/68 EEC which prohibits provisions which include situations where, although applicable irrespective of nationality, their exclusive or principal aim or effect is to keep nationals of other member states away from the employment offered. An exception is made for requirements of linguistic knowledge.

Article 141 (ex 119) of the EC Treaty, and the Equal Treatment Directive 76/207 require equal treatment between men and women in respect of pay and working conditions and apply to direct and indirect discrimination. The Burden of Proof Directive No 97/80/EC (15 December 1997) defined indirect discrimination[29]. Although this is the first definition to be found in the treaty or directive, the European Court of Justice has consistently found indirect discrimination to be in breach of article 141 unless objectively justified[30].

Affirmative action or reverse discrimination

Article 14 requires that 'the enjoyment of the rights and freedoms set forth in this convention shall be secured without discrimination'. The State therefore has positive obligations to the citizen which go beyond the negative prohibition of less favourable treatment. There are indications that the positive obligation to enable the citizen to enjoy the rights provided under the ICCPR without discrimination, extends to a duty to give effective access to such rights.

It was held in the *Belgian Linguistics* case that not all instances of differential treatment are unacceptable and that 'certain legal inequalities tend only to correct factual inequalities'. In *Airey v Ireland*[31], the applicant claimed under articles 6 and 14 that she was entitled to positive discrimination in the form of funding for a barrister so that she could enjoy effectively equal right of access to the courts. It was her case that judicial separation was more easily available to those who can afford to pay than those without financial resources. Having found the existence of a positive obligation under article 6(1) the court found it was not necessary to consider the article 14 claim[32]. As with other cases the Court having made a finding of a positive obligation under the substantive article treated the article 14 claim as superfluous[33].

In *DG & DW Lindsey v United Kingdom*[34], in the context of a tax advantage for married women it was stated that such advantage had 'an objective and reasonable justification in the aim of providing positive discrimination' to encourage married women back to work. There is no criteria for determining whether or not any particular action of reverse discrimination is permissible. Each case is decided according to whether or not the Court finds objective justification. This remains the case under Protocol 12[35].

Article 14 and the European Court of Human Rights

THE approach of the European Court of Human Rights to article 14 by and large has been cautious and favourable to the State. Article 14's impact has been limited not only by the fact that it is not a free-standing right but also by the Court's reluctance to determine an article 14 claim if it can dispose of the claim under the substantive article heading alone. There has been little willingness to challenge the grounds of justification put forward by Member States. Neither has the Court been willing to expand the suspect grounds so as to enhance protection from discrimination beyond that provided in a number of Member States. This has meant that with a few limited exceptions article 14 has not afforded protection from discrimination beyond that already found in the United Kingdom where there is already comparatively strong protection in employment against discrimination on grounds of sex, race or disability. In areas where one might look to article 14 to provide protection missing from domestic legislation such as sexual orientation or race discrimination so far unprotected by the Race Relations Act, such as immigration, article 14 has offered little to date.

The under-utilisation of article 14 was further emphasised in *Smith v United Kingdom*[36]. It was held for the first time that the ban on homosexuals in the armed forces was a violation to article 8 (right to respect for private and family life) and of article 13 (right to an effective remedy). The complaints were brought under article 8 in conjunction with article 14, but the Court having upheld the article 8 complaint made no finding on the article 14 complaint as it considered that it did not give rise to any separate issue. The case is of wide import in respect of employment outside the armed services but it is more likely that any future complaints will primarily rely on article 8 rather than article 14.

The scope of discrimination protection under the Human Rights Act

IN considering the circumstances in which article 14 or other Convention rights may assist in enhancing protection against discrimination and equal opportunities within the United Kingdom, there are two broad categories of cases. First, there are those forms of discrimination already prohibited in certain circumstances by domestic law with or without additional prohibition in EU instruments. Discrimination on the grounds of sex, race, disability, and in limited circumstances, trade union activities and industrial action, fall into this category.

Then there is discrimination arising for reasons so far unprotected in this way, or if protected only by attaching another prohibited ground as the reason for the discrimination concerned. Discrimination on grounds of sexual orientation, age or employment status would fall into this second category. However, as the grounds of discrimination are not closed, any particular set of circumstances giving rise to a substantive claim under the convention, such as article 6 (Right to a Fair Trial), article 8 (Right to Respect for Private and Family Life), or article 11 (Freedom of Assembly and Association), may be strengthened by adding an article 14 claim where it can be said that the applicant has been discriminated against compared to a person with a different status. It must also be remembered that even if the substantive claim fails, the article 14 claim may succeed. Some examples, which do not purport to be comprehensive, are given of the kind of claims where article 14 may be of use in respect of particular grounds of discrimination. Claims for gender discrimination in employment (other than sexual orientation) are less likely to be assisted by an article 14 claim in view of the EC jurisprudence.

It is not possible to be very positive as to the use of article 14 at present. Circumstances in which Convention rights may be of assistance in combating discrimination will be substantially enhanced if the Protocol 12 to the ECHR giving a free standing right to discrimination, which is considered below, is ratified. In considering in what circumstances resort to Convention rights to combat discrimination will be of assistance it is necessary to bear in mind that the European Union has made progress towards enhancing protection against discrimination in adopting a Council Directive implementing the principle of equal treatment covering race and ethnic origin, and proposing a revision to the Equal Treatment Directive of 1976 to define sexual harassment[37].

Race discrimination

Serious cases of race discrimination may fall under article 3 as in *Assenov and Others v Bulgaria*[38]. Allegations of police ill-treatment followed the arrest of a 14 year old Romani boy. Despite complaints by Assenov and his parents the State failed to investigate. The Court found violation of article 3 by reason of the State's failure to undertake an effective and official investigation and article 13 (right to an effective remedy), because of its failure to conduct a thorough and effective investigation and to provide effective access to the investigatory procedure and payment of compensation. The Court's ruling referred specifically to ill-treatment by the police or other such agents of the State. Whether ill-treatment within the employment context gives rise to such a duty is likely to depend both on its degree of seriousness and on whether the employer is a public body[39].

The Commission has attached a special importance to discrimination on grounds of race. In *East African Asians v United Kingdom*[40], applicants who were citizens of the United Kingdom and colonies challenged British immigration legislation which denied United Kingdom passport holders of Asian origin who were resident in East Africa admission to the United Kingdom. The Commission found that the legislation discriminated against the applicants on 'grounds of their colour or race' and that article 3 had been violated. The Commission found that 'a special importance should be attached to discrimination based on race', and that 'discrimination based on race could, in certain circumstances, of itself amount to degrading treatment within the meaning of article 3 of the Convention'. In an important passage the Commission ruled that 'differential treatment of a group of persons on the basis of race might therefore be capable of constituting degrading treatment when differential treatment on some other ground would raise no such question'. It was held that the challenged immigration legislation had subjected the applicants to racial discrimination and amounted to degrading treatment in violation of article 3.

The approach of the Court in *Gaygusuz v Austria*[41] where the discrimination found was on the grounds of nationality, is another indication that discrimination on the grounds of race is to be treated as a suspect category. In *Smith v United Kingdom*[42] the Court said that negative attitudes towards someone because of their race, origin or colour could not amount to sufficient justification for interference with an applicant's right. It might be argued that the focus on article 3 in the context of discrimination on the grounds of race and nationality indicates the weakness of article 14[43]. It is to be noted that the strength of article 3 is that it does not afford states a margin of appreciation unlike article 14. Though as indicated above, this distinction from other Articles should be of less importance when cases are brought before domestic courts, as then the concept of a margin of appreciation should have no application.

In circumstances in which the applicant has suffered discrimination in the enjoyment of the Convention right itself, an article 3 claim arising from race discrimination may be supported by an article 14 claim. Article 3 is unqualified so that no issue of justification arises. If there was no protection under the Race Relations Act 1976, (for example if there was doubt as to whether or not an employment relationship could be established, or whether the employer would be held liable for the relevant acts), a Convention claim might assist a claim under domestic law. Claims of race discrimination may also give rise to a violation of article 8 (Everyone has the right to respect for his private and family life, his home and correspondence). That article may be relevant in the context of racial or sexual harassment. There is no free-standing right to found a claim under the Convention against a private sector employer. However, as employment tribunals have a duty to interpret domestic legislation in a way which is compatible with convention rights, adding an article 8/14 claim when appropriate to a claim for race or sex discrimination may strengthen the case. If there is an element of race discrimination in an article 6 claim (right to a fair trial), an article 14 claim could be added.

Religion

Two further articles which may play a role combined with article 14, are article 9 (Freedom of Thought, Conscience and Religion) and article 10 (Freedom of Expression). It is to be noted that one of the glaring omissions in domestic provisions prohibiting discrimination in Britain is that there is no protection for religious discrimination. This is in contrast to Northern Ireland where the Fair Employment (Northern Ireland) Acts 1976 and 1989 prohibit discrimination on grounds of religious belief. In addition the Northern Ireland Act 1998 makes it unlawful for a public authority to discriminate on the grounds of religious belief or political opinion. There is also a duty to promote equal opportunity[44]. Neither does the EU Race Directive referred to above cover religious discrimination. This is therefore an area where the Human Rights Act may be utilised to support claims of discrimination and/or unfair dismissal or other detrimental treatment.

Article 9 claims linked where appropriate with an article 14 claim could be made. Cases brought under the Convention provide little assistance. One major difficulty is that the employee may be held to have contracted out of the right concerned by taking the employment in question. In *Choudhury v United Kingdom*[45] the Commission ruled inadmissible a claim under article 9 relating to blasphemy holding that there was no positive obligation on the State to allow individuals to bring proceedings against those who offended the sensibilities of particular groups. It did not consider the article 14 claim. However, such a narrow approach may not be followed by the domestic courts. In any particular case if the tribunal holds that it is not possible to construe domestic provisions to be consistent with article 9, that in turn on appeal and/or judicial review could lead to a declaration of incompatibility and finally a change in the law.

In Chapter 3 it is suggested that article 10 may assist in cases where the employer restricts employees choice of clothing. These may be claims which affect one gender or group defined by ethnic background or religion in which case an article 14 claim may be appropriate.

Trade union and collective rights

In Chapter 4 several restrictions on trade union and collective rights are identified that could give rise to challenges under the Human Rights Act. If an employer discriminates against a particular group of workers in respect of any such rights, for example not affording casual workers or temporary workers such rights, there may be scope for asserting there had been a violation of article 11 (1) which gives the right to workers to form and join trade unions for the protection of their interests with article 14. In *Sweden Engine Drivers' Union v Sweden*[46] the Court placed weight on the words in article 11 (1) 'for the protection of his interests', and held that those words required that in addition to being able to join a union, members of the union had the right that the trade union should be heard. In certain circumstances, there might be a combined breach of article 11 (1) and article 14, should the arrangements for consultation be discriminatory against any groups of workers, for example those working particular shifts or based outside the main workplace.

Sexual orientation

Protection from discrimination on grounds of sexual orientation has been greatly enhanced by *Smith v United Kingdom*[47] and *Lustig Prean v United Kingdom*[48] in which the European Court of Human Rights found the dismissal of a serviceman on grounds of his sexual orientation constituted a breach of privacy under article 8. In both cases although article 14 was relied upon that aspect of the claim was not determined. Cases could now be brought in the employment tribunals relying on the Sex Discrimination Act 1975 and articles 8 and 14 and requiring the tribunal to give effect to the Sex Discrimination Act in a way which is compatible with articles 8 and 14 so as to prohibit discrimination on grounds of sexual orientation. It would appear that this course of action would not be without its supporters among the judiciary, some of whom expressed the view that the ban on gays in the armed forces was contrary to convention rights[49].

Age discrimination

Another area where domestic law so far provides no overt protection against discrimination is discrimination on the grounds of age. Cases that have succeeded have done so because it has been possible to label the discrimination concerned as being on grounds of sex. In 1999 the government introduced a Code of Practice on Age Diversity in employment. The code is voluntary and there are no current plans to introduce statutory protection. The difficulty in using the Convention to raise cases of age discrimination will be finding a violation of a substantive article to which an article 14 could be added. It is likely that continuing to raise discrimination on the grounds of age as a form of sex discrimination in suitable cases is going to be the most fruitful avenue either before the domestic courts or the European Court of Justice[50].

Protocol 12

ON 26 June 2000 the Committee of Ministers of the Council of Europe adopted the text of Protocol 12 and published a draft explanatory report. It will be opened for signature on 1 November 2000. It is not yet known whether the United Kingdom will become a signatory and amend the Human Rights Act to include Protocol 12.

The preamble to the Protocol has regard to 'the fundamental principle according to which all persons are equal before the law and are entitled to equal protection of the law. It declares that the member states are 'resolved to take further steps to promote the equality of all persons through the collective enforcement of a general prohibition of discrimination' by means of the Convention. The substantive Articles provide:

Article 1 - General Prohibition of Discrimination

1 The enjoyment of any rights set forth by law shall be secured

without discrimination on any ground such as sex, race, colour, religion, political or other opinion, national or social origin, association with a national minority, property, birth or other status.

2 No one shall be discriminated against by any public authority on any grounds such as those mentioned in paragraph 1.

The protection from discrimination in the Protocol extends beyond article 14 in that paragraph 1 requires that any right set forth by law shall be secured without discrimination. In contrast, the guarantee in article 14 is restricted to the rights and freedoms set forth in the Convention. Article 14 has no equivalent to paragraph 2 which provides a general prohibition on discrimination by any public authority on any ground listed in paragraph 1 which remains non-exhaustive.

The purpose of the Protocol is specified in the accompanying report. The primary areas where it was considered there should be additional protection were race and sex discrimination. However, it was decided to achieve this by maintaining a list of specified grounds and by means of 'other status', as in article 14, making the categorisation of grounds open ended. Other grounds such as physical or mental disability, sexual orientation or age, were not added. The report states that this was not because of lack of awareness that such grounds have become particularly important in today's societies. It was considered unnecessary to add them as the list of grounds is not exhaustive and were they added it might be interpreted as weakening the case of any ground not added. This is not a convincing explanation and inevitably leaves those grounds not specified as 'second status' to the grounds expressly identified.

The term affirmative action or positive discrimination is not used. However, the report accompanying the Protocol states that measures taken to promote full and effective equality will not be prohibited by the principle of non-discrimination, provided that there is an objective and reasonable justification for them. The fact that there are disadvantaged groups or categories of persons who are disadvantaged, or the existence of de facto inequalities, may constitute justifications for adopting measures providing for specific advantages in order to promote equality, provided that the proportionality principle is respected. Such positive measures are not obligatory. The report also states that the Protocol's protection in comparison with article 14 concerns, in particular, cases where a person is discriminated against:

i in the enjoyment of any rights specifically granted to an individual under national law;

ii in the enjoyment of a right which may be inferred from a clear obligation of a public authority under national law, as where a public authority is obliged by national law to behave in a particular manner;

iii by a public authority in the exercise of a discretionary power (such as granting certain subsidies);

iv by any other act or omission by public authority (such as the behaviour of law enforcement officers when controlling a riot).

The explanatory report is guarded as to when article 1 might encompass discrimination in relations between private persons, that is to say its indirect horizontal effects. As the first paragraph is circumscribed by the reference to 'any right set forth by law', and the second limits the prohibition of discrimination to that by a 'public authority', the report concludes that positive obligations in relations between private persons would be exceptional and gives two examples of when it might arise. First, if there is a clear lacuna in the domestic law protection; and secondly, where in respect to relations between private persons the failure to provide protection might be so clear cut and grave that it might engage clearly the responsibility of the State. It would concern at the most relations in the public sphere which are normally regulated by law and for which the State has a certain responsibility, such as employment contracts or arbitrary denial of access to restaurant or other services. Purely private matters would not be affected.

The rights protected by law will include rights under statute law and common law rules. The exercise of a discretionary power by a public authority as well as those to be inferred from a clear obligation of a public authority under national law or from any other act or omission of a public authority would be covered. The protection afforded by the Protocol remains limited. It is primarily a negative obligation not to discriminate in those areas covered. It does not expressly include or define indirect discrimination. It is therefore a fairly modest extension of the ECHR guarantees. Certainly far more limited than article 26 of the ICCPR. It will, however, give more scope than article 14 if the United Kingdom becomes a signatory.

Notes

1 United Kingdom legislation prohibits discrimination on grounds of sex, colour, race, nationality, or ethnic or national origins, or disability. Sex discrimination covers discrimination against transsexuals, but not sexual orientation. Discrimination against married persons in employment is covered but not against single persons, though this is likely to the covered by the EC Equal Treatment Directive 76/207, which covers discrimination. on marital status. Discrimination on grounds of religious belief or political opinion is prohibited in Northern Ireland but not in Great Britain.

2 *Dudgeon v United Kingdom* (1982) 4 EHRR 149.

3 *Inze v Austria* (1987) 10 EHRR 394.

4 See T Choudhury, "In what respects does United Kingdom discrimination legislation fall short of the standards demanded by International Human Rights Law?", Working Paper No.2, *Independent Review of the Enforcement of United Kingdom Anti-Discrimination Legislation,* November 1999.

5 See A Lester & D Pannick *Human Rights Law and Practice* (1999), p 91.

6 The International Convention on the Elimination of All Forms of Racial Discrimination 1996 (CERD), article 2(1), places an obligation on States to ensure that neither they nor public authorities or public institutions engage in any act or practice of racial discrimination. Measures are to be taken to review governmental, national and local policies, and to amend, rescind or nullify any laws and regulations which have the effect of creating or perpetuating racial discrimination wherever it exists. The Convention on the Elimination of all Forms of Discrimination against Women (CEDAW) has similar provisions. Both require States to take appropriate measures to eliminate or bring to an end the discrimination concerned by any persons, group or organisation.

7 *Inze v Austria* (1987) 10 EHRR 394. There was no infringement of article 1 of the First Protocol considered alone but as Austrian law gave priority to legitimate over illegitimate heirs there was a violation of article 14 in combination with article 1 of the First Protocol.

8 In the *Belgian Linguistics (No.2)* case (1968) 1 EHRR 252. French-speaking parents complained that the Belgian educational system did not enable their children to be educated in French-speaking schools except if they travelled a considerable distance. They relied on article 2 of the First Protocol, together with articles 8 and 14. They only succeeded in respect of article 14, the Court holding that the rule barring access to certain schools in six communes was discriminatory and disproportionate when there was no equivalent rule for Flemish-speaking children. The Convention as such does not require a State to provide any system of education but in so far as it does (and each signatory state in fact provided a general educational system) there was a right not to be discriminated against in its provision which encompassed the right to be educated in one of the national languages. See also *Delcourt v Belgium* (1970) 10 YB 238, article 6(1) does not guarantee a right of appeal from a decision by a court. However, if a State provides a right of appeal those proceedings are governed by article 6(1) and any discrimination arising may fall under article 14.

9 (1995) 7 EHRR 471.

10 D J Harris, M O'Boyle and C Warbrick, *Law of the European Convention on*

Human Rights (1995), at pp 464-466 has a useful discussion of this issue.

11 See S Fredman "A critical review of the concept of equality in United Kingdom anti-discrimination law", Working Paper No.3, *Independent Review of the Enforcement of United Kingdom Anti-Discrimination Legislation*, November 1999.

12 In the *Belgian Linguistics* case, *op cit*, at p 284 the court held that to construe article 14 as forbidding every difference in treatment would reach absurd results. In defining the criteria to determine whether difference in treatment in the exercise of a Convention right violated the principle of equal treatment the court extracted principles from the legal practice of many democratic states to hold that there would be violation if the distinction had no objective and reasonable justification. The existence of such a justification must be assessed in relation to the aims and effects of the measure under consideration, regard being had to the principles which normally prevail in democratic societies. There must be a legitimate aim and a reasonable relationship between the means employed and the aim sought to be realised.

13 Whether this will continue to be the case will have to be seen. See *Birds Eye Walls, Case C-132/92* [1993] ECR 1-5579 (where the Advocate General took the view that both direct and indirect discrimination could be justified),and *Webb* C-32/93 [1994] ECR 1-3567.

14 (1995) 20 EHRR 205.

15 (1990) 13 EHRR 774.

16 *Belgian Linguistics* case, *op cit.*

17 (1975) 1 EHRR 578.

18 *Markx v Belgium* (1979) 2 EHRR 330, where the Court rejected the reason put forward without evidence for differential treatment on the grounds of illegitimacy, that mothers of illegitimate children were more likely to abandon them.

19 The same approach is taken as to whether or not indirect discrimination arising under the Race Relations Act 1996 or Sex Discrimination Act 1995 is justified.

20 The test applied is similar to that adopted by the ECJ in cases of indirect discrimination when the State is the alleged discriminator, see *R v Secretary of State for Employment ex parte Seymour Smith* Case C-167/97 [1999] ICR 447. For an example of the test of objective justification for sex discrimination in *Bilka-Kaufhaus GmbH v Weber von Hartz* Case 170/84 [1986] ECR 1607.

21 See Lester & Pannick, *op cit*, p 74, though it is to be noted that a substitute margin afforded by national courts to the legislature and executive might be valid.

22 This categorisation is similar to the concept of 'suspect categories' in the United States Constitution, see W McKean, *Equality and Discrimination under International Law* (1983), at pp 237-240.

23 *Rasmussen v Denmark* (1984) 7 EHRR 371 where a time limit applicable to paternity proceedings which distinguished between husbands and wives was to be found to exist in other member states and therefore did fall within the state's margin of appreciation.

24 For example, *Handyside v United Kingdom* (1976) 1 EHRR 737 (Handyside's allegation that he was prosecuted because of his political leanings were rejected) and *Abdulaziz v United Kingdom op cit.*

---

25 *James v Eastleigh Borough Council* [1989] ICR 423, per Lord Goff – "In the majority of cases, it is doubtful if it is necessary to fix upon the intention or motive of the defendant in this way and the simple 'but for' test avoids, in most cases at least, complicated questions relating to concepts such as intention, motive, reason or purpose, and the danger of confusion arising from the misuse of those illusive terms".

26 In *Marckx v Belgium* (1979) 2 EHRR 330 the Court stated that it prohibits rules which have the object of prejudicing a particular section of the population and rules which have that result.

27 Sex Discrimination Act 1975 s.1; Race Relations Act 1976 s.1. The definitions of indirect discrimination are restrictive definitions compared to the definitions in EC law in stipulating that there must be a requirement or condition so that it is not sufficient if there is merely a policy or practice.

28 *Sotgiu v Deutsche Bundespost, Case 152/73* [1974] ECR 153.

29 "Indirect discrimination shall exist where an apparently neutral provision, criterion or practice disadvantages a substantially higher proportion of the members of one sex unless that provision, criterion or practice is appropriate and necessary and can be justified by objective factors unrelated to sex."

30 *Bilka-Kaufhaus GmbH v Weber von Hartz op cit; Enderby v Frenchay Health Authority*, Case C-127/92 [1994] ICR 112, *Seymour-Smith op cit.*

31 (1979) 2 EHRR 305.

32 *ibid*, para 30.

33 A similar approach of avoiding making a finding under article 14 is found in *Vereinigung Demokratischer Osterreichs and Gubi v Austria* (1994) 20 EHRR 56.

34 (1986) 49 DR 181

35 In EC law the Equal Treatment Directive permits affirmative action in article 2(4)which provides that the Directive shall be without prejudice to measures which promote equal opportunity for men and women, in particular in removing existing inequalities which affect women's opportunities. The scope of such action has been explored in the context of appointment or promotion in a series of cases brought before the ECJ. See *Marschall v Land Nordrhein-Westfalen*, Case C-409/95 [1998] IRLR 39; *Badeck & Others, C-158/97*, IRLR 2000 432, where the German State of Hesse required public sector departments to adopt an 'advancement plan' to eliminate under-representation of women. That required that more than half of the posts should be given to women in the sector in which they are under-represented. Women would not be advantaged however in five situations including giving priority to promoting disabled persons, to long-term unemployed, or those wishing to return to full-time work after a period of part-time work. It is to be noted that such positive discrimination at the point of selection remains unlawful under the Sex Discrimination Act 1975.

36 [1999] IRLR 734 *Smith and Grady v United Kingdom* (1999) 29 EHRR 493.

37 In June 2000 the Council of Ministers unanimously adopted the European Commission proposal for a Council Directive on implementing the principal of equal treatment between persons, irrespective of racial or ethnic origin. The Race Directive was part of the proposals put forward by the Commission, based on article 13 of the Treaty of Amsterdam. Those proposals which are still under discussion included a much wider proposal for a general Framework Directive aimed at prohibiting discrimination in

employment on grounds of religion and belief, disability, age and sexual orientation, as well as racial and ethnic origin. The Race Directive defines direct and indirect discrimination, gives victims a right of redress through a judicial or administrative procedure, associated with appropriate sanctions for those who discriminate, shifts the burden of proof (in civil cases) once a prima facie case of discrimination has been made out by a complainant and accepted by the courts, provides protection against harassment and victimisation. It covers discrimination in employment and training, education and social protection, (including security and health care), social advantages, and the supply of and access to goods and services, including housing. The United Kingdom government's reaction is that only some minor changes to existing law may be necessary. It was adopted at the Council's meeting in October 2000 and member States have three years to implement it. The circumstances when Convention rights may be needed will also be diminished by the recent strengthening of race discrimination law with the Race Relations (Amendment) Act 2000 which introduces a new section 71 into the Race Relations Act 1976. It imposes a general duty on public authorities to make arrangements to secure that their functions are carried out with due regard to the need to eliminate unlawful racial discrimination and to promote equality of opportunity and good relations between persons from different racial groups.

38 Application No.874/1086, 28 October 1998 (Unreported)
39 See *Tower Boot Co Ltd v Jones* [1997] IRLR 168, for an example of conduct for which the employer was vicariously liable which might fall under article 3.
40 (1973) 3 EHRR 76.
41 (1997) 23 EHRR 365.
42 *Op cit.*
43 See J A Goldston: "Race Discrimination in Europe: Problems and Prospectives" [1999] EHRLR p 478.
44 Following the Treaty of Amsterdam, a draft Directive on covering discrimination on the grounds of religion and belief was put before the Council by the Commission in December 1999.
45 Application No.1743/90, HRLJ vol.12 No.4 p 172.
46 (1975) 1 EHRR 617. See also *National Union of Belgium Police v Belgium* (1975) 1 EHRR 578.
47 Op cit. see Chapter 2, above.
48 *Lustig-Prean and Beckett v United Kingdom* (1999) 29 EHRR 548.
49 *R v Ministry of Defence ex parte Smith* [1996] ICR 740, per Lord Bingham; at p 782
50 See *Nash v Mash* [1998] IRLR 168 where the employment tribunal referred a claim that Sections 1 and 9 of the Employment Rights Act which excludes those over normal retirement age from the right to claim unfair dismissal was indirectly discriminatory against men, to the ECJ. This and other cases are covered in M Sargeant, *Age Discrimination in Employment* (Institute of Employment Rights, 1999).

Chapter 7

Lessons from Canada: the impact of the Charter of Rights and Freedoms on labour and employment law

Judy Fudge

THE incorporation of the European Convention on Human Rights into United Kingdom domestic law[1] has created a stir among labour lawyers reminiscent of that provoked by the entrenchment of the Canadian Charter of Rights and Freedoms in 1982[2]. The *Charter* was heralded by some as introducing a brave new world to work. Optimists predicted that it could be used to assist the beleaguered labour movement and to rid employment protection legislation of the myriad exclusions that denied some of the most marginal workers basic labour standards. Other forecasts, however, were not so sanguine. Basing their assessment on the historical record of the

common law courts' treatment of workers' rights and their charac-
terisation of the *Charter* as paradigmatically liberal and individualis-
tic in orientation, pessimists predicted that it would be used to
undermine, rather than strengthen, workers' rights[3].

The entrenchment of the *Charter* triggered a great deal of litigation in the labour and employment fields. Writs were issued and
rights arguments were crafted. Unions were especially quick off the
mark, in part because the proclamation of the *Charter* coincided
with a full-scale legislative assault on public sector collective bargaining rights and a deep recession which gave employers the upper
hand in collective bargaining[4]. They invoked the freedoms of association and expression guaranteed by the *Charter* to challenge legislative restrictions on the right to strike and common law limitations on
picketing. Simultaneously, employers and individual employees
launched legal challenges to some of the cornerstones of the Canadian statutory collective bargaining regime; certification procedures, unfair labour practice provisions, and union security arrangements, including the political use of compulsory union dues, were all
impugned as infringing *Charter*-protected rights and freedoms[5]. The
Charter was also brought to bear on the individual employment law
regime. Exclusions from protective legislation were challenged by
workers and their advocates as infringing constitutional guarantees
of equal benefit and protection under the law, while employers contested protective legislation and enforcement mechanisms as unjustifiably limiting their fundamental rights and freedoms.

After 18 years with the *Charter*, the early optimism has almost
completely cooled, the most pessimistic predictions have been tem-
pered and the flood of labour-related litigation has diminished to a
trickle. With but minor, and very recent, exceptions, unions have not
been able to establish collective labour rights under the *Charter*. The
gap between the strong endorsement by the International Labour
Organisation of workers' collective rights and their absence from the
Canadian rights jurisprudence is glaring[6]. But, neither have employers and individual employees been able to deploy *Charter* rights to
unravel the key components of the statutory collective bargaining
regime. The upshot is that, despite years of litigation and millions of
dollars in legal fees, the central elements of the collective bargaining
regime have been preserved. And although its impact has been
greater in the area of individual employment law, in general, the
Charter has not exerted much influence on it as a result of the limited scope of application and the restrictive interpretation of rights
provided by the courts. Self-styled pragmatists have applauded the
courts' deference to the political compromises that legislatures and

expert tribunals have fashioned in the contested arena of labour relations[7]. However, in a context in which public sector workers' rights in particular and organised labour's strength in general have been systematically undermined, judicial deference has not been benign. Thus, while the instrumental impact of the *Charter* on workers' interests in employment and labour law has been slightly positive at best or neutral at worst, its ideological impact has been negative.

This chapter surveys the *Charter* jurisprudence in the areas of labour and employment law, concentrating on Supreme Court of Canada judgments, but referring to salient decisions of lower courts and tribunals[8], in order to determine what lessons, if any, can be drawn from the Canadian experience. Beginning with a brief overview of the structure of the Charter that contrasts it with the key features of the Human Rights Act 1998 the chapter proceeds to examine the scope of the *Charter*'s application in the labour and employment law fields. The remaining sections examine how rights have been defined, the limitations that have been accepted and remedies that have been crafted by focussing on the interests at stake in the litigation. In the conclusion, some caveats regarding drawing lessons on the basis of international comparisons will be noted.

Structure of the *Charter*

THERE is a high degree of overlap in the Human Rights Act and the *Charter* regarding the substantive rights and freedoms that are protected and pertain to the labour and employment fields[9], as well as common issues relating to scope of application and appropriate remedies. However, a distinguishing feature of the *Charter* is that it begins with a general limitation section, followed by the enumeration of the rights and freedoms it guarantees[10]. This structure differs markedly from that of the ECHR, which tailors acceptable limitations to specific rights. A second difference is the degree of detail with which the rights that are protected are expressed; the ECHR rights generally include much more detail than their Canadian counterparts. In the *Charter*, for example, s.2 declares that "everyone has the following freedoms" and subsection (d) enumerates the "freedom of association". Any limitations on that right must be justified under s.1, which is extremely broad and open-textured. By contrast, not only does article 11 of the ECHR specifically include "the right to form and to join trade unions for the protection of his [or her] interests" within the freedom of association, it goes on to identify the kinds of restrictions prescribed by law and necessary in a democratic society, including national security or public safety, etc, that are acceptable limitations on the right.

Another significant difference between the two documents is with respect to equality rights. The Canadian equality protections provide free-standing rights. In the *Charter*, s.15(1) states that "every individual is equal before and under the law and has the right to equal protection and equal benefit of the law without discrimination" and s.15(2) continues that this right "does not preclude any law, program or activity that has as its object the amelioration of conditions of disadvantaged individuals or groups". By contrast, article 14 of the ECHR is limited to the "enjoyment of rights and freedoms set forth in this Convention" and does not create a free standing right[11]. Like article 14 of the ECHR, the *Charter* prohibits discrimination generally and then goes on to enumerate specific grounds as illustrations of the types of discrimination that are prohibited. While the prohibited grounds of discrimination in the two equality provisions overlap, specifically race, sex, colour, religion and national origin, there are some telling differences. The Canadian provision lists age and mental or physical disability, which are not contained in article 14. Canadian courts have stated that the open-ended equality protection must be interpreted in light of the enumerated grounds, which they have characterised as illustrations of "ineluctable characteristics"[12]. The ECHR equality protection appears to be broader since it also includes "political or other opinion" as prohibited grounds of discrimination[13]. Moreover, unlike the *Charter*, the ECHR includes "social origin, association with a national minority, property, birth or other status".

Another major difference between the *Charter* and the Human Rights Act is how the application of the rights is expressed. The Human Rights Act describes two mechanisms of application: the first imposes a duty on courts to interpret legislation in a manner that is compatible with Convention rights and the second provides that Convention rights are directly enforceable against public authorities in domestic courts[14]. While there are some obvious interpretive issues, especially what counts as a public authority and a private function, to be resolved in order to determine the scope of application of the Convention rights in the context of United Kingdom labour and employment law, the Human Rights Act provides greater guidance than its Canadian counterpart. In Canada, the application of *Charter* rights revolves around two, very vaguely drafted, sections. The first, s.32, states that "this *Charter* applies... to the Parliament and government of Canada... and to the legislature and government of each province". The critical interpretive question is what counts as government and this has plagued Canadian courts, especially in the areas of labour and employment law. The second, s.52, simply states that "the Constitution of Canada", which includes the *Charter*, "is the supreme law of Canada" and "any law that is inconsistent with the provision of the Constitution is, to the extent of the inconsistency, of no force or effect".

This latter provision also indicates another difference in the two documents; the Canadian courts have been given much more robust powers than their United Kingdom counterparts to develop creative remedies, including striking down, suspending or amending legislation, for dealing with rights violations[15]. Moreover, a unique feature of the *Charter* is s.33, which allows provincial legislatures and the federal parliament, if they follow the appropriate procedure, to over-ride rights and freedoms entrenched in the *Charter*, with some exceptions, for up to five years at a time. Notably, one of the rare occasions upon which the over-ride was invoked was to exempt legislation that prohibited what was otherwise a lawful strike during a labour dispute[16].

Scope of application of the *Charter* to labour and employment law

THE threshold question which, to a large extent, determines the impact of constitutional rights on labour and employment law is whether the *Charter* applies. The resolution of this question depends upon the judicial interpretation of the term "government". Although the nomenclature relating to the scope of application differs in the Human Rights Act, many of the crucial issues are the same.

The most difficult question with which the courts have had to grapple is what constitutes the government for the purpose of applying the *Charter*. In some contexts, for example, where primary and secondary legislation is involved, the answer has been easy. When labour and employment-related legislation is invoked by private parties in a dispute the *Charter* applies. Such legislation can also be challenged directly on the ground that it violates *Charter*-protected rights. However, there are contexts in which the answer to this question is not self-evident and a surprising number of them have arisen with respect to employment and labour law[17]. In *Slaight Communications v Davidson*, the Supreme Court found that statutory authorities which exercise statutory discretion are subject to the *Charter*[18]. This means that the decisions and actions of statutory tribunals and statutory adjudicators that impact on labour and employment relations are subject to *Charter* scrutiny.

The contentious question of whether the *Charter* applies to the common law was largely resolved by the Supreme Court in *Dolphin*

Delivery, a case involving unlawful secondary picketing by a union[19]. The Canada Labour Code, unlike many provincial collective bargaining statutes, is silent on the issue of secondary picketing so the employer sought, and obtained, an injunction to restrain the picketing on the ground that it was unlawful as it amounted to a tort recognised by the common law. When the union argued that the injunction violated its freedom of expression guaranteed under s. 2(b) of the *Charter*, the issue arose as to whether the *Charter* applied to the activities of private actors and to judge-made common law. A unanimous Court held that the *Charter* applies only to government and that for the purposes of the *Charter* government does not include the courts. Thus, the *Charter* does not apply to litigation based on the common law between private parties nor to a court order enforcing common law rights in a dispute between private parties. The Supreme Court also stated that the *Charter* applies to a government actor relying on the common law to infringe *Charter* rights. It went on to say that although the *Charter* did not apply to disputes between private parties, this was "a distinct issue from the question whether the judiciary ought to apply and develop the principles of the common law in a manner consistent with the fundamental values enshrined in the Constitution. The answer to this must be in the affirmative"[20].

But precisely what applying *Charter* values means is far from clear. In a case dealing with a lawful strike involving government workers who engaged in primary picketing of their workplaces, including court-houses, the Supreme Court of Canada held that the *Charter* applied in a proceeding involving an ex parte injunction issued on the basis of the common law[21]. The Chief Justice of British Columbia issued, on his own motion, an injunction to restrain the picketing of court-houses on the ground that such activity constituted criminal contempt of court. The union subsequently challenged the injunction as violating its freedom of expression under the *Charter*. Despite the fact that no government actor was involved and that the only law relied upon was the common law, the court unanimously held that the *Charter* applied because the judge, in issuing the injunction, acted in a public capacity and invoked criminal law powers. Moreover, in another case involving an injunction issued on the basis of the common law to restrain secondary picketing in a private sector labour dispute, the Saskatchewan Court of Appeal set aside the injunction against picketing third party retailers on the ground that the *Charter*'s protection of freedom of expression precluded it from following an extremely controversial Ontario precedent which held that secondary picketing was illegal *per se*[22]. The majority of the court applied *Charter* values, that picketing is a form of protected expression, to the development of the common law[23]. However, the Supreme Court has been careful to insist that the *Charter* does not apply directly to private activity and that it cannot be applied in the same manner as when government activity is involved. Thus, although *Dolphin Delivery* set the outer limits of the application of the *Charter* to the common law as it is invoked by private parties, crucial interpretive questions, especially the degree to which *Charter* values should shape the common law, are yet to be resolved.

In one of a series of cases that dealt with professional employees who claimed that their employers' mandatory retirement policies infringed their *Charter* right to equality of treatment without discrimination on the basis of age, the Supreme Court set out its vision of the role of the *Charter*: "the *Charter* is essentially an instrument for checking the powers of government over the individual.... To open up all private and public action to judicial review could strangle the operation of society... and could seriously interfere with freedom of contract"[25]. It also grappled with the troublesome issue of how to define government in the context of statutory bodies or entities which inhabit the broader public sector. The majority held that the critical issue for determining whether the *Charter* applied is not the function being performed by the entity in question but whether or not it is part of the apparatus of government, which, in turn, depends on the degree to which government ministers or their officials exercised significant control over the entity's day to day operations. This test involves a case by case scrutiny of the governing statute and the relations between the entity and what are clearly government officials. Using this test, the court held that the *Charter* did not apply to universities or hospitals, but that it did apply to community colleges[26]. In *Lavigne v OPSEU*, a case involving a community college employee's *Charter* challenge of the use of compulsory dues for political purposes by the union certified to represent the bargaining unit of which he was a member, the Supreme Court of Canada confirmed the significance of the government control test and made it perfectly clear that once the *Charter* applied to a government entity it applied to all of that entity's functions regardless of whether or not a function was public or private[27]. By implication, the employment decisions, actions, policies and rules of all government entities are subject to the *Charter*.

The Supreme Court also found in *Lavigne* that the existence of permissive legislation, a provision that allowed the parties to agree to a compulsory dues check-off in the collective agreement, was not by itself sufficient to implicate the legislature as a government actor requiring *Charter* application. A ramification of this decision is that similar permissive legislation that pertains to labour relations in the private sector and provides for union security arrangements, including the closed shop, in collective agreements will not render the *Charter* applicable to collective agreements between private parties[28].

Initially there was a bright line, however difficult to discern in practice, that determined the scope of the *Charter*'s application and it was whether government action was involved. If it was, then all of the functions of the entity, including employment, were subject to *Charter* scrutiny. This obviated the need to identify whether or not the function in which the entity was engaged was public or private. However, a recent decision by the Supreme Court of Canada has complicated the determination of the scope of the *Charter*'s application. In *Eldridge v British Columbia (AG)*, the court ruled that a private entity may be subject to the *Charter* in respect of certain inherently governmental activities[29]. The *Charter* will apply to private entities in so far as they act in furtherance of or act to implement a specific government program or policy. It is not sufficient that the entity perform a public function; rather, it must be implementing a specific governmental policy or program and it will be subject to the *Charter* only with respect to those activities. This has led some commentators to speculate that "in the current context where the 'privatisation' of government services holds considerable political cache, the decision could help employees and recipients of 'governmental' services to prevent an erosion of their *Charter* rights"[30]. However, the impact of the extension of the *Charter* to private entities implementing public policies on employment law will depend upon whether the courts consider a particular private entity's employment relations as part of its public policy function.

There are several lesson that can be discerned from this aspect of *Charter* jurisprudence. Judicial decisions regarding the scope of application of the Convention will determine, to a large extent, the impact of human rights law on United Kingdom labour and employment law. However, it has been extremely difficult for the courts in Canada to come up with a principled basis for determining when the *Charter* ought to apply and this has resulted in a great deal of indeterminacy. This is also likely to be the case in the United Kingdom. Moreover, the Supreme Court has been extremely reluctant to apply the *Charter* to litigation based on the common law between private parties. Not only does this have the potential to result in more robust rights for workers employed by the government than those in the private sector, it also means that any restrictions on collective action that are based on statute are subject to *Charter* scrutiny, while those that are based upon the common law, are not. This is ironic, given that in Canada, like the United Kingdom, many of the most potent restrictions on workers' collective action are to be found in the common law.

The *Charter* and labour law

Claims brought by unions

Unions were quick to invoke the *Charter*'s guarantee of freedom of association to challenge legislative restrictions on their rights to strike and engage in collective bargaining. They argued that the *Charter*'s guarantee of freedom of association ought to be read purposively and, as such, should include not only the right to join an association to pursue common goals but also protection of the objects of the association (collective bargaining) and the means (striking) by which those objects are pursued. In 1987, the Supreme Court of Canada issued three decisions, known as 'the labour trilogy', which dealt with this argument and it was spectacularly unsuccessful[31]. In the *Alberta Reference*, which provided the reasons upon which the other two decisions were based, four of the six judges held that the freedom of association guaranteed in s.2(d) of the *Charter* did not include the right to strike. According Le Dain J, whose reasons were endorsed by two other judges, the freedom of association only encompassed the freedom to join in association for a common purpose and association activities insofar as they represented the exercise of another fundamental or constitutionally protected right or freedom. Since the rights to bargain collectively and strike were not fundamental freedoms but modern legislative rights, he held that neither were protected by the *Charter*. Going slightly further, McIntyre J stated that the freedom of association also included protection for all activities pursued in association with others that a person could lawfully pursue as an individual. Since an individual could not lawfully strike, because striking is inherently a collective activity, he held that the right to strike was not protected by the freedom of association[32].

The issue of whether the *Charter's* guarantee of freedom of association included the right to bargain collectively was decisively resolved by the Supreme Court in *Professional Institute of the Public Service of Canada (PIPS) v Northwest Territories (Commissioner)*[33]. PIPS had represented a group of federal government employees who were transferred to employment with the Northwest Territories' government. The public service labour legislation provided that a union could not be certified nor obtain bargaining rights unless it was incorporated under the legislation. The government, which had complete discretion to incorporate a union, refused to incorporate PIPS and, thus, it could not bargain collectively on behalf of its transferred members. Four of the seven judges held that the freedom of association did not protect the right to bargain collectively. According to Sopinka J, "restrictions on the activity of collective bargaining do not normally affect the ability of individuals to form or join unions"[34]. The majority concluded that the government was under no constitutional obligation to bargain collectively or to provide a statutory scheme for collective bargaining by recognition or certification.

In *Delisle v Canada (Deputy AG)*[35], the Supreme Court affirmed the narrow interpretation of freedom of association in the labour relations context. Delisle, a member of the Royal Mounted Canadian Police (RCMP) and president of an informal employee association representing RCMP officers in Quebec, challenged the exclusion of members of the RCMP from the collective bargaining legislation governing federal public service workers as a violation of freedom of association. He argued that the exclusion of RCMP members from the statutory protections regarding collective bargaining left them vulnerable to management actions designed to influence their rights to form an association and carry out its lawful activities. Writing for the majority, Bastarache J held that only the establishment of an independent employee association and the exercise in association of the lawful rights of its members are protected under s.2(d) of the *Charter*. He also stated that the fundamental freedoms protected by s.2 do not impose a positive obligation of protection or inclusion on the government, save perhaps in exceptional circumstances. Thus, there was no general obligation for the government to provide a particular legislative scheme for its employees to exercise their collective rights. However, since the RCMP is part of the government within the meaning of s.32, he went on to state that it was open for Delisle or any other party with standing to challenge directly under the *Charter* any actions by the RCMP management which interfered with the employees' freedom to join an independent employee association directly under s.2(d). But what precisely such protections against unfair labour practices would look like is far from clear.

The problem posed by the exclusion of groups of employees from collective bargaining legislation will force the Supreme Court of Canada to come to terms with the implications of its early decisions that collective bargaining is not protected by the *Charter* and the consequences of the different treatment of public and private sector employees. In *Delisle*, the court was able to assert that s.2(d) provided some remedy against employer unfair labour practices that interfered with an employee's right to join a union of her or his choice because the employer was part of government. However, in *Dunmore v Ontario (Attorney General)*[36], for which the Supreme Court has recently granted leave to appeal, this solution is not available since the employees in question, agricultural workers who have historically been excluded from Ontario's private sector collective bargaining legislation, are employed by private employers. Conceding that the right to bargain collectively was not protected by the *Charter*, the applicants argued that the exclusion of agricultural workers from collective bargaining legislation had the effect of denying them the right to form a trade union since their employers could take economic reprisals against employees who chose to join a union and had recourse to the common law to stop collective action in restraint of trade. Sharpe J, of the Ontario Court, rejected this argument: "based upon the current state of the law as elaborated in *Dolphin Delivery*, the fact that the efforts of agricultural workers to form unions will be resisted or undermined by employer's private economic power or by the assertion of their common law rights does not give rise to a *Charter* claim". He also rejected the claim that the provincial government was under a positive duty to enhance the right of freedom of association by creating a legislative scheme conducive to the enjoyment of that right. Moreover, he dismissed the argument that the applicants' right to equal protection and equal benefit of the law guaranteed by s.15(1). This was particularly important since the Supreme Court has held that s.15 does give rise to positive obligations on the government[38]. Although Sharpe J had no hesitation in finding that agricultural workers are a disadvantaged group, he found that they did not fit into the types of grounds set out in s.15, which are united by a common emphasis on personal traits and characteristics that have been the subject of stereotypical application of presumed group characteristics that deny individual human dignity. In *Delisle*, which was decided before *Dunmore*, the Supreme Court of Canada relied on similar reasoning to reject the claim that the exclusion of the RCMP officers from the federal public sector collective bargaining regimes denied them equal benefit and protection under the law as guaranteed by s.15.

The Supreme Court of Canada has, with one exception, discussed below, rejected every single claim brought by unions to protect or to extend collective bargaining and workers' collective action. In *United Nurses of Alberta v Alberta*[39], the court upheld, by a four to three majority, the lower courts' conviction of the union for criminal contempt which resulted from its failure to comply with the Alberta Labour Board order to cease and desist in its unlawful strike. The union argued that the vague and uncertain distinction between civil and criminal contempt constituted a violation of s.7 of the *Charter*, which provides that a person ought not to be deprived of liberty except in accordance with the principles of fundamental justice. For the majority, McLachlin J devised some guidelines for criminal contempt from past decisions and held that they provided a sufficiently precise definition of the offence to satisfy the requirements of fundamental justice. Cory J, writing in dissent, stated that the union's actions did not qualify as criminal contempt because it was exercising its *Charter* right to freedom of speech. Moreover, he urged the court to defer from intervening in labour relations, a position the majority had adopted in 'the labour trilogy' in refusing to constitutionalise the right to strike.

Unions have had slightly more success in invoking the *Charter*'s guarantee of freedom of expression to challenge labour law restrictions on their actions. However, that success has been profoundly qualified; the greater the activity in question resembles traditional forms of union action the less likely it is to be protected. In *Dolphin Delivery*, the Supreme Court dealt the earliest and harshest blow to unions' aspirations to use the *Charter* to enhance collective rights. Although the case, which concerned whether an injunction used to prohibit secondary picketing infringed the freedom of expression protected in s.2(b) of the *Charter*, was resolved on the ground that the *Charter* did not apply to litigation based on the common law between private parties, McIntyre J stated that peaceful picketing was a form of protected expression. Moving quickly to the s.1 analysis, which allows for the infringement of rights to the extent that it can be demonstrably justified, he asserted that secondary picketing is one of those rare cases where the elements of the s.1 analysis are obvious or self-evident and concluded that restraints on secondary picketing affecting third parties are *per se* reasonable limits[40]. The Supreme Court has the opportunity to reconsider whether the common law restrictions on secondary picketing constitute a demonstrably justifiable limitation since it gave leave to appeal *RWDSU Local 558 v Pepsi-Cola Canada Beverages (West) Ltd*[41]. In that case, the Saskatchewan Court of Appeal refused to follow the Ontario Court of Appeal and declare secondary picketing to be *per se* illegal on the grounds that *Charter* values should apply to the common law.

Despite continuing to declare that picketing is a form of expression protected under s.2(b) of the *Charter*, the Supreme Court has been hostile to traditional union picketing activities, justifying limitations on them and emphasising their coercive aspects, even when the picketing is peaceful, on every occasion when it has addressed the issue. In *BCGEU v British Columbia*[42], a unanimous court upheld the *ex parte* interim injunction which the Chief Justice of British Columbia issued, on his own motion, to prohibit altogether peaceful picketing in front of court-houses by court workers who were engaged in a lawful strike. Although the Supreme Court held that the peaceful picketing was expressive behaviour, it concluded that the injunction was justified under s.1. What was remarkable was the extent to which the Supreme Court of Canada played fast and loose with the rigorous s.1 analysis that it set out in *Oakes v R*[43]. In *Oakes*, Dickson CJC stated that the party seeking to justify a limitation on a *Charter* protected right must establish on a balance of probabilities, first, that the objective sought by the restriction is of sufficient importance to warrant overriding a constitutionally protected freedom; and second, that the restriction is proportional to the objective sought by the legislature[44]. Holding that access to the courts was an essential element of the rule of law, which was contained in the preamble to the *Charter*, in *BCGEU* Dickson CJC concluded that there was a valid objective behind the injunction. Despite the lack of any evidence that the picketing had interfered with access to the courts[45], he assumed that it "could only result in massive disruption to the court process of British Columbia". He also failed to discuss alternatives to a province-wide ban on picketing, such as limiting the number of pickets, for example.

In what is to date the only example of a union successfully arguing before the Supreme Court that the *Charter* protects a tactic unions deploy during labour disputes, Cory J, writing for a unanimous court, held that the provisions regulating picketing in the British Columbia Labour Code which prohibited peaceful consumer leafleting by a union at secondary sites were not justified limitations under s.1 of the freedom of expression protected in s.2(b)[46]. In concluding that the ban on secondary consumer leafleting was not justified, the court went to great effort to emphasise that "consumer leafleting is very different from a picket line"[47]. After elaborating several conditions to which consumer leafleting in the context of a labour dispute ought to conform in order to be considered protected expression, Cory J engaged in a detailed s.1 analysis. Characterising the objective of the legislative restrictions on picketing as minimising the impact of industrial conflict on persons who are not involved in the dispute, he concluded that the provisions did not pass the proportionality aspect of the test. As a remedy, he declared that the

---

broad definition of picketing was invalid, but suspended the declaration for six months to give the provincial government an opportunity to revise the section. In a companion case which also dealt with the legality of peaceful and carefully targeted secondary consumer leafleting under a provincial labour relations statute which regulated picketing, Iacobucci J invoked the *Charter* in order to interpret the picketing provision so as to exclude peaceful leafleting and on this basis he quashed the injunction issued by the trial judge.

Although it did not address collective bargaining or industrial dispute tactics, *Osborne v Canada (Treasury Board)*[49] is an example of the Supreme Court using the Charter to enhance workers' individual liberty by striking down restrictive legislation. At issue was the validity of provisions in the federal Public Service Employment Act which placed severe restrictions upon the freedom of federal public service workers to engage in any form of political activity "for or against" a candidate or political party. The applicants argued that the restrictions on political activity infringed their freedoms of expression and association under the *Charter*. In light of the broad definition of freedom of expression adopted by the court, Sopinka J held, on behalf of the majority, that the legislation violated s.2(b). He reasoned that although the constitutional convention of political neutrality for civil servants did not preclude a finding that s.2(b) had been infringed, it would be relevant in determining whether or not any infringement was justified under s.1. However, he found that the restrictions were not justified since they failed to meet the minimum impairment requirement of the proportionality test. But instead of "reading down" the provisions in order to preserve them, he declared them to be of no force and effect[50]. As yet, the Supreme Court has not been called upon to determine whether strikes which have a political purpose are a protected form of expression under the *Charter*, although the Ontario Labour Relations Board has ruled that although a political strike is a protected form of expression under the *Charter*, restrictions upon the timing of strikes which have the effect of rendering political strikes unlawful are justified under s.1[51].

The Supreme Court of Canada's interpretation of the *Charter* has resulted in very weak associational rights in the labour context. At most, the right to join a trade union and participate in its lawful activities are protected; however, the Supreme Court has yet to decide whether the *Charter* will provide employees any remedies against private employers who infringe upon these fundamental freedoms. It is also clear that the court does not consider that the freedoms protected in s.2 of the *Charter* require the government to take positive actions to preserve them. Moreover, the restrictive reading of s.15, which limits the right to equal protection and benefit of the law to persons whose personal traits or characteristics have been the subject of stereotypical application of presumed group characteristics that deny individual human dignity, precludes claims of discrimination on the basis of occupational status. It also remains to be seen whether the court will be able to cling to its distinction between impermissible (picketing) and permissible (leafleting) forms of expressive activity. Recently, the Quebec Court of Appeal affirmed the right of striking municipal workers to picket in front of the homes of the employer municipality's mayor, local councillors and senior managers. The court held that picket lines were a protected form of expression used by striking workers to gain public support for their position in a labour dispute and it made no difference whether the picket lines were being used to distribute informational leaflets about the strike or to carry placards expressing the union's views[52].

Claims brought by individual employees and employers

When the *Charter* was first enacted individual employees and employers brought a number of challenges against key features of the Canadian legislative collective bargaining regime on the ground that their fundamental rights and freedoms were infringed. Most were dismissed by labour boards and lower courts and few made their way to the appellate courts[53]. Of those that did, most were unsuccessful. The Supreme Court has consistently maintained a deferential stance to legislative choices in the area of labour law and, generally, has not acceded to attempts to enhance individual rights at the expense of collective bargaining.

Early appeal court jurisprudence made it clear that legislation that simply permitted unions and employers to enter into union security arrangements was not sufficient to trigger the application of the *Charter*[54]. However, Merv Lavigne, who was backed by the National Citizen's Coalition, a right-wing lobby group opposed to unions and big government, raised a novel argument. He alleged that the use of his dues, which the collective agreement between his bargaining representative and employer required to be deducted from his wages, for political purposes, constituted a violation of his freedoms of association and expression which could not be justified[55]. The majority found that the *Charter* applied because Lavigne's employer, a community college, was a government entity under the government control test and that its acquiescence to the union's request for dues to be deducted without the employee's permission was enough to amount to government action[56]. And although all seven judges on the panel upheld the use of compulsory dues by unions for non-collective bargaining purposes, their analysis of the scope of the protection provided by the *Charter* diverged widely. Three judges held that the recognition of the freedom to refrain from association is a necessary counterpart to meaningful association. According to LaForest J, instead of being distinct rights, the freedom of association and the freedom not to associate were but two sides of a bilateral freedom. Moreover, he also concluded that "the freedom of association of an individual member of the bargaining unit will be violated when he or she is compelled to contribute to causes, ideological or otherwise, that are beyond the immediate concerns of the bargaining unit". However, he found that the infringement of Lavigne's freedom of association was justified under s.1 since it was important to ensure that unions had the resources to enable them to play a role in shaping the political, economic and social context in which bargaining takes place. While McLachlin J agreed that freedom of association included the freedom not to associate, she adopted a much narrower approach than LaForest J, holding that it only protected people against ideological conformity and that compelled payments did not fall within this. By contrast, three judges, for reasons provided by Wilson J, rejected the argument that freedom of association under s.2(d) included any form of freedom not to associate.

While this decision was applauded by the labour movement because it left the political use of compelled dues intact, the failure of the Supreme Court to develop a unified approach to whether or not freedom of association includes the freedom not to associate gives cause for concern. The troubling question is whether, in cases where there is the requisite government action necessary to trigger the application of the *Charter*, forms of union security will be found to violate an employee's freedom of association. The Supreme Court will be dealing with this issue in the near future, as it gave leave to appeal in *R. v Theriault*. In that case the Superior Court of Quebec held that a workers' obligation to choose between a number of different employees' organisations for the purposes of collective negotiation within a centralised regime based on union pluralism was not an infringement of the fundamental freedom of association, even if that freedom did include the right not to associate.

The only clear *Charter* victory for employers who challenged aspects of the collective bargaining regime at the Supreme Court level was *National Bank of Canada v RCIU*[58]. In *obiter*, a majority of the court indicated that a common labour board remedial order, the requirement that an employer found to have violated the unfair labour provisions of the labour relations statute send a letter to all of its employees admitting its violations, infringed the employer's freedom of expression under the *Charter*. But, according to a subsequent case, so long as the statutory authority simply requires the employer to make factual statements, the limitation on its freedom of expression will likely be justified[59]. Moreover, the court has used the standing requirements, that the party seeking to challenge legislation on the ground that it violates *Charter*-protected rights must demonstrate a legal interest, to dismiss an action brought by the Conseil du Patronat du Quebec, a leading employers' organisation, that the anti-"scab" provision of the labour code were unconstitutional[60]. In the context of attacks to the system of collective bargaining, judicial deference to legislative policy choices has been beneficial to unions. However, it is important to note, that without the *Charter*, such challenges could not have been launched in the first place.

The *Charter* and employment law

Claims brought by employees and their advocates

Attempts to persuade adjudicators that the right to life, liberty and security of the person guaranteed by s.7 of the *Charter* should be given a broad and purposive interpretation so as to include the right to employment were dashed by the Supreme Court of Canada[61]. This meant that the most powerful ground available to employees to challenge either governmental employment decisions, actions, rules and policies or employment-related legislation was the denial of equal benefit and protection under the law as guaranteed by s.15 of the *Charter*. Moreover, unlike the fundamental freedoms guaranteed in s.2, the Supreme Court has imposed an obligation under s.15 on governments to take positive steps to end private discrimination[62]. This is important, because, although every jurisdiction in Canada has human rights statutes which prohibit discrimination on a shared core of enumerated grounds in private and public employment, not only does the list of prohibited grounds of discrimination differ between jurisdictions, some statutes may provide defences to complaints of discrimination that would not pass *Charter* scrutiny.

The equality rights jurisprudence of the Supreme Court has been in a state of flux as the court had failed to embrace a common or consistent methodology for determining whether equality rights have been breached. Some very recent cases, however, indicate that the court is developing a consensus on the appropriate approach to s.15.

Significantly, these cases addressed the validity of statutory requirements relating to age and disability status for obtaining state-provided employment-related benefits[64]. A unanimous court set out three broad question which are key to considering a s.15 challenge: first, does the law being challenged afford differential treatment; second, does the differential treatment involve one or more of the enumerated or analogous grounds; and third, does the differential treatment discriminate in a substantive sense in that it impairs an individual's dignity. This approach, while having the benefit of attracting all of the members of the Court, is restrictive from the point of view of employees and other claimants bringing equality challenges. In both cases, the claims for employment-related benefits were dismissed on the ground that the third aspect of the inquiry was not made out[65].

In cases in which the Supreme Court has found either a governmental employer's employment policy or an employment-related statute to violate the guarantee of equal benefit and protection of the law guaranteed by s.15 the controversial legal issue has been whether or not the infringement was justified and, if so, what the appropriate remedy should be. In a series of four cases released at the same time dealing with the constitutional validity of mandatory retirement policies, all members of the Supreme Court agreed that by allowing employers and workers to negotiate mandatory retirement provisions at age 65 the human rights statutes permitted discrimination by reason of age within s.15[66]. However, in all of the decisions the majority of the court held that the violation of s.15 was saved under s.1. Not only were the judges of the view that it served the public interest for the parties to negotiate their own mandatory retirement policies, they recognised a range of legitimate labour market rationales for such policies[67]. But it is possible that these rationales might not be sustained in subsequent cases, since they were framed in a way that was specific to each workplace and, as LaForest J noted, the law may change to reflect the greater value that society may attach to protecting people from age discrimination[68].

Brian Etherington has suggested that the Supreme Courts's emphasis on the values of freedom of contract and the widespread support of employers and unions for mandatory retirement policies helps to explain the contrast between its approach in the mandatory retirement cases and its far less deferential stance in a case dealing with age discrimination against those over 64 years of age in the unemployment insurance legislation[69]. In *Tétrault-Gadoury*[70] the court accepted the argument that the provisions in the former Unemployment Insurance Act which denied ordinary benefits to persons over sixty-five years of age violated s.15 in a manner which could not be justified under s.1. Although it was *obiter*, since the case was decided on the procedural issue of the jurisdiction of administrative tribunals to make *Charter* rulings, the court engaged in an extensive s.1 analysis. Accepting the importance of the government's objectives to provide a benefit system for unemployed workers that avoided the danger of double payment of social benefits and abuse by those who had decided to retire, the court concluded that the legislation was not designed with sufficient care to achieve these objectives with minimal impairment to *Charter*-protected rights[71].

While these cases dealt with direct discrimination on a prohibited ground, the equality protection contained in s.15 also prohibits indirect discrimination on a prohibited ground and discrimination on grounds analogous to those specifically enumerated. Thus, s.15 has been used to challenge some of the myriad exclusions from protective labour relations which are not, with few exceptions, expressed in terms of a directly prohibited ground of discrimination[72]. However, the scope of equality rights challenges in the context of employment law has been severely limited by the Supreme Court by virtue of its restrictive definition of what counts as analogous grounds of discrimination.

In *Schachter v Canada*, the Supreme Court accepted the claim that biological fathers were denied equal benefit of the law under s.15 by a provision in the unemployment insurance legislation that denied them parental leave benefits which were provided to adoptive fathers[73]. Yet, in *Schafer v Canada*, the Ontario Court of Appeal held that the s.15 rights of adoptive mothers were not infringed by their denial of benefits under the unemployment insurance legislation equivalent to those which mothers who gave birth to a child were entitled[74]. The Court reasoned that the additional weeks of benefit provided to mothers who gave birth was designed to permit them to recover physically from the ordeal of childbirth and thus the denial of these benefits to adoptive mothers did not constitute discrimination. Moreover, *Schachter* is especially important because of the Supreme Court's extensive discussion of the appropriate remedy – invalidity, severance or extension – for under-inclusive benefit-conferring legislation. Essentially, a court may order the extension of benefits where the class of persons to be added is relatively small in relation to those already in receipt of the benefit, but particular care must be exercised when the remedy has budgetary effects[75].

Since the majority of exclusions from employment protection legislation are framed either in terms of the employee's occupation, the industry in which the employment is located or job-related characteristics, unless it can be demonstrated that the exclusion has a discriminatory impact on a prohibited ground or that the exclusion targets personal traits or characteristics which have been the subject of stereotypical application of presumed group characteristics that deny individual human dignity the complaint of discrimination under s.15 will not be made out. Despite the absence of a Supreme Court ruling on the issue of whether an occupation which historically has been associated with social and economic disadvantage constitutes an analogous ground of discrimination, the over-whelming weight of authority is to the effect that occupational status alone does not constitute a prohibited ground of discrimination under the *Charter*[76].

In *Vriend v Alberta*, the Supreme Court held that the appropriate remedy for the unlawful exclusion of gays and lesbians, since sexual orientation was found to constitute an analogous ground of discrimination under s.15, from protection under the provincial human rights legislation was to add "sexual orientation" to the statute's list of prohibited grounds[77]. An implication of this decision is that under certain circumstances s.15 imposes an obligation to remedy private discrimination. However, the Ontario Court of Appeal has ruled that s.15 does not create a positive duty on government to enact employment equity legislation, which imposes obligations on employers to take positive steps to ensure representation of disadvantaged groups in their workforce proportional to the participation of these groups in the labour[78].

To date, the equality rights protections contained in the *Charter* have been a big disappointment to workers in the area of employment law. Only the most obvious and egregious exclusions of categories of workers, such as gays and lesbians, from employment-protection or -benefit conferring legislation have been successfully challenged[79]. So far, the only means by which it may be possible to challenge the occupational and industrial exclusions from such legislation is to demonstrate that they have an indirect discriminatory impact on workers on the basis of a prohibited ground. Moreover, the overwhelming weight of authority supports the position that s.15 will require governments to take positive steps to end private discrimination only to the extent that the inequality has been created by law.

Claims brought by employers

Employers also brought a number of challenges to employment-related legislation on the ground that their *Charter* protected rights and freedoms were infringed. With but minor exception, employment-protection legislation and the statutory powers it confers upon officials and adjudicators have survived virtually unscathed. Sunday

Chapter 7 : Lessons from Canada

closing legislation, which the Supreme Court of Canada has decided infringes the guarantee of freedom of religion in s.2(a), has survived to the extent that the government could establish a legitimate secular purpose, such as protecting vulnerable workers[80]. Yet, despite the fact that the Supreme Court upheld legislation imposing a common rest day in the retail sector, the practice of Sunday shopping is now widespread and the decisions of lower courts regarding the constitutionality of the legislation designed to regulate the practice have been unpredictable[81]. Thus, statutory holidays rooted in Christian tradition may be vulnerable to *Charter* challenge .

Conclusion

What lessons can be drawn from this summary of the Supreme Court of Canada's application of the *Charter* in Canadian labour and employment law? Most apparent is that offering grand predictions about the impact of fundamental rights and freedoms on labour and employment relations is a dangerous game. After the initial frenzy of litigation, most participants have adopted a pragmatic approach to the *Charter*, using it at the edges of what the jurisprudence has already established and to test whether the bench is willing to accept new arguments or reconsider earlier rulings. In general, the Supreme Court has upheld remedial legislation in the face of challenges by employers recognising that the government has a valid objective in alleviating the inequality of bargaining power between employers and employees. However, the promise that the *Charter* could be used to enhance workers' rights has not be borne out in the area of collective action. The narrow judicial interpretation of the freedom of association has been a grave disappointment for the labour movement. And although the *Charter* has not been used to repeal key elements of the collective bargaining regime, the Supreme Court's decisions have reinforced the message that workers' collective rights are mere legislative compromises that do not engage fundamental rights and freedoms. Even when unions win a tactical victory, they are likely to lose the larger ideological struggle. In *UFCW v KMart*, although the court stated that the restrictions on peaceful consumer leafleting at secondary sites during a labour dispute violated the constitutional guarantee of freedom of expression, it depicted peaceful picketing as coercive and, thus, suspect activity.

The equality rights provided in the *Charter* have also been a disappointment for workers and their advocates as little progress has been made in extending remedial employment legislation to groups historically excluded. Because the courts have interpreted equality rights as protecting individuals from discrimination on the basis of ineluctable characteristics, discrimination on the basis of occupation has not merited constitutional review. Whether the Supreme Court will be persuaded to expand what it considers to be analogous grounds of discrimination and accept more complex arguments relating to indirect discrimination in the area of employment law remains open.

The most significant problem, however, has been the scope of application of the *Charter*. Individual employment is based on the common law, as are the main restrictions on collective worker action. While there is the possibility that *Charter* values may impact on private employment and labour relations, it is crucial to acknowledge that the *Charter* was designed to restrict the coercive power of the state, not to remedy social disadvantage and inequality generally.

There are, however, several important factors that militate against relying too heavily on the Canadian experience as a guide for what will happen under the Human Rights Act. The text of the legislation, its timing and the legal traditions of the two countries, despite a common heritage, are very different. The ECHR specifically refers to trade unions, it was incorporated into United Kingdom domestic law after the major legislative and governmental assault on trade union power was completed, and there is the enduring influence of Europe on the interpretation of fundamental rights and freedoms. Yet, experience suggests that in common law countries, entrenched rights and freedoms have not been especially beneficial to workers[82].

Notes

1 Human Rights Act 1998.
2 Part 1 of the *Constitution Act, 1982,* being Schedule B to the *Canada Act 1982 (United Kingdom)* (hereinafter *Charter*).
3 For a summary of the various positions see B Etherington, "An Assessment of Judicial Review of Labour Laws under the Charter: Of Realists, Romantics and Pragmatists" (1992) 24 Ottawa L R 685.
4 J Fudge, "Labour, The New Constitution and Old Style Liberalism" (1988) 13 Queen's L J 61, at pp 77-8.
5 *Ibid.*
6 For recent decisions of the ILO addressing complaints against Canada with respect to the freedom of association see for example: ILCCR, Observation concerning Convention No. 87, Freedom of Association and Protection of the Right to Organize, 1948 Canada (1999); CEACR, Observation concerning Convention No. 87 (1995), ILOLEX database http://ilolex.ilo.ch:1567/public/english/50normes/infleg/iloeng/iloquery.htm.
7 P Weiler, "The Charter at Work: Reflections on the Constitutionalization of Labour and Employment Law" (1990) 40 UTLJ 118.
8 For the test for determining whether a statutory tribunal has jurisdiction to apply the *Charter,* see *Tétreault-Gadoury v Canada (Employment and Immigration Commission)* [1991] 2 SCR 22.
9 These include the freedoms of religion, expression and association, the right to life, liberty and security, and equality rights.
10 Section 1 of the *Charter* guarantees the rights and freedoms set out in it "subject only to such reasonable limits prescribed by law as can be demonstrably justified in a free and democratic society."
11 K D Ewing, "The Human Rights Act and Labour Law" (1998) 27 ILJ 275, at p 277.
12 *Andrews v Law Society of British Columbia* [1989] 1 SCR 143.
13 In *Jazairi v York University* (1999) 175 DLR (4th) 302, the Ontario Court of Appeal held, in the context of an employment-related case, that the absence of a provision in the Ontario Human Rights Code prohibiting discrimination on the basis of political opinion did not violate s.15 of the *Charter.* Leave to appeal to the Supreme Court of Canada in *Jazairi* was dismissed without reasons on 3 May 2000.
14 Ewing, *op cit* note 11.
15 For an overview of the range of remedies available to courts under s.24 of the *Charter,* see R J Sharpe and K E Swinton, *The Charter of Rights and Freedoms* (1998) Ch. 17.
16 SGEU Dispute Settlement Act, SS 1984-85-86, c. 111, s.9.
17 The Court held that professional bodies exercising regulatory power delegated by the government, such as law societies and the royal college of dental surgeons, are subject to the *Charter: Black v Law Society of Alberta* [1989] 1 SCR 591; *Rocket v Royal College of Dental Surgeons of Ontario* [1990] 2 SCR 232.
18 [1989] 1 SCR 1038.
19 *RWDSU v Dolphin Delivery Ltd* [1986] 2 SCR 573.
20 *Ibid.,* at p 603.
21 *BCGEU v British Columbia (AG)* [1988] 2 SCR 214.

22 *RWDSU, Local 558 v Pepsi-Cola Canada Beverages (West) Ltd.* (1998) 167 DLR (4th) 220 (SCA) leave to appeal to Supreme Court of Canada granted 21 October 1999.

23 The dissenting judgment stressed that the *Charter* did not apply to litigation based on the common law between private parties.

24 *Hill v Church of Scientology* [1995] 2 SCR 1130.

25 *McKinney v University of Guelph* [1990] 3 SCR 229, per LaForest J at pp 261 and 262.

26 *Ibid; Harrison v University of British Columbia* [1990] 3 SCR 451; *Stouffman v Vancouver General Hospital* [1990] 3 SCR 483; and *Douglas/Kwantlen Faculty Association v Douglas College* [1990] 3 SCR 570.

27 [1991] 2 SCR 211.

28 This confirms the approach already taken by lower courts, see Fudge, *op cit* note 4, at pp 98-108.

29 [1997] 3 SCR 624.

30 M Cornish and F Faraday, "Eldridge v British Columbia: Defining the Equality Rights of the Disabled under the Charter" (1998) 6 Charterwatch 78.

31 In *PSAC v Canada (AG)* [1987] 1 SCR 424, the union challenged wage control legislation which effectively deprived federal public service workers of collective bargaining and the right to strike for a two to three year period. In *RWDSU v Saskatchewan* [1987] 1 SCR 460, the union challenged an *ad hoc* back-to-work law which prohibited the pending strike and substituted interest arbitration to resolve the dispute. In *Reference Re Public Service Employees Relations Act (Alta.)* [1987] 1 SCR 313, unions challenged a number of Alberta statutes that placed restrictions on collective bargaining by provincial government employees, firefighters, police, and hospital workers by prohibiting strikes, restricting the scope of bargaining and imposing compulsory arbitration.

32 Although Wilson J and Dickson C J C agreed that s.2(d) included the right to strike and bargain collectively, they disagreed on what constituted reasonable limits.

33 [1990] 2 SCR 367.

34 *Ibid.,* at p 404.

35 [1999] 2 SCR 989.

36 (1997) 37 OR (3d) 287 (Ont. Ct. Gen. Div). On 2 January 1999, the Ontario Court of Appeal dismissed the appeal without reasons. However, the Supreme Court gave leave to appeal.

37 *Ibid.,* at p 300.

38 *Vriend v Alberta* [1998] 1 SCR 493.

39 [1992] 1 SCR 901; for a detailed discussion of the case see J Fudge and H Glasbeek, "Alberta Nurses v A Contemptuous Supreme Court of Canada" (1992) 4:1 Constit. Forum 1.

40 The only authority cited for the harm caused by allowing industrial disputes to have a disruptive impact on trade relations beyond the actual parties was P Weiler, *Reconcilable Differences: New Directions in Canadian Labour Law* (1980) at pp 64-5.

41 *Op cit,* note 22.

42 *Op cit,* note 21.

43 [1986] 1 SCR 103.

44 In determining proportionality, three factors must be examined: first, the measure chosen must be rationally connected to the objective; second, it must impair the right as little as reasonably possible; and, third, there must be proportionality between the importance of the objective and the deleterious effects of the restriction and between the deleterious and salutary effects of the measure.

45 H J Glasbeek, "Contempt for Workers" (1990) 28 Osgoode Hall L J 1 at p 21.

46 *United Food and Commercial Workers, Local 1518 v KMart Canada Ltd.* [1999] 2 SCR 1083.

47 *Ibid*, at p 1113. Since the ruling in *Dolphin Delivery* regarding secondary picketing was not challenged, Cory J proceeded on the basis that restrictions on secondary picketing may be justified under s.1. Thus, he stated that whether restrictions on consumer leafleting are constitutionally valid will therefore depend on whether a distinction can be drawn between conventional picketing and consumer leafleting.

48 According to Iacobucci J in *Allsco Building Products Ltd. v United Food and Commercial Workers International Union, Local 1288P* [1999] 2 SCR 1136, where a provision is open to two possible interpretations, and one would run afoul of a *Charter* right or freedom, the alternative is to be preferred.

49 [1991] 2 SCR 69.

50 Similar legislative restrictions on the political activities of public service workers at the municipal and provincial levels have been challenged under the *Charter* with varying degrees of success since the ultimate determination depends upon how the courts apply the s.1 analysis to specific restrictions. For a discussion of some of these cases see Etherington, *op cit*, note 3 at footnote 86; Weiler, *op cit*, note 7, at pp 128-130.

51 *General Motors of Canada* [1996] OLRD No. 2056, 7 June 1996.

52 In *Verdun (Ville) v Syndicat canadien de la fonction publique, section local 302* [2000] JQ no. 259, 9 February 2000, the Court balanced the targeted individuals' right to privacy, which is protected under the Quebec Charter of Human Rights, against the workers' freedom of expression by restricting the number of pickets at each home, requiring them to be a certain distance from the home and limiting the hours of the picketing activity.

53 Fudge, *op cit*, note 4.

54 *Op cit*, note 28.

55 See B Etherington "Freedom of Association and Compulsory Union Dues: Towards a Purposive Conception of a Freedom Not to Associate" (1987) 19 Ottawa L R 1; and "Lavigne v OPSEU: Moving Toward or Away From a Freedom Not to Associate?" (1991) 23 Ottawa LR 533.

56 *Lavigne, op cit*, note 27.

57 *R v Theriault* [1998] AQ no. 722: the Quebec Court of Appeal refused to review the ruling; however, the Supreme Court of Canada granted leave to appeal on 19 April 1999.

58 [1984] 1 SCR 269.

59 *Slaight, op cit*, note 18 .

60 *Conseil du Patronat du Quebec v Quebec (Attorney General)* [1991] 3 SCR 685.

61 *Walker v Prince Edward Island* [1995] 2 SCR 407.

62 *Vriend, op cit*, note 38.

63 B Ryder, "A New Era of Equality Activism?" (1998) 6 Charterwatch 76; R E Charney, "The Difference Dilemma: The Supreme Court and Equality Rights in 1997" (1998) 6 Charterwatch 81.

64 *Law v Canada (Minister of Employment and Immigration)* [1999] 1 SCR 497; *Granovsky v Canada (Minister of Employment and Immigration* [2000] SCJ No. 229.

65 However, *British Columbia (Public Service Employee Relations Commission) v BCGEU*, [1999] 3 SCR 3 does leave some room for employees to be optimistic. A unanimous Court held that occupational tests designed for firefighters which took only male physiological standards into consideration and which did not demonstrate the occupational necessity of meeting those standards were discriminatory on the basis of sex. While this case was brought under the provincial human rights code, the Court relied on *Charter* equality jurisprudence to rationalise what had previously been different approaches to direct and indirect discrimination.

66 *Op cit*, notes 25 and 26. Most human rights statutes permit mandatory retirement policies by limiting the protection against age discrimination to people between 18 and 64.

67 For a detailed discussion of the rationales offered see G England, I Christie and M Christie, *Employment Law in Canada* (1999) ch 12, B 1 and para 12.67.

68 *Ibid.*, at paras 12.68-12.69.

69 Etherington, *op cit*, note 3.

70 *Op cit*, note 8.

71 The Court indicated that the remedy it would have ordered was that the unconstitutional provisions be severed, which would have had the effect of extending the benefit.

72 England, Christie and Christie, *op cit*, note 67, at para 9.94.

73 [1992] 2 SCR 697.

74 (1997) 35 OR (3d) 1, application for leave to appeal to the Supreme Court dismissed 29 January 1998. Prior to *Schachter*, the Unemployment Insurance Act provided the same length of benefit entitlement to adoptive and birth mothers. The benefits of the former were reduced in response to the successful constitutional challenge of the scheme.

75 In *Schachter*, the Court decided that the extension remedy was not appropriate, preferring instead a temporary suspension of the declaration of invalidity in order to give the government time to amend the scheme.

76 In *Delisle, op cit*, note 35, the Court was clear that the occupation of an RCMP officer was not one which was associated with an historical disadvantage. Appeal courts have consistently refused to find occupation an analogous ground under s.15: *McDermott v Nackawic (Town)* (1989), 22 CCEL 225 NBCA); *Canada v George* (1990) 33 CCEL 121 (FCA). However, the Supreme Court of Canada may address the issue of low status and low paid occupations and whether they constitute an analogous ground in *Dunmore, op cit*, note 36.

77 *Op cit*, note 38.

78 *Ferrel v Ontario (AG)* (1998) 42 OR (3d) 97, application for leave to appeal to the Supreme Court of Canada dismissed 9 December 1999. In that case the applicants used s.15 to challenge the legislation repealing employment

equity legislation enacted by the previous government.

79 However, the results of these cases have been mixed. See L G Beaman, "Sexual Orientation and Legal Discourse: Legal Constructions of the 'Normal' Family" (1999) 14:2 Canadian Journal of Law and Society 181. See also: *M v H* [1999] 2 SCR 3 and the discussion of *M v H* in R S Echlin and J M Fantini, "Developments in Labour and Employment Law: The 1998-99 Term" (2000) 11 Supreme Court Law Review 361, at pp 376-383.

80 In *R v Big M Drug Mart* [1985] 1 SCR 295 the Court had to decide the constitutionality of the federal Lord's Day Act. As a corporate entity, the drug store could not claim freedom of religion for itself, but, since it had been prosecuted, it was allowed to challenge the constitutionality of the law. Owing to the federal division of powers, the federal government could not defend its law by reference to a secular purpose and thus it was inescapable that the legislation had a religious purpose and a coercive effect since it compelled Sunday observance. Thus, the Court declared the legislation invalid. However, in *Edwards Books and Art Ltd. v R* [1986] 2 SCR 713, the impugned provincial legislation had a secular purpose, which was to give retail workers a common day of rest, and it made some accommodation for those who for religious reasons observed a different day of rest. Although the Court held that the impact of the legislation was indirectly to discriminate against freedom of religion guaranteed under s.2(a) since Saturday observers would suffer a financial loss as they were required by the law, in most instances, to close Sunday as well, the majority, albeit for different reasons, upheld the infringement as justified under s.1.

81 See *Peel (Reg. Mun.) v Great Atlantic and Pacific Co* (1991) 91 CLLC 14,013, and *R v Hy and Zel's Inc* (1996) 96 CLLC 210-232.

82 For an overview of US workers' unhappy experience with entrenched rights as interpreted by common law judges see J G Pope, "Labor and the Constitution: From Abolition to Deindustrialization" (1987) 65 Texas Law Review 1071.

Chapter 8

Human rights at work: possibilities and problems

Damian Brown and K D Ewing

IN this chapter we pull together some of the issues which have been raised in earlier chapters of this book, and attempt to assess how the Human Rights Act might be used in the employment context. There is a need first to identify the substantive issues which the Act will raise. We do this by examining the type of employment issues which have made their way to the European Court of Human Rights and which have been raised in the domestic courts before the coming into force of the Human Rights Act. We then assess the areas where the Act is likely to bite and consider how it may be used to advance the cause of human rights at the workplace. Although much of the anticipated progress is seen to come from litigation, we should not overlook the possibility that the Act might be used to promote legislation on particular issues, or that it may be used as a basis for collective bargaining on others. We also indicate some of the problems which may arise, bearing in mind that the Act empowers everyone: not just workers and trade unions, but employers and trade union members as as well. How will employers use the Act, and what will be its implications for bodies such as the CAC? Finally, we consider the role of the courts, the rock from which this legislation will be proclaimed, or on which it will be broken.

The response of the judges is an important issue for workers and trade unions in particular, with concern about the judicial role being the source of many misgivings about the entrenchment of rights such as those contained in the ECHR. But it is widely claimed that the judges have changed and that there is not the same degree of hostility to employee rights, employment protection legislation, or trade union activities that we encountered only 25 years ago[1]. Advocates of this view point to important developments in the law relating to the contract of employment (with new implied terms which benefit workers)[2], and the open recognition by the Court of Appeal that the right to strike is a 'fundamental human right'[3]. But there are nagging doubts, fuelled by decisions such as *Associated Newspapers plc v Wilson*[4], and others, and there are concerns that the court with final authority to rule on human rights questions (the House of Lords) is very exclusive in terms of race, gender and social status. Our highest court is very unusual in that it does not and never has included any women among its number. We consider some of the implications of these issues: the Human Rights Act provides now both an opportunity and an obligation to create a Bench which is both representative and accountable, as well as independent[5].

The ECHR and labour law

A NUMBER of issues in the employment field have been raised before the European Court of Human Rights in Strasbourg. Questions have arisen under article 6 which guarantees the right to a fair trial in the determination of the individual's rights and obligations. This applies as much in the employment field as in other areas of the law, though in *Stedman v United Kingdom*[6] the European Commission of Human Rights held that the two year qualifying rule for unfair dismissal did not breach the Convention. But as we have also seen, article 8 was successfully invoked in the *Halford* case[7]. There the applicant successfully asserted her right to privacy which she claimed had been violated by her employer who intercepted telephone calls relating to litigation against the employer in which she was involved. This led to changes to require better regulation of employer surveillance practices, though not to prohibit them.

Although not fully covered in any of the preceding chapters, article 9 has also been a source of some applications in the employment field, the leading case being *Ahmad v United Kingdom*[8] where the applicant unsuccessfully sought to establish that the right to freedom of religion found there gave him a right to time off work for the purposes of religious observance on Fridays. It was held by the Commission in that case that in determining the scope and content of a Convention freedom, it was necessary to take into account 'the situation of the person claiming that freedom', including any contract of employment to which he or she was a party. In this case Mr Ahmad had entered into a standard form employment contract with the Inner London Education Authority as it then was, which required him to work a five day week with no provision for paid time off for religious observance. There is an obvious concern here that the Commission appears to be saying that it may be possible in effect to contract out of Convention rights, a concern which is all the greater for the fact that under the Human Rights Act the British courts are required to have regard to the jurisprudence of the Commission, though they are not bound by it. It would be unfortunate if Convention rights were to be diminished in this way, effectively providing employers with a simple expedient to defeat their terms[9].

Article 10 has also been relied upon unsuccessfully, most notably by NALGO members complaining about the statutory restrictions on their political activities introduced in 1989: although the Court held that these restrictions violated the freedom of expression of local government officers, they were held to be necessary in a democratic society[10]. On the other hand, journalists have successfully relied upon article 10, admittedly not against employers but against third parties who seek to compel them to reveal their sources and thereby undermine their journalistic freedom. A good example is *Goodwin v United Kingdom*[11] where a journalist was supplied with confidential information about a company called Tetra. The company obtained a High Court order requiring the journalist to disclose his source, so that the company could protect its interests by taking action against the person who had leaked the information. The Court of Appeal and the House of Lords upheld the order[12], but the European Court of Human Rights held that it breached article 10 of the ECHR. Nor could it be justified under article 10(2) as the government had tried to argue. It could not be said to be necessary for the protection of the interests of Tetra, these being well protected by an injunction which prevented the publication of the material in question.

So some success under articles 8 and 10. But not much success under the freedom of association guarantees of article 11. As we saw in chapters 4 and 5 above, there have been a number of cases in which trade unions have claimed that their rights under this provision have been violated. But remarkably, in none of these cases did the application succeed. The Court has taken the view that the right to freedom of association does not guarantee any particular form of trade union action: no right to be consulted, no right to bargain collectively, and no right to strike[13]. But it has held that the right to freedom of association includes a right not to associate, despite clear evidence that this had never been intended by those who drafted the Convention[14]. And it was also held by the Commission that the GCHQ ban did not breach article 11[15], thereby preventing the matter from being dealt with by the Court. The decision of the Commission turned on the hitherto neglected last sentence of article 11(2) which allows for restrictions to be imposed where these relate to workers engaged in the administration of the State. It may perhaps also be noted that the Committee of Independent Experts also found that there was no breach of the Social Charter in the GCHQ case, in what could not be described as its finest hour[16].

The ECHR, labour law and the domestic courts

ALTHOUGH the Convention rights have been incorporated into domestic law by the Human Rights Act 1998, it would be a mistake to overlook the extent to which the ECHR was already taken into account by the courts, and in this way given a preferred legal status, at least so far as other international treaties are concerned. As a result the ECHR has been considered in a number of cases, including a number of cases relating to labour law and employment law. Most of these have related to articles 8-11. The most significant case under article 8 is *Blackpool and the The Fylde College v NATFHE*[17] which was concerned with the duty on the union to provide the employers with the names of members who were to be balloted for industrial action. It was said by the Court of Appeal that this duty – introduced by the Trade Union Reform and Employment Rights Act 1993 and repealed by the Employment Relations Act 1999[18] – did not violate the workers' rights to privacy as expressed in article 8 of the Convention. Curiously article 8 was relied on by the government during the debates on the Employment Relations Bill[19]. Apparently trade unions could not be given details of the names and addresses of workers in a bargaining unit because to give this information without the consent of the individuals in question would breach their Convention rights[20].

The importance of article 9 was revealed in the *Ahmad* case in the Court of Appeal before the application to Strasbourg[21]. Mr Ahmad was denied 45 minutes time off work on Friday afternoons to attend a nearby Mosque for religious observance. He resigned from his job claiming that he had been constructively dismissed. The action failed, but one of the issues in the case was whether he was entitled to time off as a result of the Education Act 1944 which provided that 'no teacher shall be deprived of any emolument or be deprived of any promotion or other advantage by reason of his religious opinions or his attending religious worship'. The majority of the Court of Appeal were unwilling to construe the 1944 Act to give effect to article 9, and Lord Denning in particular was unwilling to conclude that it gave Mr Ahmad 'any right to manifest his religion on Friday afternoons in derogation of his contract of employment: and certainly not on full pay'. In view of the nature of the duty on the courts to construe legislation consistently with Convention rights, this is a conclusion which may not now be open to them, subject to the important caveat of general significance, namely whether workers will be 'free' to contract away their Convention rights.

Article 10 has already featured in a number of cases, including the *Goodwin* case about the protection of journalists' sources already discussed, where the domestic courts issued an order to compel the trainee journalist to disclose his sources under the authority of the Contempt of Court Act 1981, s.10[22], which is modelled on article 10. It has been raised also in the challenge mounted by NALGO to the ban on local government officers from taking part in prescribed political activities[23]. In that case the union's action for judicial review of the regulations was unsuccessful. But perhaps the most interesting application of article 10 to date in the domestic courts is in the *Middlebrook Mushrooms Ltd* case[24], which was concerned with an application by the company to restrain the picketing of supermarkets which were selling their produce. The action failed, and in the course of his judgment Neill LJ said that article 10 was to be borne in mind 'in all cases which involve a proposed restriction on the right of free speech'[25]. This raises questions about the current restrictions on the law of picketing in the course of trade disputes, particularly the restrictions on the location of such picketing, and the numbers who may attend. The application by the police of the code of practice would appear to be particularly vulnerable to review[26].

Some of the cases raising article 11 issues have been considered in chapter 4. But there are in fact three quite different issues which have been raised here. The first is in relation to trade union admission and expulsion. As we saw in chapter 4 the Court of Appeal attempted unsuccessfully in *Cheall v APEX*[27] to use article 11 as a source of regulation of trade union autonomy. That job has now been done by Parliament. The second is in relation to trade union recognition procedures. As we shall see in the following pages, the Court of Appeal (again) tried to use article 11 as an instrument to regulate the discretion of ACAS under the recognition procedures of the Employment Protection Act 1975. In particular it was used to prevent ACAS from refusing recognition in the interests of good

---

industrial relations[28]. But as in the *Cheall* case[29], the House of Lords reversed. Finally, article 11 was raised in the domestic legal proceedings to challenge the trade union ban at GCHQ. In that case the House of Lords held that decisions taken on the ground of national security could not be challenged by the courts. The fact that the ban was a breach of ILO Convention 87, and the possibility that it might be a breach of the ECHR (which it was later proved not to be) was dismissed as a 'minor matter'[30].

The Human Rights Act and labour law

IT is clear that many people have high hopes about the Human Rights Act 1998. In the employment field in particular it is widely anticipated that it will operate as a positive force to advance the rights of workers and trade unions[31]. In different ways the different chapters of this book have shown how the Act could have an impact, and in different ways these different chapters have shown what the nature of that impact might be.

- In chapter 2 consideration is given to the right to privacy, and whether this could be used to promote better protection of workers against surveillance by their employers[32]. The right to privacy could also be used in the absence of specific legislation to promote the rights of gay and lesbian workers, to protect them from discrimination and dismissal. As the TUC reminds us in its recent report *Straight up! Why the Law Should Protect Gay and Lesbian Workers*, 'Discrimination against lesbians and gay men because of their sexuality is widespread, often vicious, and the situation is intolerable'[33].

- In chapter 3 consideration is given to the right to freedom of expression, and whether this could be used in a range of circumstances to protect workers, from matters such as employer dress codes which are often discriminatory and stereotypical, to employee trade union and political activities, through to issues such as whistleblowing. In the last case it is true that the matter is governed by the Public Interest Disclosure Act 1998, but the Act is limited in its scope, and there are questions about whether these gaps can be filled in by a judicious use of the Human Rights Act.

- In chapters 4 and 5 consideration is given to the right to freedom of association, and whether this could be used to promote trade union rights in a number of circumstances. Could it be used to remove existing measures which permit discrimination against trade union members following the decision in the *Wilson and Palmer* case and the Ullswater amendment? Could it be used to remove existing restrictions on the autonomy of trade unionists to determine who may become and remain a member of their respective trade unions? And could it be used to create a right to strike?

Ve also considered in chapter 6 the extent to which article 14 will xtend protection from discrimination in the workplace. It was noted that this is not a general right not to be discriminated against, but a right not to be discriminated against in the application of Convention rights. Still, the grounds of prohibited discrimination are much wider than under domestic law, and there is a possibility of additional protection in the shape of Protocol 12. It is also the case that article 14 will be a useful device to support applications based on a violation of other articles of the Convention.

But in addition to identifying the areas where the Human Rights Act may be useful, it is necessary also to develop a strategy for securing the rights to be found in the Act. This could be done by legislative pressure, by collective bargaining or by litigation. So far as collective bargaining is concerned, this is not to be underestimated at this stage, particularly as there is so much uncertainty among employers about just what the Act requires. But it would be possible through collective bargaining to:

- Revise equal opportunities policies to ensure that they apply to gay and lesbian workers and to ensure that they are properly enforced;
- Promote the establishment of procedures for dealing with surveillance by employers, and revise existing procedures on whistleblowing;
- Promote the introduction of procedures to facilitate religious observance and respect for the holy days and festivals of non Christians.

There will of course be stubborn employers who will refuse to negotiate, in which case litigation will need to be contemplated. There are also existing breaches of the Convention (such as the restrictions on trade union freedoms) in relation to which collective bargaining is not appropriate. In these cases litigation will be necessary if the government cannot be convinced to bring in amending legislation to meet obligations under the Human Rights Act.

Enforcing Convention rights

SO although the Human Rights Act provides an opportunity for workers to promote their rights by litigation, there is a question about how they do so in practice. This may not always be straightforward, and there are a number of procedural hoops which may have to be jumped before a court can deal with the matter. Some of the issues are considered in chapter one above in which Professor Gearty outlines the different ways in which Convention rights may arise for consideration by the courts. As we have seen the courts and tribunals will be required to interpret legislation to give effect to Convention rights, and where this is not possible, the High Court (but not employment tribunals or the EAT) will be empowered to declare that legislation is incompatible with Convention rights, thereby in effect inviting the government to seek to change the law. This is a curious state of affairs in some respects which gives rise to some uncertainty at this stage. Take for example the Trade Union Reform and Employment Rights Act 1993, s.14 imposing restrictions on trade union admission and expulsion rules. Suppose a union wanted to challenge this provision as being incompatible with Convention rights, in order to encourage the government to think about changing the law.

Will it be necessary for the union to contrive a situation in which a worker is excluded or a member is expelled knowingly in breach of the law, on the basis that this would then allow the law to be challenged in legal proceedings brought against the union by the aggrieved party? If the application against the union is successful does this mean in effect that the union will have to compensate the individual for the violation of his or her statutory rights even though the legislation violates Convention rights? If so it would seem strange that individuals and organisations are required deliberately to put themselves offside in this way to challenge a practice which may or may not breach Convention rights. This raises the question of whether it would be possible to bring an action by way of judicial review proceedings (and not directly under the Act) for a declaration of incompatibility where it is alleged that a particular statutory provision is in breach of Convention rights. This is in effect what was done in relation to EC law in *R v Secretary of State for Trade and Industry, ex parte EOC*[34], and if permitted in relation to the Human Rights Act could significantly extend the utility of the latter, particularly if applications for judicial review could be made by someone who has an interest in the matter but is not necessarily a victim of the alleged breach.

The other issue relates to the position of workers who wish to assert their Convention rights against their employers. In some cases this may be relatively straightforward, as in the case of public sector workers: it would appear that they are entitled to enforce their Convention rights against public authorities like anyone else. So in the *Ahmad* case described above, it would now be possible for the applicant to bring an action directly against ILEA in the domestic courts to assert his Convention rights. Similarly if the facts of *Vogt v Germany*[35] were to occur in this country: it would be possible for the schoolteacher in that case dismissed because of her political views to sue to enforce her Convention rights in the domestic courts, quite apart from any remedy she might have for unfair dismissal or otherwise. Presumably it would be possible to proceed with a human rights claim, as well as the other claim. (There may also be a claim for wrongful dismissal!) But although there is an opportunity for the public sector worker to proceed in this way directly to enforce Convention rights, there remains uncertainty about what constitutes a public authority for this purpose, and the question of how to deal with workers employed by bodies with mixed public/private functions[36]. For example is a political party a public body?

But what about the private sector employee? How does he or she assert his or her Convention rights?[37] In an unfair dismissal claim it would be possible to rely on the Human Rights Act in an appropriate case as an aid to the construction of the Employment Rights Act 1996. Indeed it will be necessary for the tribunals and courts to construe the latter in a manner which is consistent with the former where possible, even if this is not the obvious construction. So someone dismissed because they are gay may be able to argue that such a dismissal is unfair, because of the operation of the Human Rights Act. But what about the situation where the employee believes that there has been a breach of the Human Rights Act in circumstances where there has not been a dismissal and no cause of action under statute to which a Convention right can be attached? An example might be the employees who claim that they are the subject of surveillance which breaches the standards in the Convention. In these cases it may be possible to argue that the conduct is a breach of an implied term of the contract, either as an incident of an existing implied term, or on the ground that compliance with Convention rights is itself an implied term of the contract[38].

The Human Rights Act and the statutory agencies

THE attention so far has focused on the possible ways in which trade unions and workers might use the Human Rights Act to protect and promote their interests. But although there may thus be some benefits to flow from the changes which the Act could require, we should not overlook its potentially disruptive effect. Public bodies in the employment field will find themselves challenged by employers and others who are unhappy with their work. In the past bodies such as the CRE have felt the full force of the judicial lash because the courts felt that they dealt unfairly with employers when conducting formal investigations[39]. In these cases the House of Lords introduced by means of the principles of natural justice a number of procedural obligations which had not been found in the Race Relations Act 1976. The Human Rights Act provides an opportunity for that process of procedural knot-tying to continue: we should not overlook the fact that employers also have human rights, bizarre though this may sound[40]. We are faced with one of the cruellest of ironies, namely employers using the Human Rights Act to constrain agencies which perhaps more than any others are genuinely responsible for promoting human rights in this country.

An indication of this potentially disruptive effect is to be found in experiences under the recognition provisions of the Employment Protection Act 1975, sections 11-16. These provisions were administered principally by ACAS, and their introduction coincided with the emergence of judicial review in its modern form. Although not concerned directly with the ECHR, the cases brought against ACAS provide a valuable insight into judicial attitudes to legislation of this kind, which the Human Rights Act may yet serve to nourish by providing additional opportunities to frustrate the operation of the new recognition legislation. It is true that the type of issues which troubled the courts are unlikely to arise again in their original form. The new statutory procedure is very different from the old one, and indeed specific steps have been taken to address the drafting failings which invited some of the litigation in the first place. So the vulnerable points will be different in the future from what they were in the past, with articles 6 (the right to a fair trial) and 10 (freedom of expression) of the Convention, and article 1 of the First Protocol (protection of private property) giving the courts something more to bite with.

Yet even though judicial review was in its infancy in the 1970s, and even though the ECHR had not been incorporated, there was enough evidence even then to indicate the Convention's scope to frustrate. In one leading case, the Convention was relied on by a trade union which was attempting to disturb established collective bargaining arrangements. In *United Kingdom Association of Professional Engineers v ACAS*[41], the union had made an unsuccessful application to ACAS for recognition. Although it could claim 79 per cent support among the workers it claimed to represent, the application was rejected because it was feared that recognition of the association would undermine well established collective bargaining procedures. The Court of Appeal was not inclined to permit practical considerations of this kind to prevail, with Lord Denning referring to article 11 and concluding that

it seems to me that these professional engineers have a right to form and join their own trade union. In this case they have exercised that right. They have formed UKAPE and they have joined it. The right is given to each one for a specific purpose – 'for the protection of his interests'. What good is that right to him, I would ask? What good is it to him if UKAPE is disabled from protecting his interests – by being refused recognition – as a result of threats by the big battalions?'[42]

For this and other reasons the Court of Appeal upheld the High Court decision quashing the ACAS report.

At one level the observations of Lord Denning are extremely heart-warming: here we have a full commitment to the principles of trade union representation and recognition. But we should keep in mind the circumstances in which these words were expressed. This was not a case in which a trade union was asserting a right against an employer. Rather it was a case in which a non TUC trade union was asserting a right against a statutory body, which had taken into account the interests of other trade unions. Although today such sentiments strongly expressed would be helpful, we ought not to lose sight of the time and circumstances in which they were expressed. But apart from being unhelpful in the short term, they were to have potentially damaging long term repercussions, leading to a successful appeal by ACAS to the House of Lords. By the time the appeal was heard the legislation had been broken by the Court of Appeal, and the government of Mrs Thatcher had been elected with a mandate to restrict trade union freedoms. The significance of the appeal for present purposes lay in the observations of Lord Scarman which were no doubt designed to be helpful at the time (though it was too late for ACAS to be helped). Lord Scarman said:

'I agree with Lord Denning that article 11 of the convention and the common law recognise and protect the right of association, which in the present context includes the right to join a trade union. But it does not follow from the existence of the right that every trade union which can show that it has members employed by a particular company or in a particular industry has a right to recognition for the purposes of collective bargaining. I would be surprised if either the Convention or the common law could be interpreted as compelling so chaotic a conclusion'[43].

The Human Rights Act, statutory recognition, and the CAC

THE CAC is clearly a public body which is bound directly to comply with the Act. If it fails to comply, it will be subject to judicial review on that ground alone. So far as the CAC is concerned, there are a number of different ways by which the Act could bite. In the first place there is the article 6 right to a fair trial in the determination of civil rights and obligations. This is a right which obstructive employers may wish to inflate to extend the length of CAC procedures, by challenging the composition of the CAC in particular cases[44], and by insisting on a greater number of hearings than is currently provided for in the Employment Relations Act 1999 in relation to any particular application[45]. For example, under paragraph 36 an application is not admissible unless the members of the union constitute at least 10 per cent of the bargaining unit, and a majority of workers in the relevant unit 'would be likely to favour recognition of the union'. There is no provision in the Act for the employer to be given a hearing to challenge the union's claims, though employers will no doubt argue that a decision to proceed with a ballot is a decision which will affect their civil rights and obligations, most notably the duties under paragraph 26 if a ballot is held. This in turn could require the employer to allow access to his or her property under the access code[46].

It seems highly predictable that employers will be heard to squeal that these are obligations (a duty to co-operate and a duty to allow access) which arise as a result of a decision of a quasi judicial body in which the employer has no right to take part as the Act is drafted. Conversely there are situations where a union may wish to insist on a hearing before certain decisions are taken by the CAC under the procedure but for which there is no provision in the procedure as drafted. The obvious example of this is in relation to paragraph 22 which provides that the CAC can order a ballot even though the union is able to show that it has majority membership in the bargaining unit. The ballot can be ordered in these circumstances on one of three grounds – all of which are highly contestable – which the union may wish to challenge. But as matters currently stand the union has no right to contest the order in a hearing before the CAC even though the evidence on which the CAC has acted may be incorrect or based on a judgement which is unsound. What is not clear is whether in these cases the union's civil rights and obligations have been prejudiced. It is certainly the case that its right to automatic recognition will be denied, and that it will be given additional obligations, not the least of which will be the costs involved in campaigning in a ballot and meeting the costs of the ballot jointly with the employer[47].

But it is not only the CAC's procedures which are vulnerable to challenge under the Human Rights Act (and in this the CAC is no different from any other public body). There is also the question of its powers, particularly those relating to trade union access to the workforce. If the employer refuses to comply with the various duties arising under paragraph 26, the CAC is empowered under paragraph 27 to order the employer 'to take such steps to remedy the failure as the CAC considers reasonable and specifies in the order'. If the employer fails to comply with any such order, the CAC may then issue a declaration that the union is recognised for the purposes of collective bargaining. There are two questions which seem calculated to arise here. The first is whether the access code is vulnerable to challenge under the Human Rights Act[48], and the second is whether any order issued to an employer by the CAC will be open to challenge. So far as the first issue is concerned, the issue here will be whether the obligation under the Code to allow trade union access to the employer's premises will be regarded as breach of the employer's right to private property in article 1 of Protocol 1. In the United States such interference with employer's property rights is not permissible as a result of rulings of the Supreme Court[49].

It is inevitable that the issue will be challenged here, though it is far less clear what the result will be[50]. But we should be in no doubt that an employer who refuses to allow a trade union access to his or her premises will almost certainly argue before the CAC that the provisions of the Code of Practice are in breach of the Human Rights Act. Over to the CAC. An employer which is then ordered by the CAC to allow trade union access to his or her premises will almost certainly look for reasons to challenge that order in judicial review proceedings: the Human Rights Act may provide that opportunity. But the constraining potential of the Act will arise in other ways, as indicated by an important decision of the Supreme Court of Canada. In *Re National Bank of Canada and Retail Clerks' International Union*[51] the employer closed a branch of the bank for anti-union reasons. The Bank was then ordered by the Labour Relations Board to send a letter to its employees informing them that henceforward the Bank would respect their rights under the Labour Relations Act. This was said by the Supreme Court to be an 'extreme measure' which violated the Bank's right to freedom of expression, as being 'totalitarian and as such alien to the tradition of free nations like Canada, even for the repression of the most serious crimes'.

The Human Rights Act and the adjudication of employment disputes

IT is not only agencies such as the EOC, CRE, DRC, ACAS or the CAC which will be affected by the Human Rights Act. So too will be the employment tribunals, the Certification Officer, and the EAT (as well as disciplinary bodies in some cases)[52]. Most obviously this will arise in the interpretation of the substantive law which they are required to deal with. For example in unfair dismissal cases, the Employment Rights Act 1996 will have to be interpreted in a way which is consistent with the Convention. So anyone dismissed on the grounds of sexuality would have a strong claim before a tribunal that the dismissal is unfair, despite existing case law to the contrary[53]. This could arise in a number of ways. The first is that it would be open to a tribunal to say that a dismissal for a reason which is contrary to Convention rights can never be a reason for dismissal under s 98 of the Act. The other possibility is that the tribunal could say that although such a reason can be a valid reason, the dismissal must be unlawful under the second limb of the section, namely that no reasonable employer could ever regard such a reason as a proper reason for dismissal. But either way, there will be a duty on the tribunals to ensure that legislation (and where appropriate the common law) is applied consistently with Convention rights[54].

But apart from substantive issues of this kind, there are also important procedural points under article 6. Issues have already arisen under the provision in article 6 guaranteeing the right to a fair and public hearing in the determination of rights and obligations[55]. Already the basis of an important decision in Scotland where the Act has been partially in force as a result of the Scotland Act 1998[56], this particular article has raised questions about whether the system of appointing employment tribunals is consistent with the additional requirement that the hearing should be before 'an independent and impartial tribunal established by law'[57]. But it is not only the question of independence. There is also the matter of delay in the processing of applications, an issue raised in *Darnell v United Kingdom*[58] where the applicant was a school caretaker whose claim for unfair dismissal against the NHS took nine years. This was held to breach article 6. There is also the suggestion that there may be a need to ensure that legal aid is available for tribunal proceedings, at least in some if not all cases. How can it be said that the unrepresented worker is being given a fair hearing if he or she is up against a specialist lawyer representing the employer on a matter of great technicality?

It is not only disputes between employers and workers in the tribunals which will be governed by the Human Rights Act. The Certification Officer will also be affected, and it is in this forum that some interesting issues could arise, for what is at stake here is a clash between the trade union's right to freedom of association on the one hand, and the various Convention rights which might be claimed by members in dispute with the union on the other. One question will be whether much of the detailed regulation of trade union financial affairs, and much of the detailed regulation of trade union elections will be subject to scrutiny on the ground that they impose disproportionate burdens on the trade union's right to freedom of association[59]. It is of course the case that the Certification Officer will be required to apply this legislation, and that a union which wishes to challenge it will have to bring an application for judicial review seeking a declaration of incompatibility. One of the consequences of the Employment Relations Act 1999 conferring jurisdiction on the CO as well as the High Court is that it may be more difficult for unions to challenge restrictive legislation if members proceed with their complaints to the former rather than the latter body[60].

Yet there may well be circumstances in which the CO will have to engage directly with the Human Rights Act. One area relates to his new jurisdiction over trade union rule book disputes. In these cases the CO may have to ensure that in a disciplinary case, for example, the union acted in a way which did not violate the Convention rights of the member. A question will arise whether it is an implied term of the contract of membership that the union does not act contrary to Convention rights. If such a term is implied, it will be difficult for a trade union to discipline a member under the rules for non participation in action (not already unlawful) where the member refused to participate for reasons of conscience, or for conduct which would lead to a breach of the member's right to freedom of expression. But any such claim by the member will have to be balanced against the legitimate claims of the union to protection of its right to freedom of association. As pointed out in chapter 4, it is already strongly arguable that statutory restrictions on trade union admission and expulsion rules breach article 11. Quite apart from issues of this kind, the CO will also wish to be mindful of article 6 in the way in which hearings are conducted.

The Human Rights Act: uncertainty and unpredictability

SO although there is scope for the application of the Human Rights Act to the employment relationship and a need to develop a litigation strategy to maximise the potential of the Act, it remains the case that there is a great deal of uncertainty and unpredictability. Uncertainty about how it will affect the employment relationship, and uncertainty about the role of the courts. But at the end of the day, the Act can really only deal with the margins of the employment relationship. It does not deal with pay, working time, holidays and the like. Clearly it provides an important opportunity to take the rights of citizenship into the workplace, such as the right not to be subject to improper surveillance, or to respect for one's religious beliefs and practices, and the right to speak out about working conditions or employer practices. But we should also bear in mind that many of the rights which are guaranteed by the Convention are heavily qúalified, and in particular they allow restrictions which are 'necessary in a democratic society' on a number of grounds, including the rights and freedoms of others. These others will include employers, other workers, and members of the public, to protect the interests of whom it may be necessary to impose limits on Convention rights.

But the difficulty here is that there is no guidance in the Act as to what is 'necessary in a democratic society' by which to judge any possible restrictions on Convention rights. There is some case law of the European Court of Human Rights but this does not advance the matter a great deal, and indeed much of the case law may not be relevant to the extent that it holds that in determining whether a restriction is necessary in a democratic society, a margin of appreciation must be allowed to member states. All of which means that there is no escape from the fact that the value of the rights in the Act and the value of the Act to workers is largely in the hands of the judges. This is another great source of uncertainty. How will the judges respond? Workers and trade unions have every right to be cautious. The observations of Lord Justice Scrutton in a lecture to University College, London law students about the Commercial Court in 1920 is no less relevant today than it was then[61]. He said:

'the habits you are trained in, the people with whom you mix, lead to your having a certain class of ideas of such a nature that, when you have to deal with other ideas, you do not give as sound and accurate judgments as you would wish. This is one of the great difficulties at present with Labour. Labour says: where are your impartial Judges? They all move in the same circle as employers, and they are all educated and nursed in the same ideas as the employers. How can a labour man or a trade unionist get impartial justice? It is very difficult sometimes to be sure that you have put yourself into a thoroughly impartial position between two disputants, one of your own class and one not of your class... The difficulty does not arise in the Commercial Court.'[62]

But people say that the judges have changed (but into what?). As pointed out in the introduction to this chapter, there is indeed some evidence of this, though the inevitable question is how much have they changed? We see the confirmation by the House of Lords of a new implied term that the employer must not act in a way which will undermine trust and confidence in the relationship with his or her employees; but a recognition in the same case that this is not likely to amount to much in terms of remedies on dismissal except in the case of highly paid workers[63]. We see acknowledgement in the Court of Appeal that the right to strike is a fundamental human right; but a holding of the Court of Appeal only two years earlier confirmed that so far as the common law is concerned, trade unions are in unlawful restraint of trade[64]. And we see the decision of the House of Lords in *Wilson and Palmer*[65], a decision reached despite the open acknowledgement by Lord Browne-Wilkinson that it would leave 'an undesirable lacuna in the protection of employees against victimisation'. The expression of regret is comforting, but a decision the other way would have been convincing. There are nevertheless a number of cases in which it is possible to detect a liberalisation of judicial attitudes in a number of areas, most notably in relation to freedom of assembly and freedom of expression[66].

It is also the case that the judges have been extensively trained about the requirements of the new Act through the Judicial Studies Board. The training has reached all parts of the system – from the highest courts to the lowest. People operating in all the specialist fields of law are fully aware of the Act and its implications, fields as diverse as social security law and insolvency law, employment law and family law. Yet the judicial challenge remains immense, as recognised by Lord Woolf of Barnes, one of the senior judges who will now be responsible for bringing the Human Rights Act to life. He said:

'Almost all the rights contained in the Convention are qualified by exceptions. Usually the rights have to be balanced against the interests of the public a whole. It is the judiciary who will have responsibility because if the right balance is not struck there will be the risk of the UK courts' decisions being disapproved on application to the European Court of Human Rights and of the new rights being devalued in the eyes of the public. If, on the other hand, the job is done well, the judiciary of this country will have the opportunity they have so far been denied to make a contribution to the international jurisprudence of human rights.'[67]

Critical to the success of the Human Rights Act is the willingness of the judges to grasp their new powers and to go beyond the rather disappointing jurisprudence, certainly in the labour field. How likely is this? How can we square the role of judges with our traditional legal theory? How will they adapt to their new role, and what should it be?

The judicial challenge

TRADITIONAL theory has it that the courts are subordinate to Parliament. Judges are not lawmakers; nor should they be. They are not involved in controversial areas of policy as this would render them vulnerable to political criticism and thus undermine their independence. However they can be said to make law in a number of different ways. In developing the common law the judges have a law making function. Judges have another role – to interpret the will of Parliament as expressed in legislation (a feat they managed to achieve for years without reference to Parliamentary material until recently). The judge interprets a statute by simply giving the words their normal meaning. If there is ambiguity the judge must look at all of the law in the area and determine what was the intention of Parliament. Even the use of plain words in a statute leaves them with considerable discretion. In *Express Newspapers Ltd v McShane*[68] Lord Diplock said this:

'When the meaning of the statutory words is plain and unambiguous it is not for the judges to invent fancied ambiguities as an excuse for failing to give effect to its plain meaning because they themselves consider that the consequence of doing so would be inexpedient or even unjust or immoral... It endangers continued public confidence in the political impartiality of the judiciary, which is essential to the continuance of the rule of law, if judges, under the guise of interpretation, provide their own preferred amendments to statutes which experience of their operation was shown to have had consequences that members of the court before whom the matter comes considers to be injurious to the public interest.'

So Lord Diplock recognised that the exercise of the interpretative function may, if exercised improperly, undermine confidence in the judiciary. Where words are ambiguous, whether genuinely or simply perceived to be so, the discretion is obviously wider. There is a third aspect of judicial law making and it is in respect of their powers to review the acts of local and central government that will now increase under the Human Rights Act.

It goes without saying that judges ought not, and in most cases do not, expressly decide cases in accordance with their individual political party opinion. But frequently the exercise of a discretion will involve a value judgment or ethical principle that can be described as a political principle. So for example, one judge may display values that indicate he is well-disposed to defer to the executive in matters of national security, another to openness and a free press. Sir John Laws has recognised that the normal exercise of the courts' discretion involves 'ethical ideals' that are not 'morally colourless'; and that it is important 'to recognise the moral force of the basis on which control of public power is effected by the unelected judges'[69]. His conclusion in 1994 was that the process of judicial review was not political as it did not encroach upon the legitimate authority of governments or other elected bodies. Whether one agrees with his conclusion at the time, he was absolutely right in asserting that judicial review would not remain static and therefore:

> 'The true differences between judicial and elective power are of the greatest importance if we are to entertain a respectable theory as to the basis on which judicial review may hereafter develop... towards offering an explicit and systematic protection of constitutional rights. Might the judges in the future, if they wish to claim a greater jurisdiction to establish and insist upon fundamental rights, affront the imperative of democracy? Might they stake a claim, however well-intentioned, which transgresses the proper bounds of their unelected power?'

Pausing there, this is not to question for the moment the nature of the value judgments, but to acknowledge the fact that they are already made and they will be substantially increased. Judges are arguably second only to politicians in the potential impact they have on the lives of the populace. They are in a special position and their powers to review and criticise the actions of democratically elected politicians have substantially increased by virtue of the Human Rights Act. Certainly the interpretative approach to the ECHR and the Human Rights Act for English judges will be radically different to that they are used to. In the process of interpretation the courts will have to approach Convention rights as 'living instrument[s]' in the 'light of present-day conditions'[70]. Lester and Pannick go further and suggest that this dynamic interpretation involves having regard to the general objects and purpose of the Convention – to maintain and promote the ideals of a democratic society. These ideals involve concepts such as 'pluralism, tolerance and broad mindedness', 'the rule of law', 'access to the courts' and 'freedom of expression'[71]. This question of the values that should inform any judicial discretion is a controversial one and, of course, one judge's notion of the restrictions on freedom of expression as are 'necessary in a democratic society' will very easily differ from another just as we can think of many different types of democratic society. Does this refer to parliamentary, liberal, participatory or presidential democracy? Lester and Pannick go on to point out that Convention case law suggests that the courts should seek to 'strike a fair balance... between the demands of the general interest of the community and the requirements of the protection of the individual's fundamental rights'[72].

This 'balance' involves the doctrine of proportionality – any restriction of a freedom guaranteed by the Convention must be proportionate to the legitimate aim pursued. We already have some degree of guidance from the case law. A measure will be proportionate if:

- it is sufficiently important to justify limiting a fundamental right;
- the measures designed to meet the legislative objective must be rationally connected to that objective;
- the means used to impair the right or freedom must be no more than is necessary to accomplish the legitimate objective – that is the more severe the effects of a measure, the more important the objective must be if it is to be justified.

This is a very sophisticated analytical process and involves judges using a set of undefined value judgments. Human rights law, after all, is about substance and purpose and not technical matters. It is one thing to hold, as the Court of Appeal recently did in *Storer v British Gas plc*[73] that an employment tribunal preliminary hearing held in a room with a key code lock on the door on it for reasons of administrative convenience breached the regulation on public hearings. It is another to hold that the right to freedom of association includes the right to strike. Can we really expect a sympathetic hearing from judges who, as recently as 1994 declared that – so far as the common law is concerned – trade unions remain 'in unreasonable restraint of trade'[74].

Reforming and guiding the judiciary

THESE new powers of the courts give rise to important questions about the composition of the judiciary, and about the need also to constrain the wide discretionary powers of the courts with clearer guidance from Parliament. So far as composition is concerned, there is a need in particular for a more pluralistic Bench – one which is more representative of the people of this country. The calls for a more representative judiciary are not new. It was Labour Party policy to modernise the judiciary, and historically the Labour Party has been particularly concerned with the unrepresentative nature of the magistracy[75]. A recent *Labour Research* survey has shown that there has been little change in the gender, ethnicity, or even educational background of the judges appointed since 1997[76]. Further details are to be found in the Appendix to this chapter. Indeed it remains the case that the highest court in this country – the House of Lords – does not have and never has had a single woman member. It is true that a judiciary differently composed in terms of gender and ethnicity is no guarantee that there will be substantial differences to substantive outcomes, though it would at least engender more public confidence when the judges foray into political questions[77]. It would also remove the bizarre spectacle of our senior human rights court being a court of 12 elderly white men with limited experience of the concerns of the people appearing before them. No amount of training can substitute for experience.

But it is easier to talk about securing a more pluralistic Bench than to achieve it. There are in fact two issues which need to be confronted. The first is the method of appointment. At the present time senior appointments are made by the Queen on the advice of the Prime Minister and the Lord Chancellor, though the latter is clearly the pivotal figure[78]. There has been some concern about the process of appointment and the secrecy which surrounds it. These procedures were nevertheless broadly endorsed recently in a report for the Lord Chancellor by Sir Leonard Peach, which made a number of proposals for reform[79]. More radical proposals for reform were made in 1991 by the IPPR which suggested that there should be a new Ministry of Justice which would be responsible for judicial appointments with clear and transparent procedures[80]. But in a sense this misses the point, or at least is not the whole point. It is to some extent immaterial who makes the appointments if the pool of candidates remains the same, solicitors or barristers. In effect what we have is a system of appointment which depends on the candidate's record of achievement in a closed labour market. Real reform of the system of judicial appointments is one which will open up the system to a much wider group of people who are not dependent on the approval of the gatekeepers in the legal system[81].

But the Human Rights Act does not simply suggest a need for a more representative and balanced judiciary, bringing a wider range of experiences to bear on decision-making. There is a need too for a greater need for guidance to the courts when they are asked to decide hard questions under the Act. This applies regardless of how the judges are appointed. The Act gives to the courts a wide discretion to determine the content of Convention rights and to determine the circumstances in which they may be constrained in the interests of a democratic society. This last issue is particularly important, with the nature and values of a democratic society to be determined by the judges themselves. But as already suggested democratic societies come in different forms: a liberal democratic society would be less tolerant of measures designed to promote equality of the many by restraining the liberty of the few than would be a social democratic society. Similarly, a liberal democratic society would be less tolerant of measures designed to promote the rights of social institutions at the expense of property rights than would be a social democratic society. There is a need to address this wide discretionary power to protect social legislation and administrative action from being undermined by the courts.

There are a number of ways by which this could be done. One would be to use other international treaties – such as ILO Conventions and the Council of Europe's Social Charter of 1961 – as an aid to the construction of Convention rights. As we saw in chapter 4, there is jurisprudence of the Strasbourg Commission and Court to the effect that these treaties are to be taken into account in the construction of the ECHR. It is important that these cases are brought to the attention of the domestic courts, which are bound to have regard to the jurisprudence of the Strasbourg bodies, even if they are not bound to follow it. But it is also important as a result that British lawyers become familiar and fluent with these other international treaties and the great social achievements which they represent, as well as the work of the supervisory bodies which give the treaties substance. The other and more radical possibility would be for the government to take the lead by giving a more formal role to the Social Charter of 1961 – the younger sibling of the ECHR – in the new constitutional architecture of the United Kingdom. The giving of a prominent place in the constitution to Charter rights as well as Convention rights would bring us into line with the great European social democracies and would clearly distinguish us from the liberal democracy of the USA, which is where we appear to be drifting by default.

Conclusion

ALTHOUGH the foregoing gives an indication of the range of issues which may arise under the Human Rights Act, the list is by no means exhaustive. The Act provides an opportunity for steps to be taken to promote the interests of workers and trade unions. The potential is fully recognised in the resolution at the TUC Conference 2000, key passages of which were expressed in the following terms:

Congress believes that trade unions should use the legislation [the Human Rights Act] to extend rights at work and calls upon the General Council to begin:

a) investigating the potential for the Act to be used to advance rights at work;

b) investigating the potential for the Act to be used to extend equality under the law for all, including lesbians and gay men;

c) promoting awareness among unions and union members of the Act and its implications within the workplace;

d) co-ordinating activity by affiliates in bringing test cases to establish the full extent of the Act's potential. If necessary affiliates should be invited to share the costs of such test cases particularly if the case has to be dealt with at the European Court of Human Rights.

Congress also notes the potential impact of the Act on the way in which businesses and public sector bodies work. Congress encourages employers to ensure that all their staff are properly trained and fully aware of the implications of the Act[82].

It is hoped that the foregoing pages of this book will indicate the type of areas where the Act could apply and the kind of issues on which substantial progress could be made. But as the TUC resolution hints at, there is a need to make it work by developing a pro-active litigation strategy, without losing sight of its potential in collective bargaining. There is a need to identify areas where the Act might be used: first where there is a gap in the statutory protection of workers which the Act might fill (as in the case of surveillance at work or gay and lesbian discrimination), or where there is legislation which is restrictive and contrary to the standards which the Human Rights Act secures (as in the case of the restraints on trade union freedom in the Trade Union and Labour Relations (Consolidation) Act 1992). But as also suggested earlier in this chapter, there is a need for careful thought about how to get these cases into court in the first place. There is a menu of options: a possibility in some cases of securing by judicial review a declaration of incompatibility, but this will be relevant only where there is already legislation in force; it may be possible in some cases to mount a test case against a public body, which if successful will put great pressure on the government to introduce legislation of universal application[83]; and it may be possible to make progress by slugging it out through the tribunals on a daily basis.

But although there are thus high hopes and great expectations, we should end on a note of caution and with a sense of realism. In the first place it is important to bear in mind that the range of Convention rights relevant to the workplace is extremely limited: it does not affect the core issues of the employment relationship such as pay and working conditions. This is the job of the Social Charter of the Council of Europe: it has not been incorporated, though it should be and as argued in chapter 4 it may have a role to play in the interpretation of Convention rights[84]. Secondly it is important to acknowledge that the Convention does not only empower workers and trade unions: it empowers everyone, including companies and employers. Although it is important not to exaggerate this dimension, we cannot overlook the fact that in other countries it has been employers who have used constitutional rights similar to Convention rights to cut back progressive legislation and to impede statutory agencies established to administer such legislation[85]. The same may happen here. And finally, there is the role of the courts, at this stage very unpredictable. However seductive and tempting the prospect of litigation may be, the cautious advice would be to take a long hard look at the judicial record in protecting workers' rights before storming the court room door, armed only with the Human Rights Act 1998.

Notes

1 The judges are also acutely aware of what is expected of them. See A Lester and D Pannick, *Human Rights Law and Practice* (1999), Introduction by Lord Woolf of Barnes.

2 Such as the duty of mutual trust and confidence, on a recent application of which see *TSB Bank plc v Harris* [2000] IRLR 157.

3 *London Underground Ltd v NUR* [1996] ICR 181 (Millett LJ).

4 [1995] 2 All ER 100.

5 On which see K D Ewing, 'A Theory of Democratic Adjudication: Towards a Representative, Accountable and Independent Judiciary' (2000) 38(3) Alta LR 1.

6 (1997) 23 EHRR CD 168.

7 *Halford v United Kingdom* (1997) 24 EHRR 523.

8 (1981) 4 EHRR 126.

9 There is a compelling sense in which this matter needs to be looked at again. We live in a multi-cultural society with many different religions and beliefs. Yet we have working practices which are based exclusively around Christian festivals and Christian observance, which are compromised only where they are commercially inconvenient (as in the case of restrictions on Sunday Trading). So we celebrate Christmas and Easter (whether we are Christians or not), but we do not celebrate the major events of other beliefs. The world of work goes on regardless. Similarly Sunday is a day of rest, justifiable on secular grounds, but with clear religious origins. But the holy days of other religions are not also regarded as universal days of rest. This is a matter about which the Human Rights Act may force changes, and may require a re-examination of the existing jurisprudence, the leading cases now being a quarter of a century old. Time has changed. There is a need to adapt working practices to accommodate different beliefs.

10 *Ahmed v United Kingdom* (1998) 29 EHRR 1.

11 (1996) 22 EHRR 123. But see *Camelot Group v Centaur Communications Ltd* [1998] 1 All ER 251.

12 See *X Ltd v Morgan Grampian (Publishers) Ltd* [1990] 2 All ER 1.

13 See *National Union of Belgian Police v Belgium* (1975) 1 EHRR 578; *Swedish Engine Drivers' Union v Sweden* (1975) 1 EHRR 617; and *Schmidt and Dahlstrom v Sweden* (1975) 1 EHRR 637.

14 *Young, James and Webster v United Kingdom* (1982) 4 EHRR 38; and *Sigurjonsson v Iceland* (1993) 16 EHRR 462.

15 *Council of Civil Service Unions v United Kingdom* (1988) 10 EHRR 269.

16 For an account of the response of the different international bodies see the extremely valuable account in G Morris, in K D Ewing, C A Gearty and B A Hepple, *Human Rights and Labour Law: Essays for Paul O'Higgins* (1994), ch 2.

17 [1994] ICR 648. An application to Strasbourg was ruled inadmissible.

18 See K D Ewing, 'Freedom of Association and the Employment Relations Act 1999' (1999) 28 ILJ 283.

19 HL Debs, 7 June 1999, col 1090.

20 This seemed a strange argument in the light of the NATFHE case, above. But it reveals the power of the Human Rights Act as a means of closing political debate on contentious issues. We must all learn to be much less

deferential to legal claims unsubstantiated by evidence.

21 [1977] ICR 490.

22 *X Ltd v Morgan Grampian (Publishers) Ltd, op cit.*

23 *NALGO v Secretary of State, The Times,* 2 December 1992.

24 *Middlebrook Mushrooms Ltd v TGWU* [1993] ICR 612.

25 *Ibid,* at p 620.

26 This would be true where the recommended 6 pickets were applied like a statutory maximum. See *Thomas v NUM (South Wales) Area* [1986] Ch 20.

27 [1982] ICR 543.

28 *UKAPE v ACAS* [1979] ICR 303. See also *EMA v ACAS* [1980] ICR 215.

29 *Cheall v APEX* [1983] ICR 398.

30 *Council of Civil Service Unions v Minister of State for the Civil Service* [1985] AC 374.

31 There is now a growing literature which includes the following: B Hepple, 'The Impact on Labour Law', in B Markenisis (ed), *The Impact of the Human Rights Bill on English Law* (1997), K D Ewing, 'The Human Rights Act and Labour Law' (1998) 27 ILJ 275, G Lightman and J Bowers, 'Incorporation of the ECHR and its Impact on Employment Law' [1998] EHRLR 560, and S Palmer, 'Human Rights: Implications for Labour Law' [2000] 59 CLJ 168.

32 The Institute of Employment Rights Code of Practice prepared by Michael Ford and included as an appendix to chapter 2 provides a valuable basis for regulation, whether in legislation or by collective bargaining.

33 For a full account of the legal position, see R Wintemute, *Sexual Orientation and Human Rights* (1995).

34 [1995] AC 1.

35 (1996) 24 EHRR 205.

36 This is an extremely difficult issue. See G Morris, 'The Human Rights Act and the Public/Private Divide in Employment Law' (1998) 27 ILJ 293.

37 For a consideration of this question (the horizontality of Convention rights), see R Buxton (2000) 116 LQR 48, H W R Wade (2000) 116 LQR 217, and A Lester and D Pannick (2000) 116 LQR 380. See also H W R Wade and C F Forsyth, *Administrative Law* (8th ed, 2000), pp 187 and 982-4.

38 But there will still be cases where Convention rights have nothing to bite on: for example the person who is refused employment by an employer for a reason which breaches Convention rights. A possible example would be the person refused employment because of his or her sexuality, unless it is possible to find a statutory route to a remedy (such as one based on the interpretation of the Sex Discrimination Act 1975).

39 See *R v CRE, ex parte Hillingdon London Borough Council* [1982] AC 779, *Re Prestige Group Ltd* [1984] 1 WLR 335.

40 See K D Ewing, 'Trade Unions and their Human Rights' (1998) 48(1) *Federation News* 1. For a recent reminder that corporations also have human rights under the Act, see *County Properties Ltd v The Scottish Ministers, The Times,* 19 September 2000.

41 [1979] ICR 303.

42 at p 317.

43 [1980] ICR 201, at p 214.

44 This has been the source of the major decisions under the Act so far from Scotland. See below. But in the context of the CAC an issue which may come

up relates to the different roles of the CAC under the procedure. Under paragraph 18, for example, the CAC has a mediation role on the determination of the bargaining unit. Under paragraph 19 this becomes an adjudicatory function if the parties fail to agree under paragraph 18. Can the same panel perform both functions without falling foul of article 6 of the ECHR?

45 For employer strategies in the United States which include the stringing out of litigation, see W B Gould, *Agenda for Reform: The Future of Employment Relationships and the Law* (1993), ch 5. See also L Dubinsky, *Resisting Union-Busting Techniques: Lessons from Quebec* (Institute of Employment Rights, 2000). For the possibility of similar tactics being deployed in this country, see *The Observer*, 4 June 2000.

46 But it also includes a duty to co-operate with the holding of the ballot and to supply personal data about workers to the CAC.

47 Another issue relates to paragraph 35 and the ability of employers to defeat a statutory claim by establishing a staff association with 'bargaining rights'. The question arises whether such a device violates the article 11 guarantee to freedom of association. See on this K D Ewing, 'Trade Union Recognition and Staff Associations – A Breach of International Labour Standards?' (2000) 29 ILJ.

48 DTI, Code of Practice: Access to Workers During Recognition and Derecognition Ballots (2000), paras 26-36.

49 See *NLRB v Babcock & Wilcox Co*, 351 US 105 (1956), and *Lechmere, Inc v NLRB*, 502 US 526 (1992).

50 For an indication of how an earlier generation of judges thought trade unions should secure access, see *Grunwick Processing Laboratories Ltd v ACAS* [1978] ICR 231.

51 (1984) 9 DLR (4th) 10.

52 *R v General Medical Council, ex parte Toth* [2000] All ER (D) 865.

53 *Saunders v Scottish National Holiday Camps Association Ltd* [1981] IRLR 277.

54 For a fuller discussion, see Ewing, 'Human Rights and Labour Law', *op cit*, pp 286-287.

55 There is some question about whether this could affect disciplinary procedures under contracts of employment, and conversely trade union disciplinary procedures. Although it is unclear whether the Act will bite in these cases, it may nevertheless apply in certain circumstances to domestic proceedings if the right to practice in a profession or occupation is at stake. See *R v General Medical Council, ex parte Toth, op cit.*

56 *Starrs v Ruxton*, 2000 JC 208. See also *Gibbs v Ruxton*, 2000 JC 258.

57 *Smith v Secretary of State for Trade and Industry* [2000] IRLR 6.

58 (1991) 69 DR 162.

59 These measures are a source of considerable administrative difficulty for some unions, with concerns being raised by the Musicians' Union at the TUC Annual Congress in 2000. For example does the right of access to the union's accounting records under the Trade Union and Labour Relations (Consolidation) Act 1992, s 30 include a right of access to personal data (apart from the salaries of leading officers as required by statute)? If so, could such access violate both articles 8 and 11? If so, will it be possible for the 1992 Act to be construed to give effect to Convention rights? It is in trenches such

as this that many of the battles around the Human Rights Act will be fought in the employment field.

60 For a very helpful account of the CO's jurisdiction, as expanded by the 1999 Act, see Annual Report of the Certification Officer 1999-2000 (2000).

61 T E Scrutton, 'The Work of the Commercial Courts' (1921) 1 CLJ 6.

62 For comment on this, see R Miliband, *The State in Capitalist Society* (1968), pp 124-130; and R Miliband, *Capitalist Democracy in Britain* (1982), pp 116-121. See also J A G Griffith, *The Politics of the Judiciary* (5th ed, 1997).

63 *Malik v Bank of Credit and Commerce International SA* [1997] ICR 606.

64 See respectively, *London Underground Ltd v NUR, op cit;* and *Boddington v Lawton* [1994] ICR 478.

65 *Associated Newspapers plc v Wilson, op cit.*

66 See especially, *DPP v Jones* [1999] 2 All ER 257, *R v Home Secretary, ex parte Simms* [1999] 3 All ER 400.

67 Lester and Pannick, *Human Rights Law and Practice, op cit,* Introduction by Lord Woolf of Barnes.

68 [1980] 1 All ER 65.

69 J Laws, *Law and Politics – No-Go Areas for Judges?,* Public Law Project Lecture, 12 May 1994.

70 *Tyrer v United Kingdom* (1978) 2 EHRR 1, at p 10.

71 Lester and Pannick, *op cit,* p 67.

72 *Sporrong v Sweden* (1982) 5 EHRR 35, at p 52, cited in Lester and Pannick, *op cit,* p 68.

73 [2000] IRLR 495.

74 *Boddington v Lawton, op cit.*

75 For full discussion of this issue, see Ewing, 'A Theory of Democratic Adjudication: Towards a Representative, Accountable and Independent Judiciary', *op cit.*

76 'Judging Labour on the Judges', *Labour Research,* June 1999.

77 On the importance of gender balance on the court, see the account by a distinguished former member of the Supreme Court of Canada, B Wilson, 'Will Women Judges Really Make a Difference?' (1990) 28 *Osgoode Hall Law Journal* 507.

78 See A W Bradley and K D Ewing, *Constitutional and Administrative Law* (12th ed, 1997), ch 18.

79 L Peach, *Judicial Appointments and QC Appointments* (1999).

80 IPPR, *The Constitution of the United Kingdom* (1991).

81 For further discussion, see Ewing, 'A Theory of Democratic Adjudication: Towards a Representative, Accountable and Independent Judiciary', *op cit.*

82 TUC, GPC Report and Composite Motions (2000), C4.

83 As happened for example when various parts of the unfair dismissal law were challenged in the courts as violating EC law.

84 The arguments for incorporating Convention rights apply with equal force to Charter rights. The arguments for incorporating the former were based mainly on the remoteness of the Strasbourg court and the British record of non-compliance. These apply to the Charter. See K D Ewing, 'Social Rights and Human Rights: Britain and the Social Charter – The Conservative Legacy' [2000] EHRLR 91

85 We have already referred to some of the cases on trade union recognition

from the USA. In Canada it was a company (not workers or consumers which used freedom of religion guarantees to strike down Sunday trading restriction), and in Ireland employers have used constitutional guarantees of private property to strike down legislation requiring workplaces to be adapted for disabled workers. It is also the case the Strasbourg Court has used article 11 only against but not also for trade unions. In Australia free speech guarantees implied into the Constitution have not extended to trade union picketing.

Appendix

The British
judiciary

Sonia McKay

A N examination of the social and economic background of Britain's judges shows that they come from a narrow sector of society and that they fail to reflect the gender or ethnic mix of the population as a whole.

The Institute of Employment Rights commissioned the Labour Research Department to conduct a survey of the British judiciary, the results of which are published below. The survey covers judicial appointments to the House of Lords, the Court of Appeal, the High Court (Queens Bench, Chancery and Family divisions), together with the Circuit Courts. The total number of judges included in the survey is 704. It covers more judges than any previous LRD survey.

Historically, Britain's judges have been male, white and elderly. The LRD survey shows that this picture remains an accurate one. Six hundred and fifty-five of the 704 judges (93 per cent) are male. There are only 49 female judges in all and the overwhelming majority (38) are at the lowest level, in the Circuit Courts. There are still no women judges in the House of Lords and only two, out of 37 judges in the Court of Appeal are female. Dame Butler-Sloss, who has been the only woman in the Court of Appeal since her appointment in 1988, has finally been joined by another woman. Dame Brenda Majorie Hale was appointed to the Court of Appeal in October 1999.

Even within the judiciary it seems that stereotypical views of what women should do remain. The only court where women occupy more than seven per cent of the judicial positions is the Family Division of the High Court. Three women judges sit alongside 14 men.

There is little evidence of change in respect of appointments to the judiciary by gender. Since the 1997 election there have been 144 judicial appointments. Of these, a remarkably high, 131 have been male appointments, representing 91 per cent of all new judicial appointments. Only 13 women have been appointed or elevated to a higher position in the judiciary in the last three years. Nine were Circuit Court appointments, three were appointed as High Court judges and one made it to the Court of Appeal. Women account for just seven per cent of all judges, just a one per cent increase in three years. At this rate it would take nearly 150 years for the gender balance to be equal.

In terms of the ethnic composition of the judiciary there is no up to date published information. In 1996 the Home Affairs Committee on Judicial Appointments Procedures said that it had received less evidence on this issue than on the gender composition of the judges but suggested that five out of the then 517 Circuit judges were from an ethnic minority. This survey has records of just four ethnic minority Circuit Court judges. Although this figure may be an underestimate, given that it is difficult to ascertain the ethnic origin of an appointee to the Circuit Court from an individual's name alone, it is certainly still the case that less than one per cent of the judiciary comes from an ethnic minority background. While Black people are disproportionately over-represented both as victims and as those convicted under the criminal law system, they are less likely to be judged upon by their peers than a white person would be.

The survey was only able to ascertain the ages of the judges, in 664 of the 704 judicial posts covered in the survey[1]. It finds that half (47 per cent) the judges are aged 60 and over and nearly a quarter (22 per cent) are over the state retirement age of 65. Eleven House of Lords judges are over state retirement age as are a quarter of the judges in the Court of Appeal. The Table gives the average ages of the judges in each of the courts surveyed.

The survey also sought to ascertain the ages of those judges appointed since the 1997 election. It would be expected that, on average, these appointees would be younger, since they are at the beginning of their period of appointment or elevation. What is surprising is that the age differences are not particularly great. Indeed, the House of Lords appointments made since 1997 actually had the effect of increasing the average age of the Law Lords. On average the new appointees are just four years younger than the overall average.

Britain's judges also tend to share a similar educational background, with a disproportionate number attending public schools, followed by Oxford or Cambridge. The survey was able to find details of the educational background of 561 judges, including all of the judges at High Court and above level, save for 12 where the details were not available. Of the 561, 387 (69 per cent) attended public schools. This compares with fewer than 10 per cent of the British population overall, which benefits from this form of education.

Of the appointments made since the 1997 election the majority had a public school background. Of the 66 appointments, where details are available, a surprisingly high 75 per cent attended public school. Even if it were the case that not a single one of the judges, whose educational details were not available, had attended a state school, the results would still show that public school backgrounds are disproportionately dominant, even among the newest appointees. This suggests that there has been no effective attempt at changing the class and economic background of Britain's judges.

From public school the judges go on their preferred route to one of the two Oxbridge universities, with Oxford slightly ahead. Where the information was available[2] it shows that 64 per cent of the judges attended one of the Oxbridge universities, including 12 Law Lords and 31 of the 37 Court of Appeal judges.

Even when looking at recent appointments, Oxbridge dominates. Where the information was available[3] the survey found that 75 per cent of the new appointments went to individuals who had attended an Oxbridge college. Most of these Oxbridge appointees are men. Only two Oxbridge women were appointed, compared to 51 men. Indeed the survey suggests that the bias in favour of Oxbridge is increasing. A similar LRD survey two years after the election found that 73 per cent of the new appointees (two per cent fewer) had been to Oxford or Cambridge.

Turning to their declared leisure pursuits, today's judges reveal a relatively narrow range of interests. Those with a passion for music are well represented, followed by those with an interest in gardening. Where it was possible to obtain the information (in 490 cases) 29 per cent have a musical bent, followed by 25 per cent who enjoy being in the garden, although in the case of a few it is more watching others, than doing it themselves, that gives the pleasure. Ten judges engage in hunting pursuits. Walking, golf, sailing and cricket are also popular pastimes and are reflected in their choice of clubs to relax in, with the MCC and Bar Yacht as firm favourites. The traditional haunt of the legal profession, the Garrick club, is still popular. About one in 14 of the judges surveyed are members, but for the superior courts, the House of Lords and Court of Appeal, the proportion of judges in membership is significantly higher, at 17 per cent.

Although the commonly held view of the judges is that they are above politics, the reality is that, for at least a minority, they have had a significant involvement in politics. Twenty-three of today's judges have actually stood for office either as a councillor or Member of Parliament. While most sit in the lower court, as Circuit judges, there are two High Court judges who have stood for political office and one Court of Appeal judge. Dame Elizabeth Butler-Sloss, sister of the former Conservative Attorney-General Michael Havers, contested both Lambeth and Vauxhall as a Conservative candidate. Mr Justice Michael Barton, recently appointed as the chair of the newly expanded Central Arbitration Committee with responsibility for the legislation on trade union recognition, contested Stratford for Labour before a switch to the SDP. Mr Justice David Anthony Poole was chair of Lawyers for the Defence of the Unborn, prior to his elevation to the High Court.

Since the 1997 election there have been three appointments to judicial posts of individuals who have had an active political career. None were Conservative appointments, two were Labour and one was Liberal.

It is difficult to obtain information about the links between freemasonry and the judiciary, but the survey shows that at least nine judges are freemasons, including two Court of Appeal judges, Sir George Mark Waller and Sir John Murray Chadwick, and Lord Millett in the House of Lords. The latter two have both served as members of the panel of the Freemasons' Commission for Appeals Courts.

Several of the judges come from a military tradition, with some receiving their training in the Navy or with the Army's legal services.

Table: Britain's judges

	Gender		Age of judges		Education	
	M	*F*	*All judges*	*Appointed since 1997*	*Attended public school[4]*	*Oxbridge*
House of Lords	100%	0%	67.1	67.5	58%	92%
Court of Appeal	95%	5%	62.0	58.9	76%	89%
High Court (QB)	93%	7%	60.1	55.9	80%	82%
High Court (CH)	94%	6%	58.1	55.5	94%	94%
High Court (Fam)	82%	18%	56.4	50.8	85%	75%
Circuit	93%	7%	59.9	53.7	66%	56%
All	**93%**	**7%**	**59.9**	**55.0**	**69%**	**64%**

Notes

1 The survey has details of the ages of all of the judges High Court and above, but does not have details of the ages of 40 of the 550 circuit judges surveyed.
2 Information on the university background of 527 of the 704 judges.
3 Information on the university background of 71 of the 144 appointments since 1997.
4 Where details were available.

Chapter 8 : Human rights at work: possibilities and problems

Appendix

The Human Rights Act 1998

Human Rights Act 1998
1998 Chapter 42

ARRANGEMENT OF SECTIONS

Introduction

Section

An Act to give further effects to rights and freedoms guaranteed under the European Convention on Human Rights; to make provision with respect to holders of certain judicial offices who become judges of the European Court of Human Rights; and for connected purposes.

[9th November 1998]

BE IT ENACTED by the Queen's most Excellent Majesty, by and with the advice and consent of the Lords Spiritual and Temporal, and Commons, in this present Parliament assembled, and by the authority of the same, as follows:

Introduction

The Convention Rights.

1. – (1) In this Act "the Convention rights" means the rights and funda-mental freedoms set out in

    (a) Articles 2 to 12 and 14 of the Convention,

    (b) Articles 1 to 3 of the First Protocol, and

    (c) Articles 1 and 2 of the Sixth Protocol,

as read with Articles 16 to 18 of the Convention.

(2) Those Articles are to have effect for the purposes of this Act subject to any designated derogation or reservation (as to which see sections 14 and 15).

(3) The Articles are set out in Schedule 1.

(4) The Secretary of State may by order make such amendments to this Act as he considers appropriate to reflect the effect, in relation to the United Kingdom, of a protocol.

(5) In subsection (4) "protocol" means a protocol to the Convention

(a) which the United Kingdom has ratified; or

(b) which the United Kingdom has signed with a view to ratification.

(6) No amendment may be made by an order under subsection (4) so as to come into force before the protocol concerned is in force in relation to the United Kingdom.

Interpretation of Convention rights.

2. - (1) A court or tribunal determining a question which has arisen in connection with a Convention right must take into account any

(a) judgment, decision, declaration or advisory opinion of the European Court of Human Rights,

(b) opinion of the Commission given in a report adopted under Article 31 of the Convention,

(c) decision of the Commission in connection with Article 26 or 27(2) of the Convention, or

(d) decision of the Committee of Ministers taken under Article 46 of the Convention,

whenever made or given, so far as, in the opinion of the court or tribunal, it is relevant to the proceedings in which that question has arisen.

(2) Evidence of any judgment, decision, declaration or opinion of which account may have to be taken under this section is to be given in proceedings before any court or tribunal in such manner as may be provided by rules.

(3) In this section "rules" means rules of court or, in the case of proceedings before a tribunal, rules made for the purposes of this section-

(a) by the Lord Chancellor or the Secretary of State, in relation to any proceedings outside Scotland;

(b) by the Secretary of State, in relation to proceedings in Scotland; or

(c) by a Northern Ireland department, in relation to proceedings before a tribunal in Northern Ireland-

(i) which deals with transferred matters; and

(ii) for which no rules made under paragraph (a) are in force.

Legislation

Interpretation of legislation.

3. - (1) So far as it is possible to do so, primary legislation and subordinate legislation must be read and given effect in a way which is compatible with the Convention rights.

(2) This section-

  (a) applies to primary legislation and subordinate legislation whenever enacted;

  (b) does not affect the validity, continuing operation or enforcement of any incompatible primary legislation; and

  (c) does not affect the validity, continuing operation or enforcement of any incompatible subordinate legislation if (disregarding any possibility of revocation) primary legislation prevents removal of the incompatibility.

Declaration of incompatibility.

4. - (1) Subsection (2) applies in any proceedings in which a court determines whether a provision of primary legislation is compatible with a Convention right.

(2) If the court is satisfied that the provision is incompatible with a Convention right, it may make a declaration of that incompatibility.

(3) Subsection (4) applies in any proceedings in which a court determines whether a provision of subordinate legislation, made in the exercise of a power conferred by primary legislation, is compatible with a Convention right.

(4) If the court is satisfied-

  (a) that the provision is incompatible with a Convention right, and

  (b) that (disregarding any possibility of revocation) the primary legislation concerned prevents removal of the incompatibility,

it may make a declaration of that incompatibility.

(5) In this section "court" means-

  (a) the House of Lords;

  (b) the Judicial Committee of the Privy Council;

  (c) the Courts-Martial Appeal Court;

  (d) in Scotland, the High Court of Justiciary sitting otherwise than as a trial court or the Court of Session;

  (e) in England and Wales or Northern Ireland, the High Court or the Court of Appeal.

(6) A declaration under this section ("a declaration of incompatibility")-

  (a) does not affect the validity, continuing operation or enforcement of the provision in respect of which it is given; and

  (b) is not binding on the parties to the proceedings in which it is made.

Right of Crown to intervene.

5. - (1) Where a court is considering whether to make a declaration of incompatibility, the Crown is entitled to notice in accordance with rules of court.

(2) In any case to which subsection (1) applies-

  (a) a Minister of the Crown (or a person nominated by him),

  (b) a member of the Scottish Executive,

  (c) a Northern Ireland Minister,

(d) a Northern Ireland department,

is entitled, on giving notice in accordance with rules of court, to be joined as a party to the proceedings.

(3) Notice under subsection (2) may be given at any time during the proceedings.

(4) A person who has been made a party to criminal proceedings (other than in Scotland) as the result of a notice under subsection (2) may, with leave, appeal to the House of Lords against any declaration of incompatibility made in the proceedings.

(5) In subsection (4)

"criminal proceedings" includes all proceedings before the Courts-Martial Appeal Court; and "leave" means leave granted by the court making the declaration of incompatibility or by the House of Lords.

Public authorities

Acts of public authorities.

6. - (1) It is unlawful for a public authority to act in a way which is incompatible with a Convention right.

(2) Subsection (1) does not apply to an act if

(a) as the result of one or more provisions of primary legislation, the authority could not have acted differently; or

(b) in the case of one or more provisions of, or made under, primary legislation which cannot be read or given effect in a way which is compatible with the Convention rights, the authority was acting so as to give effect to or enforce those provisions.

(3) In this section "public authority" includes-

(a) a court or tribunal, and

(b) any person certain of whose functions are functions of a public nature,

but does not include either House of Parliament or a person exercising functions in connection with proceedings in Parliament.

(4) In subsection (3) "Parliament" does not include the House of Lords in its judicial capacity.

(5) In relation to a particular act, a person is not a public authority by virtue only of subsection (3)(b) if the nature of the act is private.

(6) "An act" includes a failure to act but does not include a failure to-

(a) introduce in, or lay before, Parliament a proposal for legislation; or

(b) make any primary legislation or remedial order.

Proceedings.

7. - (1) A person who claims that a public authority has acted (or proposes to act) in a way which is made unlawful by section 6(1) may-

(a) bring proceedings against the authority under this Act in the appropriate court or tribunal, or

(b) rely on the Convention right or rights concerned in any legal proceedings, but only if he is (or would be) a victim of the unlawful act.

(2) In subsection (1)(a) "appropriate court or tribunal" means such court or tribunal as may be determined in accordance with rules; and proceedings against an authority include a counterclaim or similar proceeding.

(3) If the proceedings are brought on an application for judicial review, the applicant is to be taken to have a sufficient interest in relation to the unlawful act only if he is, or would be, a victim of that act.

(4) If the proceedings are made by way of a petition for judicial review in Scotland, the applicant shall be taken to have title and interest to sue in relation to the unlawful act only if he is, or would be, a victim of that act.

(5) Proceedings under subsection (1)(a) must be brought before the end of
> (a) the period of one year beginning with the date on which the act complained of took place; or
>
> (b) such longer period as the court or tribunal considers equitable having regard to all the circumstances,

but that is subject to any rule imposing a stricter time limit in relation to the procedure in question.

(6) In subsection (1)(b) "legal proceedings" includes
> (a) proceedings brought by or at the instigation of a public authority; and
>
> (b) an appeal against the decision of a court or tribunal.

(7) For the purposes of this section, a person is a victim of an unlawful act only if he would be a victim for the purposes of Article 34 of the Convention if proceedings were brought in the European Court of Human Rights in respect of that act.

(8) Nothing in this Act creates a criminal offence.

(9) In this section "rules" means
> (a) in relation to proceedings before a court or tribunal outside Scotland, rules made by the Lord Chancellor or the Secretary of State for the purposes of this section or rules of court,
>
> (b) in relation to proceedings before a court or tribunal in Scotland, rules made by the Secretary of State for those purposes,
>
> (c) in relation to proceedings before a tribunal in Northern Ireland
> > (i) which deals with transferred matters; and
> >
> > (ii) for which no rules made under paragraph (a) are in force, rules made by a Northern Ireland department for those purposes, and
>
> includes provision made by order under section 1 of the Courts and Legal Services Act 1990.

(10) In making rules, regard must be had to section 9.

(11) The Minister who has power to make rules in relation to a particular tribunal may, to the extent he considers it necessary to ensure that the tribunal can provide an appropriate remedy in relation to an act (or proposed act) of a public authority which is (or would be) unlawful as a result of section 6(1), by order add to
> (a) the relief or remedies which the tribunal may grant; or

(b) the grounds on which it may grant any of them.

(12) An order made under subsection (11) may contain such incidental, supplemental, consequential or transitional provision as the Minister making it considers appropriate.

(13) "The Minister" includes the Northern Ireland department concerned.

Judicial remedies.

8. - (1) In relation to any act (or proposed act) of a public authority which the court finds is (or would be) unlawful, it may grant such relief or remedy, or make such order, within its powers as it considers just and appropriate.

(2) But damages may be awarded only by a court which has power to award damages, or to order the payment of compensation, in civil proceedings.

(3) No award of damages is to be made unless, taking account of all the circumstances of the case, including

(a) any other relief or remedy granted, or order made, in relation to the act in question (by that or any other court), and

(b) the consequences of any decision (of that or any other court) in respect of that act,

the court is satisfied that the award is necessary to afford just satisfaction to the person in whose favour it is made.

(4) In determining

(a) whether to award damages, or

(b) the amount of an award,

the court must take into account the principles applied by the European Court of Human Rights in relation to the award of compensation under Article 41 of the Convention.

(5) A public authority against which damages are awarded is to be treated

(a) in Scotland, for the purposes of section 3 of the Law Reform (Miscellaneous Provisions) (Scotland) Act 1940 as if the award were made in an action of damages in which the authority has been found liable in respect of loss or damage to the person to whom the award is made;

(b) for the purposes of the Civil Liability (Contribution) Act 1978 as liable in respect of damage suffered by the person to whom the award is made.

(6) In this section

"court" includes a tribunal;

"damages" means damages for an unlawful act of a public authority; and

"unlawful" means unlawful under section 6(1).

Judicial acts.

9. - (1) Proceedings under section 7(1)(a) in respect of a judicial act may be brought only

(a) by exercising a right of appeal;

(b) on an application (in Scotland a petition) for judicial review; or

(c) in such other forum as may be prescribed by rules.

(2) That does not affect any rule of law which prevents a court from being the subject of judicial review.

(3) In proceedings under this Act in respect of a judicial act done in good faith, damages may not be awarded otherwise than to compensate a person to the extent required by Article 5(5) of the Convention.

(4) An award of damages permitted by subsection (3) is to be made against the Crown; but no award may be made unless the appropriate person, if not a party to the proceedings, is joined.

(5) In this section

"appropriate person" means the Minister responsible for the court concerned, or a person or government department nominated by him;

"court" includes a tribunal;

"judge" includes a member of a tribunal, a justice of the peace and a clerk or other officer entitled to exercise the jurisdiction of a court;

"judicial act" means a judicial act of a court and includes an act done on the instructions, or on behalf, of a judge; and

"rules" has the same meaning as in section 7(9).

Remedial action

Power to take remedial action.

10. - (1) This section applies if

(a) a provision of legislation has been declared under section 4 to be incompatible with a Convention right and, if an appeal lies

(i) all persons who may appeal have stated in writing that they do not intend to do so;

(ii) the time for bringing an appeal has expired and no appeal has been brought within that time; or

(iii) an appeal brought within that time has been determined or abandoned; or

(b) it appears to a Minister of the Crown or Her Majesty in Council that, having regard to a finding of the European Court of Human Rights made after the coming into force of this section in proceedings against the United Kingdom, a provision of legislation is incompatible with an obligation of the United Kingdom arising from the Convention.

(2) If a Minister of the Crown considers that there are compelling reasons for proceeding under this section, he may by order make such amendments to the legislation as he considers necessary to remove the incompatibility.

(3) If, in the case of subordinate legislation, a Minister of the Crown considers-

(a) that it is necessary to amend the primary legislation under which the subordinate legislation in question was made, in order to enable the incompatibility to be removed, and

(b) that there are compelling reasons for proceeding under this section,

he may by order make such amendments to the primary legislation as he considers necessary.

(4) This section also applies where the provision in question is in subordinate legislation and has been quashed, or declared invalid, by reason of incompatibility with a Convention right and the Minister proposes to proceed under paragraph 2(b) of Schedule 2.

(5) If the legislation is an Order in Council, the power conferred by subsection (2) or (3) is exercisable by Her Majesty in Council.

(6) In this section "legislation" does not include a Measure of the Church Assembly or of the General Synod of the Church of England.

(7) Schedule 2 makes further provision about remedial orders.

Other rights and proceedings

Safeguard for existing human rights.

11. A person's reliance on a Convention right does not restrict

(a) any other right or freedom conferred on him by or under any law having effect in any part of the United Kingdom; or

(b) his right to make any claim or bring any proceedings which he could make or bring apart from sections 7 to 9.

Freedom of expression.

12. - (1) This section applies if a court is considering whether to grant any relief which, if granted, might affect the exercise of the Convention right to freedom of expression.

(2) If the person against whom the application for relief is made ("the respondent") is neither present nor represented, no such relief is to be granted unless the court is satisfied-

(a) that the applicant has taken all practicable steps to notify the respondent; or

(b) that there are compelling reasons why the respondent should not be notified.

(3) No such relief is to be granted so as to restrain publication before trial unless the court is satisfied that the applicant is likely to establish that publication should not be allowed.

(4) The court must have particular regard to the importance of the Convention right to freedom of expression and, where the proceedings relate to material which the respondent claims, or which appears to the court, to be journalistic, literary or artistic material (or to conduct connected with such material), to

(a) the extent to which

(i) the material has, or is about to, become available to the public; or

(ii) it is, or would be, in the public interest for the material to be published;

(b) any relevant privacy code.

(5) In this section

"court" includes a tribunal; and

"relief" includes any remedy or order (other than in criminal proceedings).

Freedom of thought, conscience and religion.

13. - (1) If a court's determination of any question arising under this Act might affect the exercise by a religious organisation (itself or its members collectively) of the Convention right to freedom of thought, conscience and religion, it must have particular regard to the importance of that right.

(2) In this section "court" includes a tribunal.

Derogations and reservations

Derogations.

14. - (1) In this Act "designated derogation" means

(a) the United Kingdom's derogation from Article 5(3) of the Convention; and

(b) any derogation by the United Kingdom from an Article of the Convention, or of any protocol to the Convention, which is designated for the purposes of this Act in an order made by the Secretary of State.

(2) The derogation referred to in subsection (1)(a) is set out in Part I of Schedule 3.

(3) If a designated derogation is amended or replaced it ceases to be a designated derogation.

(4) But subsection (3) does not prevent the Secretary of State from exercising his power under subsection (1)(b) to make a fresh designation order in respect of the Article concerned.

(5) The Secretary of State must by order make such amendments to Schedule 3 as he considers appropriate to reflect

(a) any designation order; or

(b) the effect of subsection (3).

(6) A designation order may be made in anticipation of the making by the United Kingdom of a proposed derogation.

Reservations.

15. - (1) In this Act "designated reservation" means

(a) the United Kingdom's reservation to Article 2 of the First Protocol to the Convention; and

(b) any other reservation by the United Kingdom to an Article of the

---

Appendix

Convention, or of any protocol to the Convention, which is designated for the purposes of this Act in an order made by the Secretary of State.

(2) The text of the reservation referred to in subsection (1)(a) is set out in Part II of Schedule 3.

(3) If a designated reservation is withdrawn wholly or in part it ceases to be a designated reservation.

(4) But subsection (3) does not prevent the Secretary of State from exercising his power under subsection (1)(b) to make a fresh designation order in respect of the Article concerned.

(5) The Secretary of State must by order make such amendments to this Act as he considers appropriate to reflect

(a) any designation order; or

(b) the effect of subsection (3).

Period for which designated derogations have effect.

16. - (1) If it has not already been designated derogations withdrawn by the United Kingdom, a designated derogation ceases to have effect for the purposes of this Act

(a) in the case of the derogation referred to in section 14(1)(a), at the end of the period of five years beginning with the date on which section 1(2) came into force;

(b) in the case of any other derogation, at the end of the period of five years beginning with the date on which the order designating it was made.

(2) At any time before the period

(a) fixed by subsection (1)(a) or (b), or

(b) extended by an order under this subsection,

comes to an end, the Secretary of State may by order extend it by a further period of five years.

(3) An order under section 14(1)(b) ceases to have effect at the end of the period for consideration, unless a resolution has been passed by each House approving the order.

(4) Subsection (3) does not affect-

(a) anything done in reliance on the order; or

(b) the power to make a fresh order under section 14(1)(b).

(5) In subsection (3) "period for consideration" means the period of forty days beginning with the day on which the order was made.

(6) In calculating the period for consideration, no account is to be taken of any time during which-

(a) Parliament is dissolved or prorogued; or

(b) both Houses are adjourned for more than four days.

(7) If a designated derogation is withdrawn by the United Kingdom, the Secretary of State must by order make such amendments to this Act as he considers are required to reflect that withdrawal.

Periodic review of designated reservations.

17. - (1) The appropriate Minister must review the designated reservation referred to in section 15(1)(a)

(a) before the end of the period of five years beginning with the date on which section 1(2) came into force; and

(b) if that designation is still in force, before the end of the period of five years beginning with the date on which the last report relating to it was laid under subsection (3).

(2) The appropriate Minister must review each of the other designated reservations (if any)

(a) before the end of the period of five years beginning with the date on which the order designating the reservation first came into force; and

(b) if the designation is still in force, before the end of the period of five years beginning with the date on which the last report relating to it was laid under subsection (3).

(3) The Minister conducting a review under this section must prepare a report on the result of the review and lay a copy of it before each House of Parliament.

Judges of the European Court of Human Rights
Appointment to European Court of Human Rights.

18. - (1) In this section "judicial office" means the office of

(a) Lord Justice of Appeal, Justice of the High Court or Circuit judge, in England and Wales;

(b) judge of the Court of Session or sheriff, in Scotland;

(c) Lord Justice of Appeal, judge of the High Court or county court judge, in Northern Ireland.

(2) The holder of a judicial office may become a judge of the European Court of Human Rights ("the Court") without being required to relinquish his office.

(3) But he is not required to perform the duties of his judicial office while he is a judge of the Court.

(4) In respect of any period during which he is a judge of the Court

(a) a Lord Justice of Appeal or Justice of the High Court is not to count as a judge of the relevant court for the purposes of section 2(1) or 4(1) of the Supreme Court Act 1981 (maximum number of judges) nor as a judge of the Supreme Court for the purposes of section 12(1) to (6) of that Act (salaries etc.);

(b) a judge of the Court of Session is not to count as a judge of that court for the purposes of section 1(1) of the Court of Session Act 1988 (maximum number of judges) or of section 9(1)(c) of the Administration of Justice Act 1973 ("the 1973 Act") (salaries etc.);

(c) a Lord Justice of Appeal or judge of the High Court in Northern Ireland is not to count as a judge of the relevant court for the purposes of section 2(1) or 3(1) of the Judicature (Northern Ireland) Act

1978 (maximum number of judges) nor as a judge of the Supreme Court of Northern Ireland for the purposes of section 9(1)(d) of the 1973 Act (salaries etc.);

(d) a Circuit judge is not to count as such for the purposes of section 18 of the Courts Act 1971 (salaries etc.);

(e) a sheriff is not to count as such for the purposes of section 14 of the Sheriff Courts (Scotland) Act 1907 (salaries etc.);

(f) a county court judge of Northern Ireland is not to count as such for the purposes of section 106 of the County Courts Act Northern Ireland) 1959 (salaries etc.).

(5) If a sheriff principal is appointed a judge of the Court, section 11(1) of the Sheriff Courts (Scotland) Act 1971 (temporary appointment of sheriff principal) applies, while he holds that appointment, as if his office is vacant.

(6) Schedule 4 makes provision about judicial pensions in relation to the holder of a judicial office who serves as a judge of the Court.

(7) The Lord Chancellor or the Secretary of State may by order make such transitional provision (including, in particular, provision for a temporary increase in the maximum number of judges) as he considers appropriate in relation to any holder of a judicial office who has completed his service as a judge of the Court.

Parliamentary procedure

Statements of compatibility.

19. - (1) A Minister of the Crown in charge of a Bill in either House of Parliament must, before Second Reading of the Bill

(a) make a statement to the effect that in his view the provisions of the Bill are compatible with the Convention rights ("a statement of compatibility"); or

(b) make a statement to the effect that although he is unable to make a statement of compatibility the government nevertheless wishes the House to proceed with the Bill.

(2) The statement must be in writing and be published in such manner as the Minister making it considers appropriate.

Supplemental

Orders etc. under this Act.

20. - (1) Any power of a Minister of the Crown to make an order under this Act is exercisable by statutory instrument.

(2) The power of the Lord Chancellor or the Secretary of State to make rules (other than rules of court) under section 2(3) or 7(9) is exercisable by statutory instrument.

(3) Any statutory instrument made under section 14, 15 or 16(7) must be laid before Parliament.

(4) No order may be made by the Lord Chancellor or the Secretary of State under section 1(4), 7(11) or 16(2) unless a draft of the order has been laid before, and approved by, each House of Parliament.

(5) Any statutory instrument made under section 18(7) or Schedule 4, or to which subsection (2) applies, shall be subject to annulment in pursuance of a resolution of either House of Parliament.

(6) The power of a Northern Ireland department to make

    (a) rules under section 2(3)(c) or 7(9)(c), or

    (b) an order under section 7(11),

is exercisable by statutory rule for the purposes of the Statutory Rules (Northern Ireland) Order 1979.

(7) Any rules made under section 2(3)(c) or 7(9)(c) shall be subject to negative resolution; and section 41(6) of the Interpretation Act Northern Ireland) 1954 (meaning of "subject to negative resolution") shall apply as if the power to make the rules were conferred by an Act of the Northern Ireland Assembly.

(8) No order may be made by a Northern Ireland department under section 7(11) unless a draft of the order has been laid before, and approved by, the Northern Ireland Assembly.

Interpretation, etc.

    21. - (1) In this Act-

        "amend" includes repeal and apply (with or without modifications);

        "the appropriate Minister" means the Minister of the Crown having charge of the appropriate authorised government department (within the meaning of the Crown Proceedings Act 1947);

        "the Commission" means the European Commission of Human Rights;

        "the Convention" means the Convention for the Protection of Human Rights and Fundamental Freedoms, agreed by the Council of Europe at Rome on 4th November 1950 as it has effect for the time being in relation to the United Kingdom;

        "declaration of incompatibility" means a declaration under section 4;

        "Minister of the Crown" has the same meaning as in the Ministers of the Crown Act 1975;

        "Northern Ireland Minister" includes the First Minister and the deputy First Minister in Northern Ireland;

        "primary legislation" means any-

          (a) public general Act;

          (b) local and personal Act;

          (c) private Act;

          (d) Measure of the Church Assembly;

          (e) Measure of the General Synod of the Church of England;

          (f) Order in Council

            (i) made in exercise of Her Majesty's Royal Prerogative;

            (ii) made under section 38(1)(a) of the Northern Ireland Constitution Act 1973 or the corresponding provision of the Northern Ireland Act 1998; or

(iii) amending an Act of a kind mentioned in paragraph (a), (b) or (c);

and includes an order or other instrument made under primary legislation (otherwise than by the National Assembly for Wales, a member of the Scottish Executive, a Northern Ireland Minister or a Northern Ireland department) to the extent to which it operates to bring one or more provisions of that legislation into force or amends any primary legislation;

"the First Protocol" means the protocol to the Convention agreed at Paris on 20th March 1952;

"the Sixth Protocol" means the protocol to the Convention agreed at Strasbourg on 28th April 1983;

"the Eleventh Protocol" means the protocol to the Convention (restructuring the control machinery established by the Convention) agreed at Strasbourg on 11th May 1994;

"remedial order" means an order under section 10;

"subordinate legislation" means any

(a) Order in Council other than one

(i) made in exercise of Her Majesty's Royal Prerogative;

(ii) made under section 38(1)(a) of the Northern Ireland Constitution Act 1973 or the corresponding provision of the Northern Ireland Act 1998; or

(iii) amending an Act of a kind mentioned in the definition of primary legislation;

(b) Act of the Scottish Parliament;

(c) Act of the Parliament of Northern Ireland;

(d) Measure of the Assembly established under section 1 of the Northern Ireland Assembly Act 1973;

(e) Act of the Northern Ireland Assembly;

(f) order, rules, regulations, scheme, warrant, byelaw or other instrument made under primary legislation (except to the extent to which it operates to bring one or more provisions of that legislation into force or amends any primary legislation);

(g) order, rules, regulations, scheme, warrant, byelaw or other instrument made under legislation mentioned in paragraph (b), (c), (d) or (e) or made under an Order in Council applying only to Northern Ireland;

(h) order, rules, regulations, scheme, warrant, byelaw or other instrument made by a member of the Scottish Executive, a Northern Ireland Minister or a Northern Ireland department in exercise of prerogative or other executive functions of Her Majesty which are exercisable by such a person on behalf of Her Majesty;

"transferred matters" has the same meaning as in the Northern Ireland Act 1998; and

"tribunal" means any tribunal in which legal proceedings may be brought.

(2) The references in paragraphs (b) and (c) of section 2(1) to Articles are to Articles of the Convention as they had effect immediately before the coming into force of the Eleventh Protocol.

(3) The reference in paragraph (d) of section 2(1) to Article 46 includes a reference to Articles 32 and 54 of the Convention as they had effect immediately before the coming into force of the Eleventh Protocol.

(4) The references in section 2(1) to a report or decision of the Commission or a decision of the Committee of Ministers include references to a report or decision made as provided by paragraphs 3, 4 and 6 of Article 5 of the Eleventh Protocol (transitional provisions).

(5) Any liability under the Army Act 1955, the Air Force Act 1955 or the Naval Discipline Act 1957 to suffer death for an offence is replaced by a liability to imprisonment for life or any less punishment authorised by those Acts; and those Acts shall accordingly have effect with the necessary modifications.

Short title, commencement, application and extent.

22. - (1) This Act may be cited as the Human Rights Act 1998.

(2) Sections 18, 20 and 21(5) and this section come into force on the passing of this Act.

(3) The other provisions of this Act come into force on such day as the Secretary of State may by order appoint; and different days may be appointed for different purposes.

(4) Paragraph (b) of subsection (1) of section 7 applies to proceedings brought by or at the instigation of a public authority whenever the act in question took place; but otherwise that subsection does not apply to an act taking place before the coming into force of that section.

(5) This Act binds the Crown.

(6) This Act extends to Northern Ireland.

(7) Section 21(5), so far as it relates to any provision contained in the Army Act 1955, the Air Force Act 1955 or the Naval Discipline Act 1957, extends to any place to which that provision extends.

SCHEDULES
Schedule 1
THE ARTICLES

PART I THE CONVENTION

RIGHTS AND FREEDOMS

ARTICLE 2 RIGHT TO LIFE

1. Everyone's right to life shall be protected by law. No one shall be deprived of his life intentionally save in the execution of a sentence of a court following his conviction of a crime for which this penalty is provided by law.

2. Deprivation of life shall not be regarded as inflicted in contravention of

this Article when it results from the use of force which is no more than absolutely necessary:

(a) in defence of any person from unlawful violence;

(b) in order to effect a lawful arrest or to prevent the escape of a person lawfully detained;

(c) in action lawfully taken for the purpose of quelling a riot or insurrection.

ARTICLE 3 PROHIBITION OF TORTURE

No one shall be subjected to torture or to inhuman or degrading treatment or punishment.

ARTICLE 4 PROHIBITION OF SLAVERY AND FORCED LABOUR

1. No one shall be held in slavery or servitude.

2. No one shall be required to perform forced or compulsory labour.

3. For the purpose of this Article the term "forced or compulsory labour" shall not include:

(a) any work required to be done in the ordinary course of detention imposed according to the provisions of Article 5 of this Convention or during conditional release from such detention;

(b) any service of a military character or, in case of conscientious objectors in countries where they are recognised, service exacted instead of compulsory military service;

(c) any service exacted in case of an emergency or calamity threatening the life or well-being of the community;

(d) any work or service which forms part of normal civic obligations.

ARTICLE 5 RIGHT TO LIBERTY AND SECURITY

1. Everyone has the right to liberty and security of person. No one shall be deprived of his liberty save in the following cases and in accordance with a procedure prescribed by law:

(a) the lawful detention of a person after conviction by a competent court;

(b) the lawful arrest or detention of a person for non-compliance with the lawful order of a court or in order to secure the fulfilment of any obligation prescribed by law;

(c) the lawful arrest or detention of a person effected for the purpose of bringing him before the competent legal authority on reasonable suspicion of having committed an offence or when it is reasonably considered necessary to prevent his committing an offence or fleeing after having done so;

(d) the detention of a minor by lawful order for the purpose of educational supervision or his lawful detention for the purpose of bringing him before the competent legal authority;

(e) the lawful detention of persons for the prevention of the spreading of infectious diseases, of persons of unsound mind, alcoholics or drug addicts or vagrants;

(f) the lawful arrest or detention of a person to prevent his effecting an unauthorised entry into the country or of a person against whom action is being taken with a view to deportation or extradition.

2. Everyone who is arrested shall be informed promptly, in a language which he understands, of the reasons for his arrest and of any charge against him.

3. Everyone arrested or detained in accordance with the provisions of paragraph 1(c) of this Article shall be brought promptly before a judge or other officer authorised by law to exercise judicial power and shall be entitled to trial within a reasonable time or to release pending trial. Release may be conditioned by guarantees to appear for trial.

4. Everyone who is deprived of his liberty by arrest or detention shall be entitled to take proceedings by which the lawfulness of his detention shall be decided speedily by a court and his release ordered if the detention is not lawful.

5. Everyone who has been the victim of arrest or detention in contravention of the provisions of this Article shall have an enforceable right to compensation.

ARTICLE 6 RIGHT TO A FAIR TRIAL

1. In the determination of his civil rights and obligations or of any criminal charge against him, everyone is entitled to a fair and public hearing within a reasonable time by an independent and impartial tribunal established by law. Judgment shall be pronounced publicly but the press and public may be excluded from all or part of the trial in the interest of morals, public order or national security in a democratic society, where the interests of juveniles or the protection of the private life of the parties so require, or to the extent strictly necessary in the opinion of the court in special circumstances where publicity would prejudice the interests of justice.

2. Everyone charged with a criminal offence shall be presumed innocent until proved guilty according to law.

3. Everyone charged with a criminal offence has the following minimum rights:

(a) to be informed promptly, in a language which he understands and in detail, of the nature and cause of the accusation against him;

(b) to have adequate time and facilities for the preparation of his defence;

(c) to defend himself in person or through legal assistance of his own choosing or, if he has not sufficient means to pay for legal assistance, to be given it free when the interests of justice so require;

(d) to examine or have examined witnesses against him and to obtain the attendance and examination of witnesses on his behalf under the same conditions as witnesses against him;

(e) to have the free assistance of an interpreter if he cannot understand or speak the language used in court.

ARTICLE 7 NO PUNISHMENT WITHOUT LAW

1. No one shall be held guilty of any criminal offence on account of any act or omission which did not constitute a criminal offence under national or international law at the time when it was committed. Nor shall a heavier penalty be imposed than the one that was applicable at the time the criminal offence was committed.

2. This Article shall not prejudice the trial and punishment of any person for any act or omission which, at the time when it was committed, was criminal according to the general principles of law recognised by civilised nations.

ARTICLE 8 RIGHT TO RESPECT FOR PRIVATE AND FAMILY LIFE

1. Everyone has the right to respect for his private and family life, his home and his correspondence.

2. There shall be no interference by a public authority with the exercise of this right except such as is in accordance with the law and is necessary in a democratic society in the interests of national security, public safety or the economic well-being of the country, for the prevention of disorder or crime, for the protection of health or morals, or for the protection of the rights and freedoms of others.

ARTICLE 9 FREEDOM OF THOUGHT, CONSCIENCE AND RELIGION

1. Everyone has the right to freedom of thought, conscience and religion; this right includes freedom to change his religion or belief and freedom, either alone or in community with others and in public or private, to manifest his religion or belief, in worship, teaching, practice and observance.

2. Freedom to manifest one's religion or beliefs shall be subject only to such limitations as are prescribed by law and are necessary in a democratic society in the interests of public safety, for the protection of public order, health or morals, or for the protection of the rights and freedoms of others.

ARTICLE 10 FREEDOM OF EXPRESSION

1. Everyone has the right to freedom of expression. This right shall include freedom to hold opinions and to receive and impart information and ideas without interference by public authority and regardless of frontiers. This Article shall not prevent States from requiring the licensing of broadcasting, television or cinema enterprises.

2. The exercise of these freedoms, since it carries with it duties and responsibilities, may be subject to such formalities, conditions, restrictions or penalties as are prescribed by law and are necessary in a democratic society, in the interests of national security, territorial integrity or public safety, for the prevention of disorder or crime, for the protection of health or morals, for the protection of the reputation or rights of others, for preventing the disclosure of information received in confidence, or for maintaining the authority and impartiality of the judiciary.

ARTICLE 11 FREEDOM OF ASSEMBLY AND ASSOCIATION

1. Everyone has the right to freedom of peaceful assembly and to freedom of association with others, including the right to form and to join trade unions for the protection of his interests.

2. No restrictions shall be placed on the exercise of these rights other than such as are prescribed by law and are necessary in a democratic society in the interests of national security or public safety, for the prevention of disorder or crime, for the protection of health or morals or for the protection of the rights and freedoms of others. This Article shall not prevent the imposition of lawful restrictions on the exercise of these rights by members of the armed forces, of the police or of the administration of the State.

ARTICLE 12 RIGHT TO MARRY

Men and women of marriageable age have the right to marry and to found a family, according to the national laws governing the exercise of this right.

ARTICLE 14 PROHIBITION OF DISCRIMINATION

The enjoyment of the rights and freedoms set forth in this Convention shall be secured without discrimination on any ground such as sex, race, colour, language, religion, political or other opinion, national or social origin, association with a national minority, property, birth or other status.

ARTICLE 16 RESTRICTIONS ON POLITICAL ACTIVITY OF ALIENS

Nothing in Articles 10, 11 and 14 shall be regarded as preventing the High Contracting Parties from imposing restrictions on the political activity of aliens.

ARTICLE 17 PROHIBITION OF ABUSE OF RIGHTS

Nothing in this Convention may be interpreted as implying for any State, group or person any right to engage in any activity or perform any act aimed at the destruction of any of the rights and freedoms set forth herein or at their limitation to a greater extent than is provided for in the Convention.

ARTICLE 18 LIMITATION ON USE OF RESTRICTIONS ON RIGHTS

The restrictions permitted under this Convention to the said rights and freedoms shall not be applied for any purpose other than those for which they have been prescribed.

PART II THE FIRST PROTOCOL

ARTICLE 1 PROTECTION OF PROPERTY

1. Every natural or legal person is entitled to the peaceful enjoyment of his possessions. No one shall be deprived of his possessions except in the public interest and subject to the conditions provided for by law and by the general principles of international law. The preceding provisions shall not,

however, in any way impair the right of a State to enforce such laws as it deems necessary to control the use of property in accordance with the general interest or to secure the payment of taxes or other contributions or penalties.

ARTICLE 2 RIGHT TO EDUCATION
No person shall be denied the right to education. In the exercise of any functions which it assumes in relation to education and to teaching, the State shall respect the right of parents to ensure such education and teaching in conformity with their own religious and philosophical convictions.

ARTICLE 3 RIGHT TO FREE ELECTIONS
The High Contracting Parties undertake to hold free elections at reasonable intervals by secret ballot, under conditions which will ensure the free expression of the opinion of the people in the choice of the legislature.

PART III THE SIXTH PROTOCOL ARTICLE

ARTICLE 1 ABOLITION OF THE DEATH PENALTY
The death penalty shall be abolished. No one shall be condemned to such penalty or executed.

ARTICLE 2 DEATH PENALTY IN TIME OF WAR
A State may make provision in its law for the death penalty in respect of acts committed in time of war or of imminent threat of war; such penalty shall be applied only in the instances laid down in the law and in accordance with its provisions. The State shall communicate to the Secretary General of the Council of Europe the relevant provisions of that law.

Schedule 2
REMEDIAL ORDERS

Orders

1. - (1) A remedial order may

(a) contain such incidental, supplemental, consequential or transitional provision as the person making it considers appropriate;

(b) be made so as to have effect from a date earlier than that on which it is made;

(c) make provision for the delegation of specific functions;

(d) make different provision for different cases.

(2) The power conferred by sub-paragraph (1)(a) includes

(a) power to amend primary legislation (including primary legislation other than that which contains the incompatible provision); and

(b) power to amend or revoke subordinate legislation (including subordinate legislation other than that which contains the incompatible provision).

(3) A remedial order may be made so as to have the same extent as the legislation which it affects.

---

(4) No person is to be guilty of an offence solely as a result of the retro-spective effect of a remedial order.

Procedure

2. No remedial order may be made unless

(a) a draft of the order has been approved by a resolution of each House of Parliament made after the end of the period of 60 days beginning with the day on which the draft was laid; or

(b) it is declared in the order that it appears to the person making it that, because of the urgency of the matter, it is necessary to make the order without a draft being so approved.

Orders laid in draft

3. - (1) No draft may be laid under paragraph 2(a) unless

(a) the person proposing to make the order has laid before Parliament a document which contains a draft of the proposed order and the required information; and

(b) the period of 60 days, beginning with the day on which the document required by this sub-paragraph was laid, has ended.

(2) If representations have been made during that period, the draft laid under paragraph 2(a) must be accompanied by a statement containing

(a) a summary of the representations; and

(b) if, as a result of the representations, the proposed order has been changed, details of the changes.

Urgent cases

4. - (1) If a remedial order ("the original order") is made without being approved in draft, the person making it must lay it before Parliament, accompanied by the required information, after it is made.

(2) If representations have been made during the period of 60 days beginning with the day on which the original order was made, the person making it must (after the end of that period) lay before Parliament a statement containing

(a) a summary of the representations; and

(b) if, as a result of the representations, he considers it appropriate to make changes to the original order, details of the changes.

(3) If sub-paragraph (2)(b) applies, the person making the statement must

(a) make a further remedial order replacing the original order; and

(b) lay the replacement order before Parliament.

(4) If, at the end of the period of 120 days beginning with the day on which the original order was made, a resolution has not been passed by each House approving the original or replacement order, the order ceases to have effect (but without that affecting anything previously done under either order or the power to make a fresh remedial order).

---

5. In this Schedule

"representations" means representations about a remedial order (or proposed remedial order) made to the person making (or proposing to make) it and includes any relevant Parliamentary report or resolution; and

"required information" means

(a) an explanation of the incompatibility which the order (or proposed order) seeks to remove, including particulars of the relevant declaration, finding or order; and

(b) a statement of the reasons for proceeding under section 10 and for making an order in those terms.

Calculating periods

6. In calculating any period for the purposes of this Schedule, no account is to be taken of any time during which

(a) Parliament is dissolved or prorogued; or

(b) both Houses are adjourned for more than four days.

Schedule 3

DEROGATION AND RESERVATION

PART I DEROGATION

The 1988 notification

The United Kingdom Permanent Representative to the Council of Europe presents his compliments to the Secretary General of the Council, and has the honour to convey the following information in order to ensure compliance with the obligations of Her Majesty's Government in the United Kingdom under Article 15(3) of the Convention for the Protection of Human Rights and Fundamental Freedoms signed at Rome on 4 November 1950.

There have been in the United Kingdom in recent years campaigns of organised terrorism connected with the affairs of Northern Ireland which have manifested themselves in activities which have included repeated murder, attempted murder, maiming, intimidation and violent civil disturbance and in bombing and fire raising which have resulted in death, injury and widespread destruction of property. As a result, a public emergency within the meaning of Article 15(1) of the Convention exists in the United Kingdom.

The Government found it necessary in 1974 to introduce and since then, in cases concerning persons reasonably suspected of involvement in terrorism connected with the affairs of Northern Ireland, or of certain offences under the legislation, who have been detained for 48 hours, to exercise powers enabling further detention without charge, for periods of up to five days, on the authority of the Secretary of State. These powers are at present to be found in Section 12 of the Prevention of Terrorism (Temporary Provisions) Act 1984, Article 9 of the Prevention of Terrorism (Supplemental Temporary Provisions) Order 1984 and Article 10 of the Prevention of Terrorism (Supplemental Temporary Provisions) (Northern Ireland) Order 1984.

Section 12 of the Prevention of Terrorism (Temporary Provisions) Act 1984 provides for a person whom a constable has arrested on reasonable grounds of suspecting him to be guilty of an offence under Section 1, 9 or 10 of the Act, or to be or to have been involved in terrorism connected with the affairs of Northern Ireland, to be detained in right of the arrest for up to 48 hours and thereafter, where the Secretary of State extends the detention period, for up to a further five days. Section 12 substantially re-enacted Section 12 of the Prevention of Terrorism (Temporary Provisions) Act 1976 which, in turn, substantially re-enacted Section 7 of the Prevention of Terrorism (Temporary Provisions) Act 1974.

Article 10 of the Prevention of Terrorism (Supplemental Temporary Provisions) (Northern Ireland) Order 1984 (SI 1984/417) and Article 9 of the Prevention of Terrorism (Supplemental Temporary Provisions) Order 1984 (SI 1984/418) were both made under Sections 13 and 14 of and Schedule 3 to the 1984 Act and substantially re-enacted powers of detention in Orders made under the 1974 and 1976 Acts. A person who is being examined under Article 4 of either Order on his arrival in, or on seeking to leave, Northern Ireland or Great Britain for the purpose of determining whether he is or has been involved in terrorism connected with the affairs of Northern Ireland, or whether there are grounds for suspecting that he has committed an offence under Section 9 of the 1984 Act, may be detained under Article 9 or 10, as appropriate, pending the conclusion of his examination. The period of this examination may exceed 12 hours if an examining officer has reasonable grounds for suspecting him to be or to have been involved in acts of terrorism connected with the affairs of Northern Ireland.

Where such a person is detained under the said Article 9 or 10 he may be detained for up to 48 hours on the authority of an examining officer and thereafter, where the Secretary of State extends the detention period, for up to a further five days.

In its judgment of 29 November 1988 in the Case of *Brogan and Others,* the European Court of Human Rights held that there had been a violation of Article 5(3) in respect of each of the applicants, all of whom had been detained under Section 12 of the 1984 Act. The Court held that even the shortest of the four periods of detention concerned, namely four days and six hours, fell outside the constraints as to time permitted by the first part of Article 5(3). In addition, the Court held that there had been a violation of Article 5(5) in the case of each applicant.

Following this judgment, the Secretary of State for the Home Department informed Parliament on 6 December 1988 that, against the background of the terrorist campaign, and the over-riding need to bring terrorists to justice, the Government did not believe that the maximum period of detention should be reduced. He informed Parliament that the Government were examining the matter with a view to responding to the judgment. On 22 December 1988, the Secretary of State further informed Parliament that it remained the Government's wish, if it could be achieved, to find a judicial process under which extended detention might be reviewed and where appropriate authorised by a judge or other judicial officer. But a further period of reflection and consultation was necessary before the Government could bring forward a firm and final view.

Since the judgment of 29 November 1988 as well as previously, the Government have found it necessary to continue to exercise, in relation to terrorism connected with the affairs of Northern Ireland, the powers described above enabling further detention without charge for periods of up to 5 days, on the authority of the Secretary of State, to the extent strictly required by the exigencies of the situation to enable necessary enquiries and investigations properly to be completed in order to decide whether criminal proceedings should be instituted. To the extent that the exercise of these powers may be inconsistent with the obligations imposed by the Convention the Government has availed itself of the right of derogation conferred by Article 15(1) of the Convention and will continue to do so until further notice.

Dated 23 December 1988.

The 1989 notification

The United Kingdom Permanent Representative to the Council of Europe presents his compliments to the Secretary General of the Council, and has the honour to convey the following information.

In his communication to the Secretary General of 23 December 1988, reference was made to the introduction and exercise of certain powers under section 12 of the Prevention of Terrorism (Temporary Provisions) Act 1984, Article 9 of the Prevention of Terrorism (Supplemental Temporary Provisions) Order 1984 and Article 10 of the Prevention of Terrorism (Supplemental Temporary Provisions) (Northern Ireland) Order 1984.

These provisions have been replaced by section 14 of and paragraph 6 of Schedule 5 to the Prevention of Terrorism (Temporary Provisions) Act 1989, which make comparable provision. They came into force on 22 March 1989. A copy of these provisions is enclosed.

The United Kingdom Permanent Representative avails himself of this opportunity to renew to the Secretary General the assurance of his highest consideration.

23 March 1989.

PART II RESERVATION

At the time of signing the present (First) Protocol, I declare that, in view of certain provisions of the Education Acts in the United Kingdom, the principle affirmed in the second sentence of Article 2 is accepted by the

United Kingdom only so far as it is compatible with the provision of efficient instruction and training, and the avoidance of unreasonable public expenditure.

Dated 20 March 1952

Made by the UK Permanent Representative to the Council of Europe.

Schedule 4
JUDICIAL PENSIONS

Duty to make orders about pensions

1. - (1) The appropriate Minister must by order make provision with respect to pensions payable to or in respect of any holder of a judicial office who serves as an ECHR judge.

(2) A pensions order must include such provision as the Minister making it considers is necessary to secure that-

(a) an ECHR judge who was, immediately before his appointment as an ECHR judge, a member of a judicial pension scheme is entitled to remain as a member of that scheme;

(b) the terms on which he remains a member of the scheme are those which would have been applicable had he not been appointed as an ECHR judge; and

(c) entitlement to benefits payable in accordance with the scheme continues to be determined as if, while serving as an ECHR judge, his salary was that which would (but for section 18(4)) have been payable to him in respect of his continuing service as the holder of his judicial office.

Contributions

2. A pensions order may, in particular, make provision

(a) for any contributions which are payable by a person who remains a member of a scheme as a result of the order, and which would otherwise be payable by deduction from his salary, to be made otherwise than by deduction from his salary as an ECHR judge; and

(b) for such contributions to be collected in such manner as may be determined by the administrators of the scheme.

Amendments of other enactments

3. A pensions order may amend any provision of, or made under, a pensions Act in such manner and to such extent as the Minister making the order considers necessary or expedient to ensure the proper administration of any scheme to which it relates.

Definitions

4. In this Schedule-

"appropriate Minister" means

(a) in relation to any judicial office whose jurisdiction is exercisable exclusively in relation to Scotland, the Secretary of State; and

(b) otherwise, the Lord Chancellor;

"ECHR judge" means the holder of a judicial office who is serving as a judge of the Court;

"judicial pension scheme" means a scheme established by and in accordance with a pensions Act;

"pensions Act" means

(a) the County Courts Act Northern Ireland) 1959;

(b) the Sheriffs' Pensions (Scotland) Act 1961;

(c) the Judicial Pensions Act 1981; or

(d) the Judicial Pensions and Retirement Act 1993; and

"pensions order" means an order made under paragraph 1.

IER's latest publications

The Institute operates a dual pricing policy: the lower price is the cost to subscribers, members, trade unions and students, the second is the cost for other purchasers.

LABOUR LAW REVIEW 2000
by Rebecca Tuck and Jeremy McMullen QC

(price £3/£10) The 2000 *Review* looks at the Employment Relations Act 1999: the right to be accompanied in grievance and disciplinary hearings; the various family friendly policies; rights of part time workers and disabled workers; issues of discrimination related to age, race and gender and how the courts are interpreting transfer rights under the TUPE Regulations. (September 2000)

CHALLENGING DISABILITY DISCRIMINATION AT WORK
by Mary Stacey and Andrew Short

(price £6.50/£20) December 2000 will be the fourth anniversary of the coming into force of the employment provisions of the Disability Discrimination Act 1995. The publication looks at the meaning of disability, the scope of the protection offered and how it compares to sex and race discrimination laws, and considers the positive duty on employers to make reasonable adjustments to assist disabled people and we look at discrimination by victimisation. (August 2000)

COMPARATIVE NOTES 5: RESISTING UNION-BUSTING TECHNIQUES: LESSONS FROM QUEBEC
by Laura Dubinsky

(price £5/£10) The recognition procedure recently introduced in the UK closely resembles the statutory procedures operating in Canada. According to this booklet, Canadian unions have experienced acute difficulties with the legislation, most notably in the form of union-busting techniques developed by employers in their attempts to deny union recognition. The author considers whether the UK legislation is open to the same union-busting techniques and offers suggestions on how UK unions can learn from the Canadian experiences to defeat attempts at union-busting in the UK. (July 2000)

THE PRISON OFFICERS' ASSOCIATION AND THE RIGHT TO STRIKE
by John Hendy QC, Damian Brown and Graham Watson

(price £6.50/£20) The Prison Officers' Association is a trade union which has a unique characteristic in British law: it is denied the right to call industrial action. This booklet considers the denial of that fundamental human right in its legal context and concludes that, especially in the absence of an effective and impartial means of binding resolution of disputes in the course of collective bargaining, the denial of the right to strike renders the UK in breach of its obligations under international laws which it has ratified and by which it is bound. (June 2000)

EMPLOYMENT RIGHTS: BUILDING ON FAIRNESS AT WORK

(price £5/£10) The Institute of Employment Rights was invited by a number of trade unions to consider what steps might be taken in the future to build on the new fairness at work legislation. In responding to that invitation we hope that this book will help inform the debate about how to continue the development of employment law in a manner consistent with a number of core values, including in particular: (i) social justice, (ii) equality of opportunity, (iii) democracy and citizenship, (iv) human rights, and (v) fairness at work. (March 2000)

CHALLENGING RACE DISCRIMINATION AT WORK
by Karon Monaghan

(price £8/£30) This timely publication provides a comprehensive guide to the complexities of UK race discrimination law. The book is designed to help trade union reps challenge race discrimination at work and includes an overview of the Race Relations Act together with detailed chapters on identifying and proving race discrimination in the workplace through to bringing a complaint to an Employment Tribunal. (March 2000)

COMPARATIVE NOTES 4: TRADE UNION RIGHTS IN SOUTH AFRICA: THE LABOUR RELATIONS ACT 1995
by Roger Welch

(price £5/£10) The Labour Relations Act was introduced in South Africa in 1995 and has since helped to transform that country from an apartheid authoritarian state into a multiracial democracy. The LRA has been proclaimed as being amongst the world's most progressive labour legislation and the author argues that British trade unions should look to the provisions of the LRA to inform their argument about the need to bring UK employment law back into line with international standards. (February 2000)

REGULATING HEALTH AND SAFETY AT WORK: THE WAY FORWARD edited by Phil James and Dave Walters

(price £12/£24) This book represents the outcome of a two year project involving around 30 health and safety specialists including academics, lawyers and trade unionists. This project represents the most comprehensive review of health and safety law and practice since the Robens Committee met 25 years ago. The book includes policy ideas on issues ranging from the level and type of regulation required; the role and responsibility of employers and worker representatives in delivering a safe working environment; enforcement strategies and questions relating to compensation and rehabilitation. (December 1999)

AGE DISCRIMINATION IN EMPLOYMENT by Malcolm Sargeant

(price £6.50/£20) This booklet highlights the way age discrimination manifests itself, it outlines why a policy on age discrimination is needed by looking at the economic and civil implications of discrimination and considers the possibility of future proposals emanating from Europe. It goes on to consider the process by which government policy developed and outlines the main proposals contained in the Code of Practice. Finally the report argues that a voluntary code, while welcome, is not enough and puts forward a case for full statutory protection through legislation. (November 1999)

COMPARATIVE NOTES 3: DEVELOPING RECOGNITION AND REPRESENTATION IN THE UK: HOW USEFUL IS THE US MODEL? by Brian Towers

(price £5/£10) Professor Towers assesses how far the new British statutory recognition procedure will contribute towards a revival of British trade union representation and collective bargaining in the light of the experience of the United States where a similar procedure operates. (September 1999)

THE FAIRNESS AT WORK BILL. IS IT FAIR? WILL IT WORK

(price £5/£10) A transcribed report of the conference organised by the Institute in March 1999

OBSERVATIONS ON TRADE UNION RECOGNITION IN BRITAIN AND AUSTRALIA

(price £2.50/£4) The text of an Occasional Lecture given by Jeff Shaw QC, Australian Attorney General, in June 1999.

COMPARATIVE NOTES 2: RESOLVING EMPLOYMENT RIGHTS DISPUTES THROUGH MEDIATION: THE NEW ZEALAND EXPERIENCE AND ACAS ARBITRATION
by Susan Corby

(price £5/£10) The Employment Rights (Dispute Resolution) Act 1998 introduced arbitration as an alternative to Tribunals for resolving unfair dismissal disputes. This booklet looks at the differences between conciliation, mediation and arbitration as forms of alternative dispute resolution. (May 1999)

FAIRNESS AT WORK AND TRADE UNION RECOGNITION: PAST COMPARISONS AND FUTURE PROBLEMS by Lord McCarthy

(price £6.50/£20) This publication looks at the role of the Central Arbitration Committee (CAC) and offers a number of informed suggestions on how the proposed new rights of recognition might be strengthened. (March 1999)

SURVEILLANCE AND PRIVACY AT WORK by Michael Ford

(price £6.50/£20) Surveillance is as old as work itself. At present UK law offers little protection and while the Data Protection Act and the Human Rights Act may offer some limited protection in the future, it would be naïve to hope that a statutory right to privacy could reverse the spread and intensification of surveillance. This publication concludes that rather than depending on a general law of privacy, a better strategy for workers would be to press for legal rights to information, consultation and enforced bargaining about surveillance. (December 1998)

A SOCIAL CLAUSE FOR LABOUR'S CAUSE: GLOBAL TRADE AND LABOUR STANDARDS – A CHALLENGE FOR THE NEW MILLENNIUM by David Chinn

(price £6.50/£20) This publication is produced in association with trade unionists in Australia and looks at how unions can strengthen international labour standards by linking them to international trade through the use of social clauses. To do this effectively, the author argues that we need to move away from the 'social dumping' argument and argue for a social dimension to the global economy. (July 1998)

LOW PAY AND THE MINIMUM WAGE
by Sanjiv Sachdev and Frank Wilkinson

(price £6.50/£20) The authors highlight the positive contribution a

---

national minimum wage can make to the economy if set at a high enough level. They provide figures about the effects of a minimum wage across different industries and occupations. The authors refute the argument that a NMW will cause job losses or inflation and warn that setting a minimum wage too low may deal with the worst excesses of employer power but will fail to tackle the economic problems underpinning the economy. (May 1998)

IN DEFENCE OF TRADE UNIONISM by Jim Mortimer

(price £5/£10) The text of a lecture given by Jim Mortimer (with an introduction by John Hendy QC) to celebrate the 10th anniversary of the Institute. (April 1998)

COMPARATIVE NOTES 1: TRADITION AND CHANGE IN AUSTRALIAN LABOUR LAW by Anthony Forsyth

(price £5/£10) This is the first in a series of comparative papers outlining how labour law operates in other countries and highlighting lessons to be learned from the experiences of workers from around the world. (April 1998)

WORKING LIFE – A NEW PERSPECTIVE ON LABOUR LAW edited by Keith Ewing

(price £12) Running to around 350 pages this is the most comprehensive and far reaching report ever produced on this topic. Compiled by over 50 experts in their fields – eminent academics, lawyers and senior trade unionists – this work provides a framework of reform and alternatives with proposals to extend democracy, opportunity and justice at work. (September 1996)

THE GUIDE TO "WORKING LIFE – A NEW PERSPECTIVE ON LABOUR LAW"

(price £6/£20) A summary, suitable for trade union schools and activists, of the report described above. (September 1996)

A COMPLETE LIST OF AVAILABLE PUBLICATIONS IS POSTED ON OUR WEBSITE **WWW.IER.ORG.UK**